Essential Biology

Ecology
&
Population Biology

3rd edition

STERLING
Education

3   2   1

ISBN-13: 979-8-8855717-9-1

Sterling Education materials are available at quantity discounts.
Contact info@sterling–prep.com

Sterling Education
6 Liberty Square #11
Boston, MA 02109

© 2024 Sterling Education

Published by Sterling Education

 Printed in the U.S.A.

STERLING
Education

From the foundations of a living cell to the complex mechanisms of gene expression, *Essential Biology Self-Teaching Guides* are a comprehensive compendium of clearly explained texts to learn and master multifaceted biology topics.

These guides provide a detailed review of essential biological processes of living systems. Develop a better understanding of cell and molecular biology, mechanisms of cell metabolism, plants and photosynthesis, evolution and natural selection, ecology and population biology. Learn the principles of genetics, microbiology, classification and diversity, as well as structure and function of anatomical systems. Reinforce your learning by working through the practice questions and detailed explanations.

Created by highly qualified biology instructors, researchers, and education specialists, these books empower readers by helping them increase their understanding of biology.

We sincerely hope that these guides are valuable for your learning.

230731akp

Featured on

Eukaryotic Cell & Cellular Metabolism

Molecular Biology & Genetics

Nervous & Endocrine Systems

Circulatory, Respiratory & Immune Systems

Digestive & Excretory Systems

Muscle, Skeletal & Integumentary Systems

Reproduction & Development

Microbiology

Plants & Photosynthesis

Evolution, Classification & Diversity

Ecology & Population Biology

Visit our Amazon store

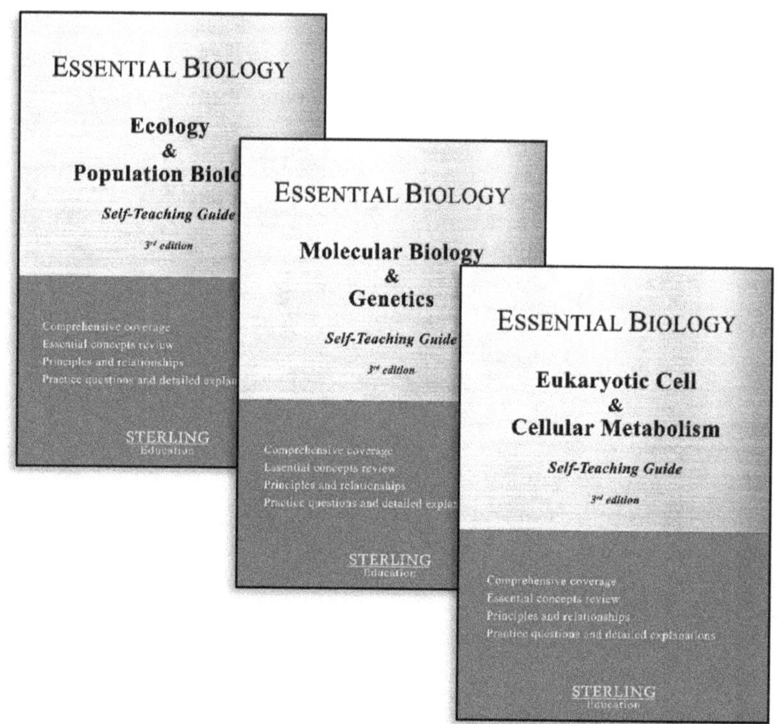

Electronic Structure & Periodic Table

Chemical Bonding

States of Matter & Phase Equilibria

Stoichiometry

Solution Chemistry

Chemical Kinetics & Equilibrium

Acids & Bases

Chemical Thermodynamics

Electrochemistry

Visit our Amazon store

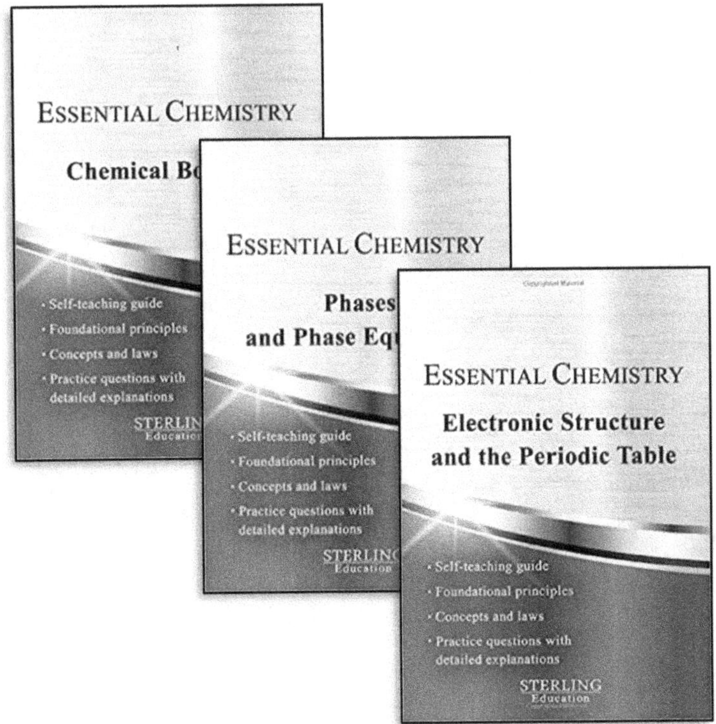

Kinematics and Dynamics

Equilibrium and Momentum

Force, Motion, Gravitation

Work and Energy

Fluids and Solids

Waves and Periodic Motion

Light and Optics

Sound

Electrostatics and Electromagnetism

Electric Circuits

Heat and Thermodynamics

Atomic and Nuclear Structure

Visit our Amazon store

Chemistry

Physics

Cell and Molecular Biology

Organismal Biology

American History

American Law

American Government and Politics

Comparative Government and Politics

World History

European History

Psychology

Environmental Science

Human Geography

Visit our Amazon store

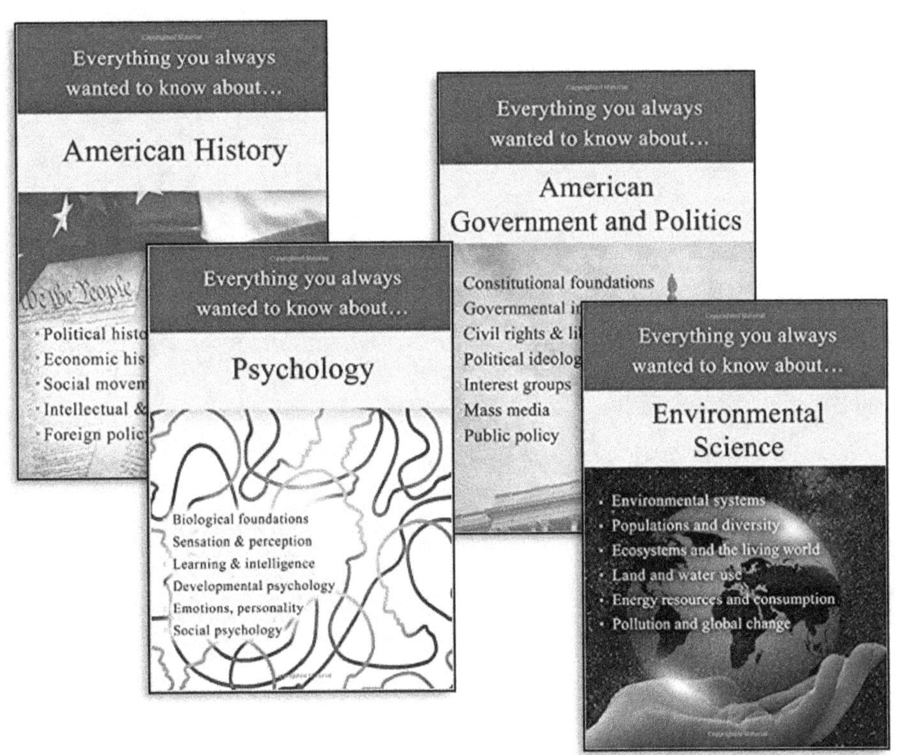

Page intentionally left blank

Table of Contents

REVIEW: Ecosystems, Biosphere & Conservation Biology **15**

Energy Flow and Nutrient Cycles **17**
Photoautotrophs and chemoautotrophs 17
Heterotrophs 17
Energy flow and thermodynamics 17
Primary producers' trophic levels 18
Secondary consumers' trophic levels 18
Complex ecosystem interactions 19
Primary productivity 19

Ecological Pyramids **21**
Food webs 21
Ecological efficiency 22
Energy reclamation 22
Pyramid numbers, energy and biomass 22
Energy and biomass pyramids 23

Biogeochemical Cycles **25**
Nutrient cycles 25
Water cycle 25
Carbon cycle 26
Greenhouse gases 27
Nitrogen cycle 27
Nitrification 27
Denitrification 28
Acid rain and photochemical smog 28
Phosphorus cycle 28
Phosphorus recycling 29

Atmosphere **31**
Climate 31
Water moderates temperature 31
Hadley, Polar and Ferrel cells 31
Coriolis effect 32
Topography and climate 33
Water affects climate 33

Table of Contents (*continued*)

REVIEW: Ecosystems, Biosphere & Conservation Biology (*continued*)

Biosphere **35**

    Distinct environmental conditions 35

    Atmosphere 35

    Biosphere 36

Terrestrial Biomes **37**

    Tundra 37

    Coniferous forests 37

    Taiga 38

    Temperate deciduous forests 38

    Tropical forests 38

    Shrublands 39

    Grasslands 40

    Savannas 40

    Deserts 41

    Latitude and elevation relationships 41

Aquatic Biomes **43**

    Freshwater and saltwater biomes 43

    Estuaries 43

    Oceans 43

    Plankton and zooplankton 44

    Streams and rivers 44

    Ponds and lakes 44

Aquatic Biomes' Structures **45**

    Lake zones 45

    Lake stratifications 45

    Oligotrophic and eutrophic lakes 46

    Continental shelf 46

    Ocean zones 47

    Neritic zone 47

    Oceanic zone 48

Table of Contents (*continued*)

REVIEW: Ecosystems, Biosphere & Conservation Biology (*continued*)

    Pelagic and photic zones 48

    Aphotic zone 48

    Seabed 49

    Oceanic zone and filter feeders 49

    Hydrothermal vents 49

Biodiversity **51**

    Biodiversity preservation 51

    Species and genetic biodiversity 51

    Biodiversity hotspots 51

    Value of biodiversity 52

    Sustainable ecosystems 52

Conservation Biology **53**

    Ecotourism 53

    Causes of extinction 53

    Habitat degradation and fragmentation 53

    Unsustainable exploitation 54

Climate Change **55**

    Soil and water pollution 55

    Light, noise and genetic pollution 55

    Extinction 55

    Indicator species 56

    Flagship and umbrella species 56

Conservation **57**

    Preservation and remediation 57

    Regulating activities 57

    Habitat restoration 58

    Pollution controls 58

    Ecosystem conservation 58

Table of Contents (*continued*)

REVIEW: Populations & Community Ecology **61**

Ecology of Populations **63**

Ecological hierarchy 63

Habitats and community 63

Ecosystems and biosphere 63

Population ecology and dispersal 64

Physiological stress 64

Environmental resistance 64

Carrying capacity 64

Limiting factors 65

Population cycle 65

Population Growth Models **67**

Discrete growth 67

Continuous growth 67

Exponential growth 67

Biotic potential 67

Logistic growth curves 68

Stable equilibrium 68

Deceleration phase 68

Population Diagrams **69**

Age structure diagrams 69

Expanding population diagrams 69

Stable and declining population diagrams 69

Population diagrams 69

Mortality patterns 70

Life tables 70

Survivorship curves 71

Population Size Constraints **73**

Intrinsic and extrinsic factors 73

Life history patterns 73

r-selection growth 73

K-selection growth 74

Human population growth 74

Developing countries' growth 75

Ecological footprints 76

Table of Contents (*continued*)

REVIEW: Populations & Community Ecology (*continued*)

Community Ecology **77**
    Communities 77
    Community composition 77
    Community models 78
    Community structure 78
    Niche theory 79
    Generalists *vs.* specialists 79
    Competition between populations 79
    Resource partitioning 80

Predation–Prey Interactions **81**
    Predation 81
    Predator-prey cycling 81
    Coevolution 82
    Predation defenses 82

Symbiosis **83**
    Symbiotic relationships 83
    Parasitism 83
    Commensalism 83
    Mutualism 84
    Essential mutualism 84

Community Dynamics **85**
    Community development 85
    Climax communities 85
    Dynamic steady state 86
    Climatic climax theory 86

Succession and Biodiversity **87**
    Succession models 87
    Community biodiversity 87
    Keystone predators 88
    Island communities 88
    Heterogeneity 89
    Invasive species 89

Table of Contents (*continued*)

PRACTICE QUESTIONS & DETAILED EXPLANATIONS **93**

    Practice Questions: Ecosystems, Biosphere & Conservation Biology....... **95**

    Detailed Explanations: Ecosystems, Biosphere & Conservation Biology.. **109**

    Practice Questions: Populations & Community Ecology........................ **131**

    Detailed Explanations: Populations & Community Ecology................... **147**

Annotated Glossary... **175**

REVIEW

Ecosystems, Biosphere
&
Conservation Biology

Energy Flow and Nutrient Cycles

Ecological Pyramids

Biogeochemical Cycles

Atmosphere

Biosphere

Terrestrial Biomes

Aquatic Biomes

Aquatic Biomes' Structures

Biodiversity

Conservation Biology

Climate Change

Conservation

Page intentionally left blank

Energy Flow and Nutrient Cycles

Photoautotrophs and chemoautotrophs

Ecosystem includes a biotic community and its abiotic environment.

Biotic communities are organized by which organisms fuel their metabolic activities.

Autotrophs are the basis of an ecosystem and feed *heterotrophs*.

Autotrophs synthesize *organic compounds* using energy from the sun or inorganic compounds.

Autotrophs include photoautotrophs and chemoautotrophs.

Photoautotrophs (e.g., algae, cyanobacteria) use photosynthesis, converting solar energy into organic compounds (e.g., glucose, fructose).

Chemoautotrophs are bacteria that *oxidize* inorganic compounds (e.g., ammonia, nitrite, sulfide) to generate organic compounds.

Chemoautotrophs are rare and typically in caves, *hydrothermal ocean vents*, and *environments lacking light.*

Heterotrophs

Heterotrophs must obtain nutrients by consuming other organisms.

Herbivores feed on autotrophs and are typically prey animals for carnivores and omnivores.

Detritivores degrade organic matter and recycle energy and nutrients within the ecosystem.

The smallest detritivores, such as fungi and bacteria, are *decomposers*; many are *saprotrophs.*

Saprotrophs digest organic matter externally by secreting enzymes into the surrounding environment and absorbing degraded products.

Energy flow and thermodynamics

Ecosystems are characterized by nutrient production, movement, consumption, and recycling.

Nutrients are *chemical energy* flowing throughout the system in predictable ways governed by the laws of thermodynamics.

> *First law of thermodynamics*: *energy can neither be created nor destroyed.*

> *Second law of thermodynamics*: *entropy* (disorder) *increases*, heat moves from hot to cold and energy transformations *lose energy to the environment.*

Energy flow is assembled into the *food chain* of a community.

Primary producers' trophic levels

Trophic levels are the food chains that describe how organisms feed.

Arrows in the food chain show the direction of energy flow.

The *greater the energy pathways* in a food web, the more *stable* the community.

At the base of every food chain are autotrophs as *primary producers.*

Primary producers are responsible for *primary production,* creating organic compounds using energy from the sun or inorganic compounds.

Chemical energy created by primary production nourishes producers and other organisms in the food chain.

Chemical energy can be quantified by *biomass* or the amount of organic material in an area.

Biomass may be living or dead; the requirement is to contain *usable energy.*

Secondary consumers' trophic levels

Herbivores consuming primary producers are *primary consumers.*

Those organisms which consume the primary consumers are *secondary consumers,* and so on.

Typically, food chains do not exceed the level of a tertiary consumer.

At the top of the food chain are *apex predators,* with no natural predators.

For example, a primary producer in a food chain may be a carrot plant.

Its direct predator, the eastern cottontail rabbit, is a primary consumer.

Red fox is a *secondary consumer,* and golden eagle is a *tertiary consumer* and *apex predator.*

However, golden eagles often prey on rabbits in addition to foxes.

An ecosystem involves many food chains interconnected into a food web.

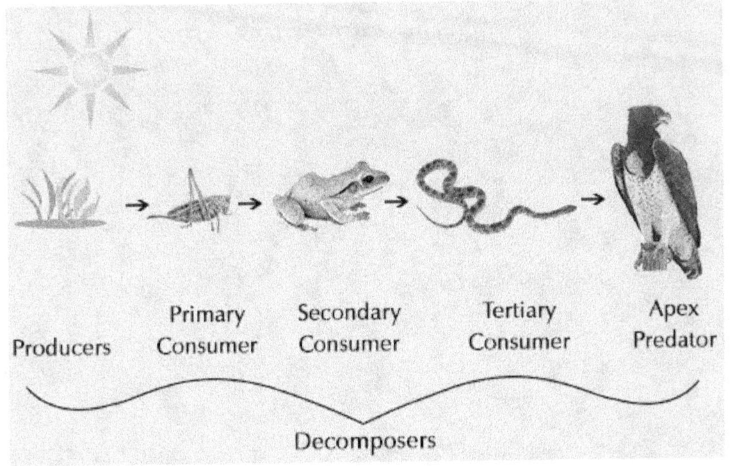

Food chain from producers and consumers to apex predator

Complex ecosystem interactions

Linear food chains fail to capture *complex ecosystem interactions.*

Detritivores are challenging to place on a food web and are often conceptualized as separate.

Grazing food webs do not include detritivores; it places primary producers at the basal level.

Detrital food webs place detritivores at the bottom.

Food webs begin when producers receive energy from the sun through photosynthesis.

Primary productivity

Gross primary productivity is the total amount of energy they generate via photosynthesis.

However, producers must use this energy to fuel their metabolism.

Net primary productivity passed to heterotrophs is unused energy.

Due to the *second law of thermodynamics*, energy is *lost at each trophic level* because organisms lose *heat* through *cellular respiration* (synthesizing ATP).

Organic matter remains *undigested* at each trophic level and is lost as waste.

Detritivores help recycle undigested organic matter and release energy from these substances.

Notes for active learning

Notes for active learning

Ecological Pyramids

Food webs

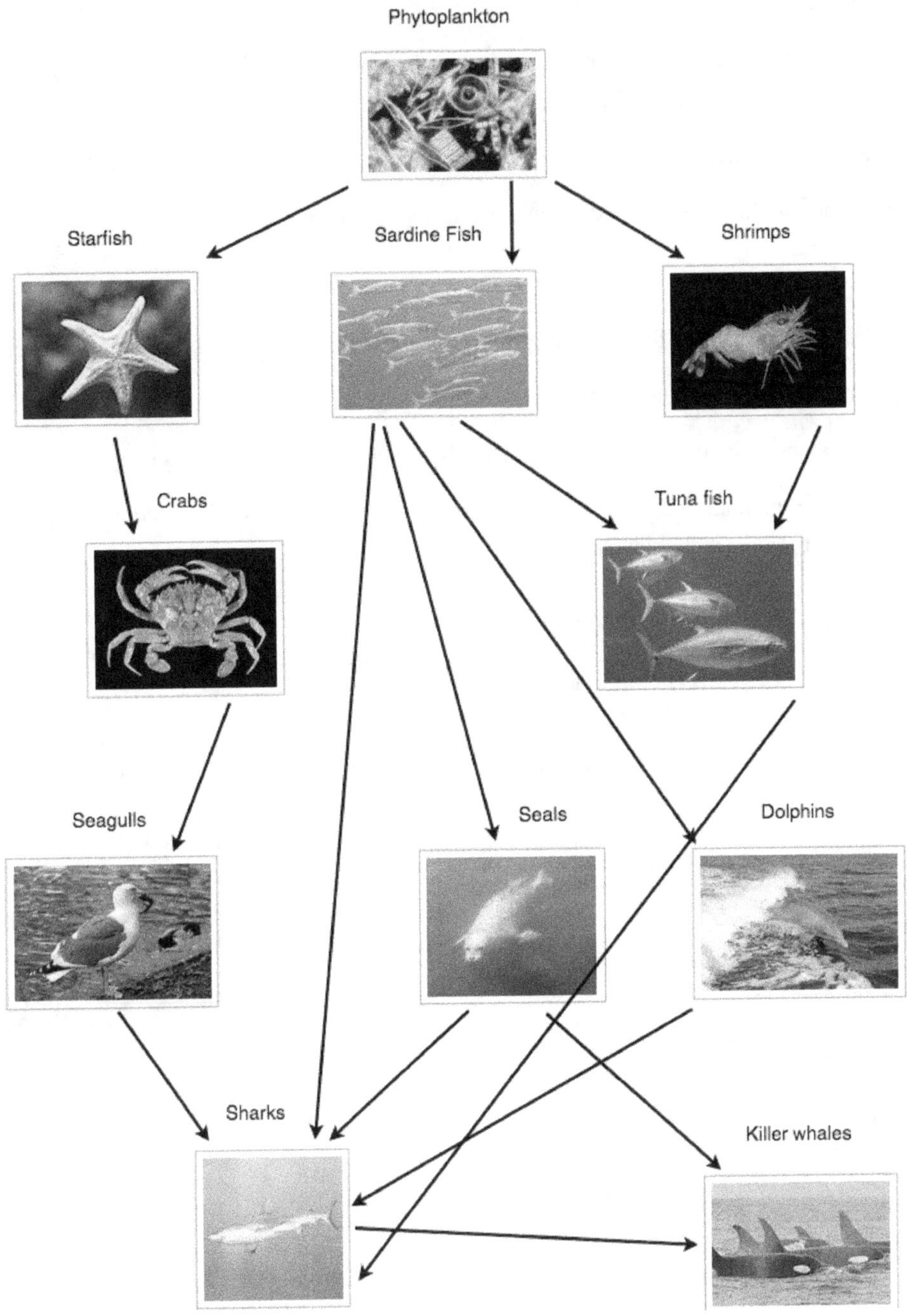

Food web from phytoplankton producers through primary, secondary, and tertiary consumers

Ecological efficiency

Ecological efficiency is the proportion of energy at each trophic level transferred to the next.

About 90% of an organism's energy is consumed for metabolism, and only 10% passes to the next trophic level.

For example, 1,000 kilograms of plant biomass supports 100 kg of primary consumers, 10 kg of secondary consumers, and 1 kg of tertiary consumers.

Massive biomass is needed at the lower levels to support the apex predators at the top.

This rapid energy loss is why food chains rarely have more than four links.

Energy reclamation

Ecological pyramids show food web trophic levels by energy, biomass, or number of species.

Energy and biomass are greatest at the primary producer and lowest at the apex predator level.

Energy reclamation by decomposers dramatically increases the ecosystem's efficiency.

Apex predator populations are the least stable and most heavily impacted by population fluctuations at lower trophic levels.

Pyramid numbers, energy and biomass

	Wolf ↑ Rabbit ↑ Plant	Ladybug ↑ Aphid ↑ Plant	Wasp ↑ Caterpillar ↑ Plant
Number of organisms at each trophic level			
Mass of biological material at each trophic level			
Energy passing through trophic levels			

Ecological pyramids; the ecological pyramid of numbers, the pyramid of energy, and the pyramid of biomass

Energy and biomass pyramids

Pyramid base is the producer trophic level, with increased consumer trophic levels.

Ecological pyramid of numbers is the number of organisms at each trophic level.

Pyramid of energy is how much energy each level generates.

Pyramid of biomass is the amount of living material (i.e., biomass) produced by a given area or volume at each trophic level.

Most pyramids resemble a typical upright triangle, but pyramids may have inversion at times.

For example, this occurs if an herbivore population feeds on a fast-growing producer, keeping its biomass low in comparison.

Notes for active learning

Biogeochemical Cycles

Nutrient cycles

Nutrients such as water, carbon, nitrogen, and phosphorus are limited in supply.

Biogeochemical cycles recycle nutrients from the ecosystem's biotic and abiotic components.

Reservoirs and exchange pools are abiotic components of biogeochemical cycles.

Reservoir stores a nutrient for long periods, perhaps hundreds, thousands, or millions of years.

Nutrients flow through living organisms (i.e., the biotic community).

Nutrients in the reservoir are accessible by an exchange pool, which is temporary storage.

Water cycle

Hydrologic cycle is water movement in Earth's crust, atmosphere, water bodies, and organisms.

At a basic level, the hydrologic cycle involves evaporating water from freshwater and saltwater bodies, which condenses and falls as precipitation.

Some water flows below Earth's surface and becomes *groundwater* in *aquifers*.

Water table is the depth at which an aquifer is saturated with water.

Some groundwater seeps to the surface, forming freshwater bodies or moving into the ocean.

Freshwater is a renewable resource of about 3% of the world's water supply.

Freshwater becomes unavailable when *consumption exceeds supply* or *becomes polluted*.

Groundwater is an example of a biogeochemical reservoir, about 20% of the world's freshwater.

Freshwater bodies and atmosphere exchange pools store available water for organisms.

Polar region ice and water in the deep oceans are reservoirs, like groundwater.

Carbon cycle

Carbon cycle is the exchange of carbon between organisms and their environment.

Terrestrial organisms and marine mammals exchange CO_2 directly with the atmosphere.

Aquatic organisms that do not breathe air do this exchange indirectly by inhaling or exhaling *dissolved carbon dioxide* (CO_2) as bicarbonate (HCO_3^-).

Terrestrial and aquatic autotrophs uptake carbon, convert it into organic compounds and cycle through the food web.

As heterotrophs respire, they return carbon dioxide (CO_2) to the air and water.

Photosynthesis and respiration occur at relatively equal rates, keeping the cycle balanced.

Organisms return carbon as organic compounds in the form of waste or from their decomposing bodies, which detritivores recycle.

Some organic compounds are not decomposed but preserved as coal, oil, and natural gas fossils.

Global reservoirs of the carbon cycle are fossil fuels and bicarbonate that remain deep in the oceans or are trapped as limestone.

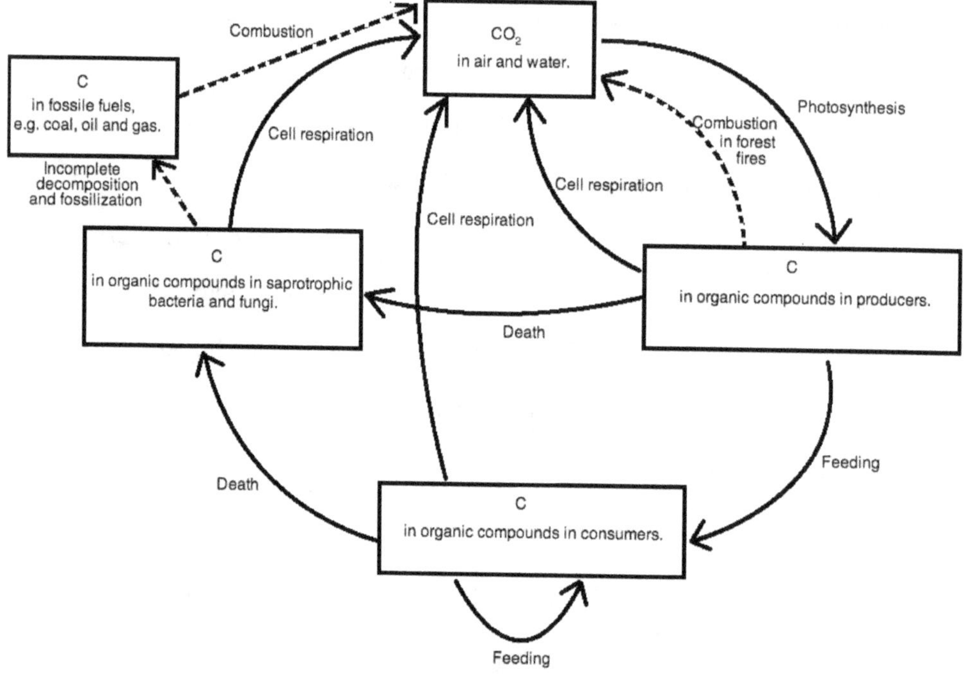

Carbon cycle exchanges carbon among organisms and the atmosphere

Greenhouse gases

Carbon dioxide (CO_2) is one of three *greenhouse gases* that increase atmospheric temperature.

Solar energy reaches the Earth and warms the planet, but a significant amount should be reflected, primarily as infrared radiation.

Burning fossil fuels and forests cause additional carbon dioxide to enter the atmosphere.

Oil spills are *carbon pollution*, releasing millions of gallons into oceans yearly.

Greenhouse gases absorb reflected infrared radiation and trap it in the atmosphere, causing a rise in atmospheric temperatures.

Carbon dioxide interferes with the exchange between photosynthesis and respiration and alters the carbon cycle.

Nitrogen cycle

Nitrogen gas (N_2) makes up 78% of the atmosphere and is vital for plant and animal growth.

Nitrogen is in amino acids, nitrogenous bases, and nucleotides ATP and $NADP^+$.

Migration of nitrogen throughout its various forms is the *nitrogen cycle*.

Plants rely on relationships with certain bacteria to convert nitrogen into forms they can use by nitrogen fixation.

Nitrogen is absorbed by plants as ammonium (NH_4^+) or nitrate (NO_3^{-1}).

Nitrification

Nitrogen-fixing bacteria may live within plant roots or freely in the soil and water; reducing nitrogen gas into ammonium which the plant absorbs.

Ammonium can be created from the urea in animal waste.

Bacteria further convert ammonium (NH_4^+) into nitrate (NO_3^{-1}) by *nitrification*.

Two-step nitrification process requires bacteria to convert ammonium to nitrite (NO_2^-), and other bacteria convert nitrite (NO_2^-) to nitrate (NO_3^{-1}).

Nitrogen converts to nitrate when lightning or cosmic radiation provides energy for a reaction between atmospheric nitrogen and oxygen.

Denitrification

Denitrification refers to converting nitrate to unusable nitrous oxide (N_2O) and nitrogen gas, thus completing the nitrogen cycle. A class of bacteria performs *denitrification*.

Human fertilizer production has altered the nitrogen cycle, adding ammonium to the soil.

Runoff from nitrogen-rich fields results in the over-enrichment (*eutrophication*) of lakes.

Eutrophication causes large algal blooms, overtaking ecosystems and killing other organisms.

Acid rain and photochemical smog

Burning plants and fossil fuels adds atmospheric nitrogen oxide, contributing to air pollution.

Acid deposition is when emissions combine with atmospheric water vapor to form acids that precipitate and acidify soil and lakes.

Nitrogen oxides react with hydrocarbons in the atmosphere to form *photochemical smog,* which contains dangerous compounds that cause respiratory distress.

Photochemical air pollutants can accumulate near the ground due to *thermal inversions,* in which warm air traps cold air just above the Earth's surface.

Phosphorus cycle

Phosphorus cycle is when plants take up phosphate ions (PO_4^{3-} and HPO_4^{2-}) available in the soil, primarily from weathering rocks.

However, while most phosphorus is in sediments, phosphorus that runs off into water bodies is incorporated into organic compounds by algae.

Phosphate is the *limiting nutrient* in most ecosystems, and organisms rapidly take up phosphate.

Animals eat producers and incorporate phosphates into phospholipids, ATP, and nucleotides.

Phosphorous recycling

Decay of organisms and *animal waste decomposition* make phosphate ions available.

However, phosphate incorporated into teeth, bones, and shells does not decay for long periods.

Like other biogeochemical cycles, humans have disrupted the phosphorus cycle.

Phosphorus cycle is disrupted primarily by mining phosphate ore and runoff from livestock waste and fertilized fields.

Human and animal sewage contributes to phosphate in water bodies, polluting water and leading to *eutrophication*.

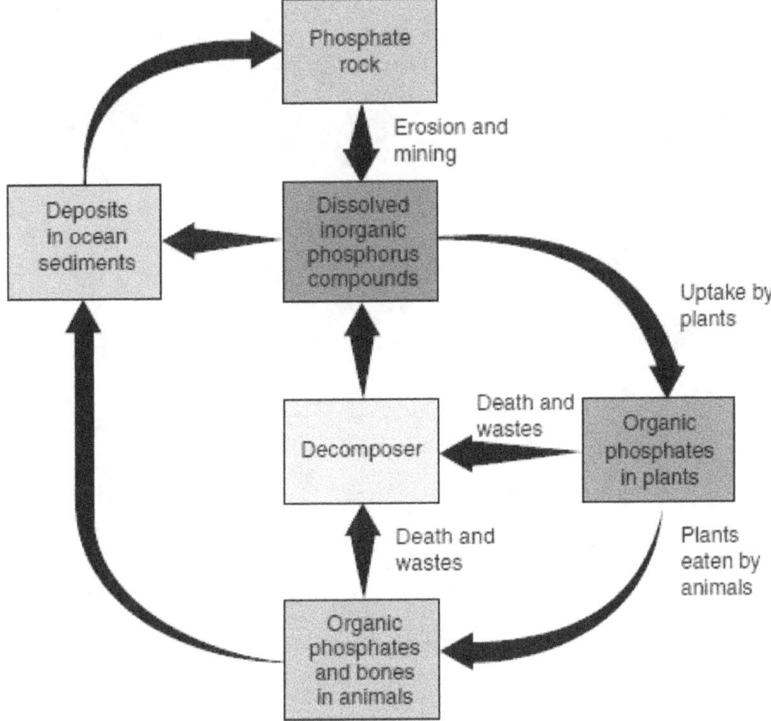

Phosphorus cycle is when plants take up released phosphorous, primarily from soil

Notes for active learning

Atmosphere

Climate

Climate is the prevailing weather in a region, primarily dictated by temperature and rainfall.

Climate involves complex interactions among factors, primarily solar radiation due to the tilt of the Earth, topography, and the presence (or absence) of nearby water bodies.

Water and air circulate through oceans and the atmosphere, creating powerful climatic effects and driving weather conditions.

Tropics are the hottest region because the sun's rays strike the equator.

Since the Earth is a sphere, sunlight strikes the higher and lower latitudes at an angle, lessening the effect of the light.

Earth tilts on its axis, causing one pole to receive more sunlight than the other depending on Earth's position in its journey around the sun.

Seasons are caused by these changes in sunlight throughout the year.

Water moderates temperature

Ocean water is warmest at equator and coldest at poles due to the distribution of the sun's rays.

As air equilibrates with the temperature of the water below, warm air moves from the equator toward colder latitudes, removing heat.

Moisture evaporating into the air carries heat energy.

Movement of air caused by the oceans creates *winds*.

Cooling and warming of air drive *circulation cells,* the closed circuits of wind circulation.

Hadley, Polar and Ferrel cells

Hadley cell forms as warm, moist air rises at the equator and flows northward, high above Earth's surface, causing hot, humid conditions in the tropics.

At about 30° N, the air cools and sinks, absorbing moisture and causing desert conditions.

After it descends, the air circles south to the equator, traveling close to the Earth's surface.

*Polar cell*s are to the north as warm air rises at about 60° N.

Air flows northward as it cools and descends at the pole (90° N), causing dry, frigid conditions.

Air moves south to 60° N to continue this cycle.

Air of the Hadley cell sinking at 30° N and Polar cell air rising at 60° N drives the circulation of an intermediate cell, the *Ferrel cell.*

*Ferrel cell*s have sinking air at 30° N flowing north across the Earth's surface to about 60° N and rising as it warms.

Air moves south to 30° N and cools, restarting the cycle.

Hadley, Ferrel, and Polar cells are in the same sequence south of the equator.

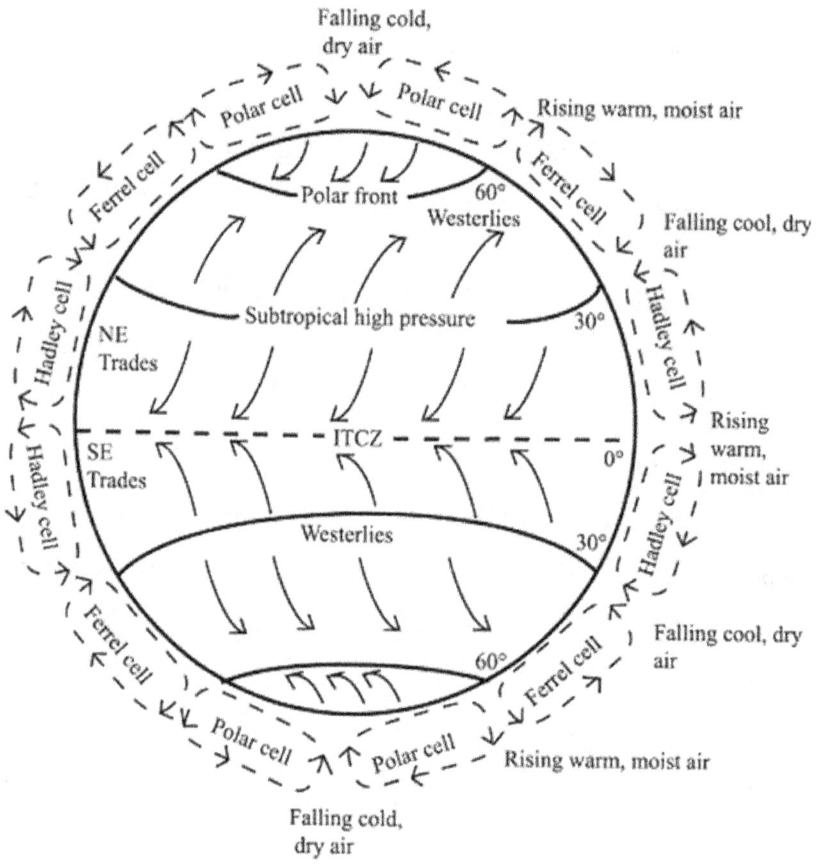

Hadley, Ferrel, and Polar cells influence atmospheric circulation

Coriolis effect

Coriolis effect is due to Earth's rotation when air does not move north to south but is deflected east or west.

Coriolis effect influences circulation cells and *wind belts,* which encircle the globe.

Six wind belts exist on Earth.

Trade winds on either side of the equator, *westerlies* in the temperate regions between 30° and 60° N and S, and weak *polar easterlies* between 60° and 90° N and S.

Topography and climate

Topography is the physical features of the land, which can tremendously affect climate.

Mountains can cause *rain shadows* in certain areas.

Air blowing over a mountain is forced to rise, cooling the land. It is dry when the air descends on the leeward side of a mountain range.

The windward side, therefore, receives moist air, producing more rainfall.

For example, rainfall on the windward side of the Hawaiian Islands is 750 cm but 50 cm in the rain shadow.

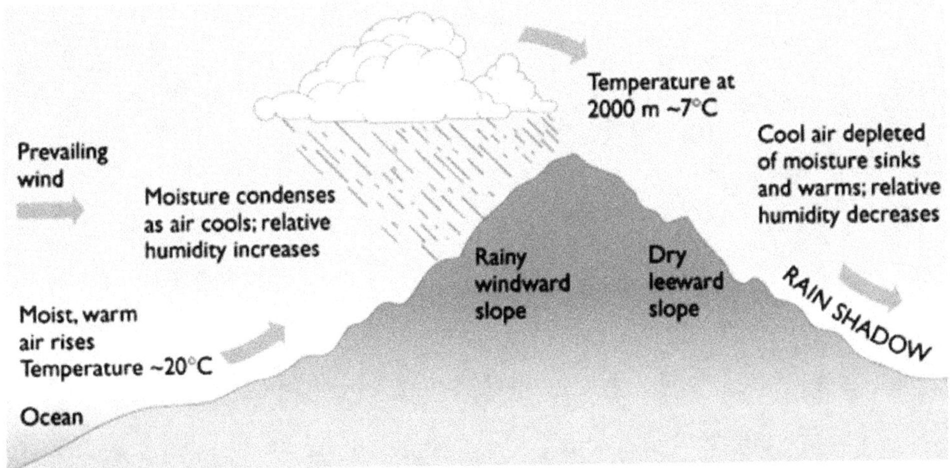

Mountains cause rain shadows, with one side experiencing significantly more rainfall

Water affects climate

Oceans regulate land temperatures since water retains heat and cools land masses.

During the day, the land heats, and warm air rises, allowing cool sea breezes to blow inland and replace the rising air.

At night, the land cools, and the cold air sinks, blowing out to sea.

Water has an excellent capacity for heat regulation; it has high *specific heat* and *absorbs energy*.

Water modulates temperature, with coastal areas cooler than inland.

Water also minimizes temperature differences between day and night.

Notes for active learning

Notes for active learning

Biosphere

Distinct environmental conditions

Earth can be divided into layers, each with distinct environmental conditions.

Geosphere is the solid portion of Earth's surface, including the cryosphere and lithosphere.

Cryosphere contains all frozen water on Earth; most are found at the poles.

Lithosphere is the rocky surface of Earth extending down about 100 kilometers, comprising the crust and the upper mantle.

Hydrosphere is the total amount of Earth's water, including the surface, underground and the air, and can be liquid, vapor, or ice.

On Earth's surface, liquid water exists as oceans, lakes, and rivers; it covers three-quarters of the lithosphere.

Hydrosphere supports a vast diversity of life and regulates global temperatures by absorbing and slowly releasing substantial amounts of heat.

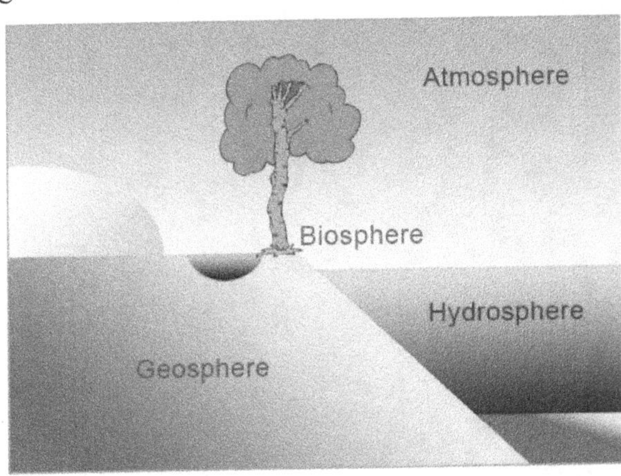

The intersection of the geosphere, hydrosphere, atmosphere, and biosphere

Atmosphere

Atmosphere is the gaseous layer around Earth, which helps regulate temperatures by insulating the Earth from the frigid temperatures of outer space.

Atmosphere is held by Earth's gravity and concentrated near the Earth's surface.

Major atmospheric gases are nitrogen (N) and oxygen (O_2).

Nitrogen (N) is more than 75% of the atmosphere and is essential for plant and animal growth.

About 20% of the atmosphere is oxygen (O_2) necessary for cellular respiration (ATP production) and is the protective ozone barrier absorbing damaging solar radiation.

Atmospheric gases are carbon dioxide (CO_2), water vapor (H_2O), and noble gases argon (Ar) and neon (Ne).

Biosphere

Interacting with the geosphere, the atmosphere, and the hydrosphere is the *biosphere.*

Biosphere is a thin layer that comprises all biomass on Earth; biosphere is the *global ecosystem.*

Biosphere has large *biomes* characterized by climate that supports a unique community of plants and animals.

Biomes change with *latitude* as well as *elevation.*

For example, tundra yields coniferous and deciduous forests from the poles toward the equator.

This same tree sequence can be observed from a mountain peak to ground elevation.

Terrestrial Biomes

Tundra

Alpine tundra is at the top of all high mountains, even the equator.

Tundra is near the north and south pole, where there is no exposure to rock or ice-covered seas.

Tundra covers about 20% of Earth's surface, including Greenland, Scandinavia, Siberia, northern Canada, Antarctica's coasts, and surrounding islands.

Tundra is characterized by a cold, dry climate that receives less than 20 cm of annual rainfall.

Tundra would be defined as a desert if not for the water provided by melting snow.

Except for alpine tundra, most tundra has a perpetually frozen layer of *permafrost* soil.

Tundra is a poor plant environment due to high winds, short growing seasons, and permafrost.

Trees cannot grow in the tundra, but short woody shrubs can survive as they flower and seed quickly during sunlight.

In summer, the ground of the tundra is covered with bogs, marshes, and streams, with abundant grasses and mosses.

Tundra has low biodiversity; few animals are adapted to live in the tundra year-round.

Tundra supports insects and migratory birds and mammals (e.g., shorebirds, wolves, and reindeer) during summer.

Coniferous forests

Coniferous forests have a milder climate than the tundra and higher annual precipitation.

Conifers are primarily spruce, fir, hemlock, and pine trees.

Evergreens are adapted to a snowy, dry climate with thick, protective leaves or needles.

Mountainous coniferous forests are *montane coniferous forests.*

Coniferous forests are divided into biomes, depending on convention.

Coniferous forest biome is a taiga or boreal forest just below the tundra, extending across northern Europe, Asia, and North America, making up 30% of its forest cover.

Coniferous forest is the largest land biome and only exceeded in coldness and dryness by tundra.

Soil does not contain permafrost but is thin and nutrient poor.

Soil is acidic and covered by lichens, mosses, and fallen needles.

Taiga

Taiga supports greater animal diversity than the tundra, with hundreds of bird species and many year-round large mammals such as bears, wolves, moose, elk, and bison.

Taiga supports many small mammals, including beavers, hares, and squirrels.

Unlike the tundra, cold-blooded reptiles and amphibians can survive in the taiga.

At the latitudes or elevations below the taiga are *temperate coniferous forests.*

They have milder summers and winters than taiga and higher precipitation.

Temperate coniferous forests are found throughout Europe, Asia, North America, and South America, including evergreens of the taiga and cedars, redwoods, juniper, and deciduous trees.

The understory is larger and more diverse, with various shrubs and herbaceous plants.

Temperate deciduous forests

Temperate deciduous forests are at latitudes lower than coniferous forests, primarily in eastern North America, eastern Asia, and much of Europe.

They have four well-defined seasons, with a growing season between 140 and 300 days.

Climate is moderate, with mild winters and appreciable rainfall, about 75 to 150 cm per year.

Deciduous trees are characterized by leaves that shed in the fall and regrow in the spring.

Deciduous forests support a wide variety of life, including countless birds, mammals, amphibians, and reptiles.

Deciduous forests are well-stratified, with large, mature trees shading saplings, shrubs, herbaceous plants, lichens, and mosses.

A well-developed understory is possible because of the broad leaves of deciduous trees, which allow sunlight to penetrate the canopy.

Major tree species in a typical deciduous forest are maples, oaks, and elms.

Tropical forests

Tropical forests are at or near the equator and can be subdivided into several categories, depending on the biome classification system.

Tropical rainforests are within 30° north and south of the equator in South America, Central America, Africa, India, Southeast Asia, and Oceania.

They have a warm climate and abundant rainfall, from 190 to 1,000 cm per year.

Tropical rainforests are warm and humid year-round, with slight changes between seasons.

Tropical rainforests are the highest diversity of land biomes, with many insects.

Colorful birds and amphibians are abundant, as are snakes and lizards.

Primates and other mammals are in rainforests. The largest carnivores are big cats, such as jaguars and leopards.

The forest is highly stratified, with a tall canopy of evergreens and a dense understory.

Forest floor has rich soil but sustains few plants due to the heavy shade.

Tropical rainforest found on high mountains is a *montane rainforest* or *cloud forest* with a frigid climate compared to lowland tropical rainforests.

Tropical seasonal forest is among the largest biomes; warm year-round with long, dry seasons.

Other tropical forests are drier and have a mix of deciduous and evergreen trees. They are north and south of equatorial rainforest belts in Africa, India, Southeast Asia, and South America.

Tropical seasonal forests are less diverse than tropical rainforests but have much fauna.

Biome often gives way to grasslands.

Shrublands

Shrubland (or *scrubland*) is dominated by short, woody shrubs with thick evergreen leaves.

Shrubs are highly resistant to forest fires and drought since shrubland is characterized by hot, dry summers and mild winters.

Seeds of many plants in the shrubland require heat from fires to induce germination.

Shrublands found throughout California and along coasts in South America, Western Australia, and the Mediterranean are *chaparral.*

Chaparral is adapted to the climate, with extensive roots and large leaves that retain water.

Chaparral comprises oaks, manzanitas, sages, and other short, thorny shrubs in California.

Xeric shrubland is drier shrubland mixed with interior desert regions.

American West and desert regions in Asia, South America, and Africa have large expanses of xeric shrubland.

Grasslands

Grasslands are arid but receive greater than 25 cm of annual rainfall.

Grasslands are too wet for desert and too dry for forests, once covering 40% of Earth's surface.

Grasslands are now significantly diminished since their rich soil is ideal for agriculture.

Grasslands are adapted to droughts, flooding, fires, and grazing from herbivores.

Temperate grasslands and *tropical grasslands* are two types of grassland.

Temperate grasslands have a mild climate with low and predictable diversity.

Temperate grasslands are located throughout North America, South America, Eurasia, and South Africa, including *prairies, pampas, steppes,* and *veldts.*

Many temperate grassland animals are large grazing mammals like bison and antelope.

Other grassland prey animals are primarily birds and rodents, preyed on by coyotes, foxes, lynxes, wolves, snakes, and predatory birds.

Temperate grasslands divide into *tall-grass* and *short-grass* regions.

Tall grasslands can support trees, are more humid and milder, and are found in the lowlands.

Short grasslands are drier, cannot support trees, and may be found in cold highlands (e.g., steppes of Russia and Ukraine).

Short grasslands often mix with deserts and shrublands.

Savannas

Tropical grasslands are *savannas* containing some trees but are mostly open.

Tropical grasslands have a relatively cool, dry season followed by a hot, rainy one.

Well-known savannas are in Africa, also found in South America and Australia.

Savannas have higher biodiversity than temperate grasslands, the largest variety of herbivores.

Insect life in savannas is plentiful and varied.

Antelopes, zebras, wildebeests, water buffalo, elephants, and giraffes make their homes in savannas and large carnivores like lions, cheetahs, hyenas, and leopards.

Deserts

Deserts are about 30° north and south of equator, where dry air descends from the Hadley cell.

They have less than 25 cm of annual rainfall and lack cloud cover.

The absence of clouds makes the days hot and the nights cold.

Due to their inhospitable conditions, deserts have some of the *lowest biodiversity*.

Most desert animals are small insects, reptiles, birds, and rodents since a large size is a problem for heat regulation.

However, large birds, camels, kangaroos, and coyotes are in various deserts.

Desert plants are highly adapted to heat and drought, but some deserts, such as the Sahara, are nearly devoid of vegetation.

Well-known deserts are in low, interior regions, but a desert may be near coasts or at high altitudes as *cold deserts*.

Researchers may classify tundra as a *polar desert* since it supports little life and is dry.

Latitude and elevation relationships

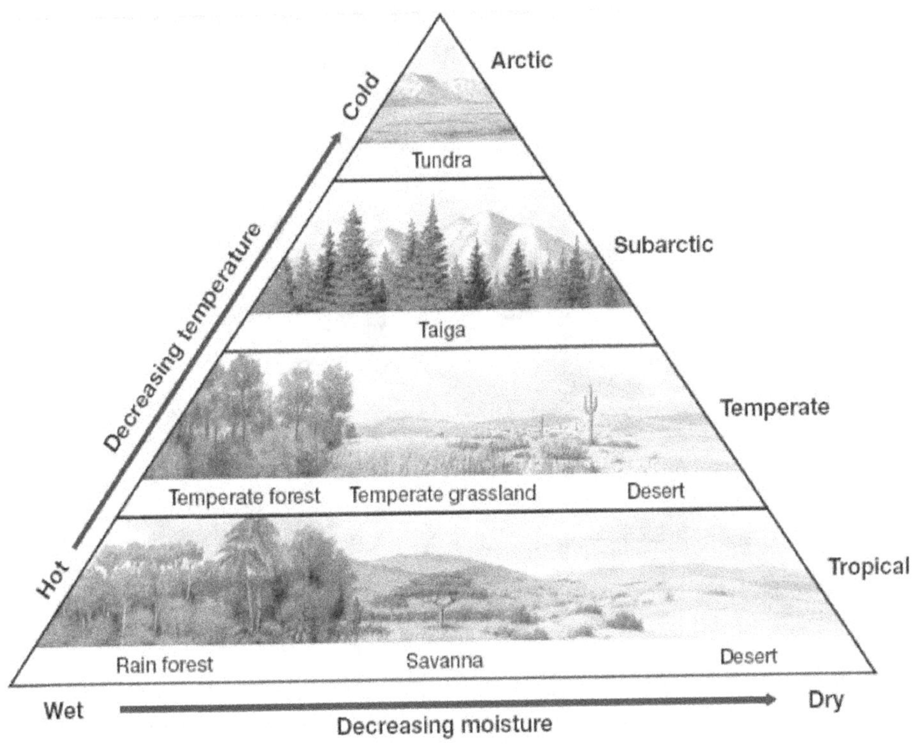

Terrestrial biomes changes relate to latitude and elevation

Notes for active learning

Notes for active learning

Aquatic Biomes

Freshwater and saltwater biomes

Aquatic biomes comprise most of Earth's biosphere, classified as freshwater or saltwater.

Wetlands may be freshwater, saltwater (i.e., marine), or a mix known as *brackish.*

Marshes, swamps, and bogs are aquatic biomes such as wetlands on coastlands across the globe.

Aquatic biomes have incredible diversity, with countless amphibians, reptiles, and birds.

Hydrophytes, plants adapted to live in water, are in abundance.

Estuaries

Estuaries are where a freshwater river merges with the ocean.

Estuaries may be bays, lagoons, inlets, sound, or partially enclosed aquatic bodies.

Estuaries are brackish but considered marine biomes because they are essential to the seas and intertwined with *wetlands*.

Over half of the marine fish are born or raised in estuaries.

Estuaries are provided with nutrients from rivers, ocean tides, and decayed vegetation, making them rich environments supporting much aquatic *flora* (i.e., plants) and *fauna* (i.e., animals).

Estuaries are a unique biome dramatically threatened by habitat destruction and pollution, leading to the collapse of many vital ecosystems.

Oceans

Oceans comprise the other marine biome.

Ocean water movement is influenced by temperature, the friction of surface winds, salinity, and *Coriolis effect*; factors combine to create ocean currents.

Since ocean currents are bounded by land, they move in a circular path,

> *counterclockwise* currents in the Northern Hemisphere

> *clockwise* currents in the Southern Hemisphere

Circular currents are vital to regulating ocean temperatures and the global climate.

Currents induce *upwelling,* circulating cold, nutrient-rich waters to the surface.

Ocean regions that experience upwelling are typically the most diverse and productive because they fuel the activities of *plankton,* a large group of free-swimming microorganisms.

Plankton and zooplankton

Plankton is the basis of aquatic food chains because they are a food source for many organisms.

Phytoplankton is microscopic photosynthetic algae.

Zooplankton is animals that feed on plankton.

Phytoplankton creates the most primary productivity in oceans, with macroalgae, cyanobacteria, and hydrophytes.

Plankton is in freshwater biomes, including lakes, ponds, rivers, and streams.

Streams and rivers

Streams and rivers are connected to ecosystems and can exhibit remarkable spatial heterogeneity. They contain salt in less than 1% concentration.

Headwaters of the river are cool, clear, and well-oxygenated.

Nutrient content and species diversity increase as the river travels towards the sea or a lake.

Water at river's mouth is murkiest from sediment accumulation, which affects light penetrance.

River mouths may have lower diversity, lower oxygen, and lower productivity.

Plant life in rivers and streams must *anchor tightly* to the riverbed.

Ponds and lakes

Lakes and ponds have *limited diversity* due to their *isolation* from other regions. They lack currents and have stable, permanent life forms.

In calmer waters, bottom-dwellers can be found that stay in place.

In fast-moving waters, nearly all animals are fish that traverse great distances.

Aquatic plants, algae, insects, mollusks, crustaceans, amphibians, and fishes may be in lakes.

Birds and reptiles like turtles, snakes, or crocodiles prey on these organisms.

Aquatic Biomes' Structures

Lake zones

Lakes are divided into four zones defined by their depth and distance from the shore.

Littoral zone includes shallow areas closest to shore, where warm water is penetrated by light.

Plants root themselves in the lakebed in this region and support animals such as mollusks, crustaceans, insects, amphibians, and small fishes.

Many larval organisms are reared in nurseries of the littoral zone.

Limnetic zone is the sunlit area in the open waters of lakes and is home to many plankton and fish. Most photosynthesis occurs here.

Profundal zone is below the limnetic zone in deeper waters with larger fish, turtles, and snakes.

Many birds dive into the profundal zone to capture prey.

There is little photosynthesis because sunlight cannot sufficiently penetrate the deeper waters.

Benthic zone is at the bottom of a pond or lake with soft sediment and little sunlight.

Benthic zone is inhabited by organisms that tolerate low oxygen levels, including worms, mollusks, and crustaceans.

Filter feeders thrive on the debris which falls from the higher zones.

Lake stratifications

In temperate latitudes, deep lakes are stratified depending on the season.

Surface waters are warm in summer due to the sun's heat, while the depths are cold.

Thermocline, a layer of abrupt temperature change, separates these layers.

In winter, this is reversed, with the depths remaining temperate due to insulation by surface ice and the surface being cold since it is closest to the frigid outside temperatures.

In fall and spring, changing temperatures cause mixing that returns the lake to a uniform temperature without a significant thermocline.

Lake animals adapt to seasonal changes and migrate to different depths for favorable conditions.

Oligotrophic and eutrophic lakes

Lakes can be classified from *oligotrophic* (nutrient-poor) to *eutrophic* (nutrient-rich).

Oligotrophic lakes cannot sustain much plant life and have low levels of primary productivity; consequently, fish dominates them.

Oligotrophic lakes have clear waters and are often in cold, alpine regions.

Eutrophic lakes have high productivity and can support many plants that outcompete fish.

Eutrophication produces massive algal blooms, which deplete oxygen during decomposition, creating *hypoxic* (i.e., lack of oxygen) conditions that kill animals.

An influx of nutrients can change an oligotrophic lake into a eutrophic lake.

Mesotrophic lakes have moderate nutrient levels and can sustain plant and animal life.

Continental shelf

Oceans are bordered by continents, each situated on a *continental shelf.*

Continental crust extends under the water for a distance from the coast.

After several hundred meters, the *continental crust* drops off rapidly, forming a steep, downward *continental slope.*

Continental rise follows the *continental slope;* contrary to the name, this region slopes downward, albeit less steeply than the slope.

The rise levels into the vast *abyssal plain,* the bottom of most of the world's oceans.

Prominent ridges and deep trenches mark it.

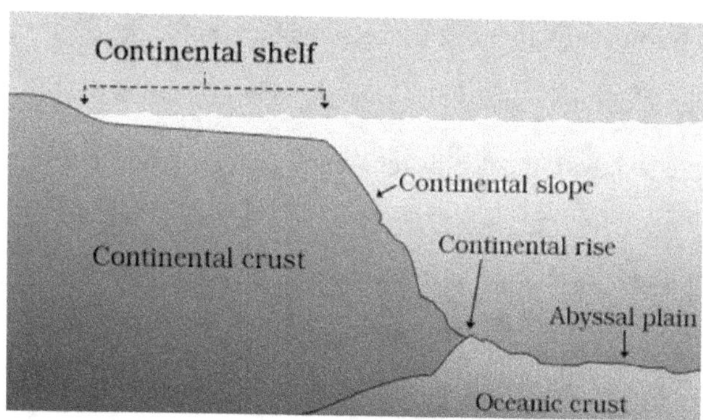

Oceans are characterized by the continental shelf with the continental crust sloping downward

Ocean zones

Ocean zones are much larger and more complex than lake zones.

Rather than the entire littoral zone, scientists refer to the *intertidal zone,* an area periodically covered and uncovered by water.

Changing sea levels due to tides presents a challenge to intertidal organisms.

Organisms must anchor themselves to rocks, hide in crevices or burrow in the sediment to avoid desiccation and being swept away.

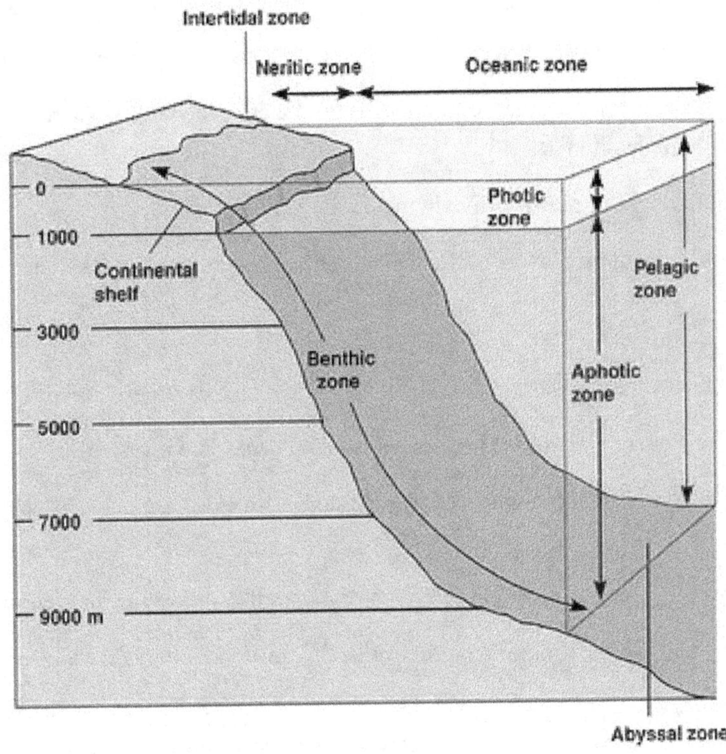

Ocean with zones at respective depths

Neritic zone

Neritic zone is where the water deepens past the intertidal zone, but the continental shelf continues below.

Neritic zone is highly productive because sunlight and nutrients are relatively abundant. It is well-oxygenated and has stable conditions, suitable for most ocean life.

Organisms from microscopic plankton to large fish are in the neritic zone and vast coral reefs.

Coastal zone marks the boundary between the shore and the open ocean.

Oceanic zone

Oceanic zone is when the continental shelf drops off into a slope; this marks the open seas.

It is vast and sustains various sea life, though relatively minor compared to the neritic zone.

The largest sea animals, whales, sharks, and giant fishes are in the oceanic zone, while smaller animals and plankton are in the surface waters.

Pelagic and photic zones

Pelagic zone has waters of the ocean that are neither close to the bottom nor the shore.

Pelagic waters are vertically stratified by light levels throughout neritic and oceanic zones.

Photic zone extends from the surface to about 1000 meters deep and is where photosynthesis occurs due to phytoplankton activity.

Fish, jellies, dolphins, and seaweed live in the photic zone.

Apex predators in the upper waters of the photic zone include sharks, mackerels, and tunas.

Aphotic zone

Aphotic zone (below the photic zone) is where no photosynthesis occurs because of darkness.

It extends to the abyssal plain 6,000 meters below and deeper into massive ocean trenches.

Aphotic zone is poorly lit and dominated by predators with excellent photoreceptors and low-light adaptations.

Prey organisms often have translucent or red coloring, well-disguised in dark waters.

Familiar squids and sperm whales are in this zone, but most inhabitants are poorly understood.

Carnivores, filter feeders, or scavengers feed on dead organisms falling from above.

Many animals release occasional flashes of light to communicate or attract prey at these depths.

Seabed

Benthic zone is the seabed, which may be exposed to air in the intertidal zone or thousands of meters below the surface at the abyssal plain of the oceanic zone.

Benthic organisms live on or in sediment, often anchoring to the underlying substrate.

Sediment may be sandy, rocky, muddy, or silty.

Seabed is covered with coral in many areas.

As marine snow, benthic organisms rely on organic and inorganic nutrients falling from above.

Oceanic zone and filter feeders

Intertidal, littoral, and neritic zones receive sunlight and support a varied food web with seaweed and filter feeders at the first trophic level.

Starfish, crustaceans, mollusks, and bottom-dwelling fish occupy the upper trophic levels.

Oceanic zone of the benthic zone receives no sunlight and is without photosynthetic organisms.

Instead, filter feeders and scavengers feed on marine snow.

Starfish, crustaceans, mollusks, and bottom-dwelling fish are on the continental slope and rise.

There is much diversity of microbes but little *macrofauna* on the pitch-black abyssal plain.

Sponges, worms, sea lilies, and other invertebrates; a few filter feeders and scavengers (i.e., feed on dead organisms) are in the oceanic zone.

Hydrothermal vents

Oceanic zones have intense pressure and are extremely cold, except where *hydrothermal vents* expel superheated, sulfurous water.

Hydrothermal vents support *chemosynthetic bacteria*, tube worms, and clams.

Hydrothermal vents are a fissure on the seabed where geothermally heated water discharges.

Hydrothermal vents are active *volcanoes* where *tectonic plates* move apart on the seabed.

Hydrothermal vents have been hypothesized for *life formation* and survival of primitive life.

Notes for active learning

Biodiversity

Biodiversity preservation

Conservation biology applies ecology and social sciences to preserving Earth's biodiversity.

Conservation biology stresses that biodiversity is vital for humans and organisms and strives to prevent extinction due to habitat destruction, pollution, invasive species, and overexploitation.

Conservation biology emphasizes practical applications, but there is an appreciable effort focused on the intrinsic value of nature to human cultures.

Species and genetic biodiversity

Biodiversity describes several concepts.

Species diversity is the variety of species living in each area.

5 to 100 million species exist on Earth, and only a fraction has been cataloged.

Genetic diversity describes alleles within the gene pool.

Genetic diversity is the ultimate measure of biodiversity but is challenging to evaluate.

Genetic diversity maintains fitness and adaptability.

Loss of genetic variation is an *extinction risk*.

Landscape diversity is the interacting ecosystems in a region.

Homogenous landscapes support a limited diversity of species, like isolated landscapes.

Biodiversity hotspots

Biodiversity hotspots are regions with unusually high species concentrations.

Biodiversity is not evenly distributed but is highest in the tropics and lowest at the poles.

Biodiversity hotspots may be detected by widespread field studies providing accurate counts of species diversity but are labor-intensive.

Conservation biologists focus on *biodiversity hotspots* to maximize effectiveness.

Hotspot regions are a fraction of Earth's area but may contain 60% of all species.

Examples of biodiversity hotspots are the Mediterranean, Amazon rainforest, and Madagascar.

Biodiversity hotspots are characterized by endemic species unique to that area.

Biodiversity frontiers such as the deep sea have more species than previously suspected.

Value of biodiversity

Biodiversity provides *ecological services*; economic, scientific, aesthetic, or ethical.

Diversity strengthens an ecosystem and makes it healthier, increasing the efficiency of services.

For example, a greater diversity of crop plants increases yield, while greater fish diversity keeps fisheries stable and productive.

Natural products are essential for manufacturing material goods.

For example, plastics, rubber, and lumber are materials derived from the environment.

Economic benefits include food, oxygen, clothing, medicine, fuel, and consumer products.

Rainforests have billions of dollars of potential medications, and many have been discovered.

Fossil fuels, such as coal, oil, and natural gas, are generated by decomposed organisms.

Sustainable ecosystems

Nature offers valuable *pest control, pollination, soil maintenance*, and *biogeochemical cycles*.

Without technology, humans rely on the environment to purify water, break down pollutants, trap carbon dioxide, provide oxygen, and recycle organic compounds into edible food.

Some ecosystem services are lifesaving.

River and wetland ecosystems are buffers against flooding, storm surges, and extreme weather.

Trees are important because they are the largest providers of O_2 and remove atmospheric CO_2.

Trees and plants hold soil and prevent erosion that clogs reservoirs, creates landslides, chokes coastal ecosystems, and destroys fisheries.

Deforestation worsens the issue of global warming by reducing the carbon dioxide sink.

Conservation Biology

Ecotourism

Tourism of natural environments (or *ecotourism*) is a multi-billion-dollar industry.

Several cities and countries base an entire economy on ecotourism.

If these natural resources are threatened, it causes debilitating economic collapses.

Humans are deeply impacted by aesthetic loss and ethical conflict.

Erosion and extinctions threaten plants, animals, and natural habitats, thus, human culture.

Causes of extinction

Significant threats to biodiversity cause species extinctions.

Research shows that potent catalysts of extinction are habitat loss, introduced or invasive species, overexploitation of flora and fauna, and pollution.

Habitat loss may be caused by destruction, fragmentation, or degradation.

Typical habitat loss includes human destruction.

For example, clearing forests for agriculture, draining wetlands, diverting rivers, building dams, mining, trawling ocean floors with fishing nets, and urbanization cause habitat loss.

Unfortunately, biodiversity hotspots are often the most threatened by habitat loss.

For example, tropical rainforests are being cleared at an unsustainable rate.

Threatened biomes include grasslands, deciduous forests, wetlands, estuaries, and oceans.

Habitat degradation and fragmentation

Habitat degradation is indirect habitat loss by pollution, climate change, and exotic species.

Habitat fragmentation usually results from urban sprawl and infrastructure, which can divide an area into fragments too small to support a species.

Fragmentation hinders migration, which is crucial for the maintenance of diversity.

For example, an invasive herbivore weakens grasses used as a habitat by native species.

Exotic species are introduced accidentally or deliberately into new ecosystems.

Human circumvention of natural barriers transports alien species to new environments.

Ecosystems evolve with their native organisms in balance; introducing new species disrupts the food chain and may lead to extinction.

Unsustainable exploitation

Overexploitation is when harvesting wild populations become unsustainable.

For example, animals may be overexploited for food, hides, furs, ivory, pets, or sport.

One-third of fisheries are overexploited; tigers and elephants have been hunted near extinction.

Plants are typically overexploited for food, building materials, medicine, and agriculture.

Overexploitation hinders an ecosystem's ability to recover even decades after it ceases.

Climate Change

Soil and water pollution

Pollution is the introduction of harmful elements into an ecosystem; it results in greenhouse gases, acid deposition, disease, and other ill effects.

For example, air pollution is caused by exhaust from factories and motor vehicles.

Soil and water pollution typically result from agricultural, industrial, and sewage runoff, containing pesticides, heavy metals, oil, fertilizers, animal wastes, and toxic chemicals.

Littering trash is physical pollution that affects the land and water.

However, pollution may take the abstract form of *light* and *noise pollution*.

Light, noise and genetic pollution

Noise pollution interferes with natural communication between animals, particularly sonar.

Over-illumination in cities disorients animals and impacts their circadian rhythms, migration patterns, and reproduction.

Genetic pollution is caused by human interference with the genetic diversity of a population.

Genetic pollution can destabilize the population, decimate its fitness, and even decimate it.

For example, breeding or engineering hybrids, homogenizing the gene pool, or introducing species that affect the natural (i.e., wild-type or native) population.

Extinction

Extinction is exacerbated by *climate change*.

For example, global warming melts ice caps, increasing seas and destroying coastal habitats.

Global warming warms the seas and increases pH, threatening many aquatic species.

Coral reefs are suffering from temperature and acidity shock.

Global warming promotes the growth of pests and pathogens, increasing disease rates.

Climate change alters *global weather patterns*, causing extreme weather events which destroy habitats and kill wild populations.

Suitable climate regions shift rapidly, faster than organisms migrate or adapt; allowing exotic species to outcompete native species in changing environments.

Indicator species

Indicator species studies are a straightforward but sometimes misleading method, highlighting certain conditions of an ecosystem that may otherwise go undetected.

For example, the presence of spotted owls indicates a stable, old-growth forest, while the bleaching of corals indicates acidic waters.

Indicator species are often *keystone species*, which can be valuable targets for conservation since they prevent the extinction of several species.

Endemic, rare, and endangered species merit the immediate attention of conservation efforts. Many of these organisms become *flagship species,* adored by humans for looks or symbolism.

Flagship and umbrella species

Flagship species are mostly mammals, such as polar bears and giant pandas, and can be a powerful tool for mobilizing conservation.

Many vitally important invertebrate and plant species are ignored in favor of flagship species.

Umbrella species spread over habitat range, often flagship, keystone, or indicator species.

Because the umbrella species has a wide range and is easily observable, targeting the conservation of the umbrella species assures the conservation of species.

For example, spotted owls require habitat protection and old-growth forests in North America. Old-growth forests have hundreds of species that benefit from spotted owl conservation.

Conservation

Preservation and remediation

Conservation efforts use *cost-benefit analysis*, statistical models, and detailed proposals.

For example, *population viability analysis* measures how much habitat a species needs. This guides conservationists to balance the costs of habitat preservation with species benefits.

Governments take on conservation efforts if they are efficient and effective. An effective way to involve governments is by describing the practical, monetary advantages of acting; providing specific actions requested.

IUCN Red List describes the conservation status of thousands of organisms, with categories such as *least concern, vulnerable, endangered,* and *extinct.*

For example, governmental conservation efforts include hunting and fishing laws, creating nature preserves, sustainable building practices, and development restrictions.

Regulating activities

Hunting, poaching, and fishing may be banned outright or only restricted for a species.

Sustainable hunting and fishing practices aim to prevent the overexploitation of biodiversity.

Conservation aimed at *invasive* or *introduced species* often culls populations of problem species. This can be costly, difficult, and often requires ongoing effort.

Introducing a *new* exotic species which preys on the problematic one can be effective if done carefully, and scientists can be confident it will not exacerbate.

Habitat loss is the leading cause of extinction; *habitat preservation* is critical for conservation.

One challenging but essential way to protect biodiversity is to restore a degraded habitat to its former health.

Habitat restoration

Habitat restoration falls under *restoration ecology*, studying strategies to restore ecosystems.

Planting vegetation may reduce erosion; for example, controlled burns can clear species.

The goal of habitat restoration is to return the habitat to its natural state and ensure it can be maintained without human intervention.

Habitat restoration often takes the form of nature preserves, where species and their environment are protected from human interference.

Wildlife corridors are a recent technique to connect habitats fragmented by land development.

Preserves and *corridors* are often selected using *gap analysis,* which overlays land-use maps with species maps to highlight areas where biodiversity is high but unprotected or fragmented.

For example, habitat loss can be prevented by low-impact development, reduction of logging and mining, and pollution control.

Of course, it is better to be proactive rather than reactive.

Pollution controls

Pollution control is a facet of conservation that received significant attention and international agreement in the *Kyoto Protocol* (1997).

Kyoto Protocol treaty targeted climate change, a critical frontier of conservation, primarily in reducing greenhouse gases and pollutants.

For example, pollution can be mitigated by enacting eco-friendly policies, waste management, cleanup, recycling, and innovative technologies that reduce old, harmful substances.

Ecosystem conservation

The most effective conservation is *in situ,* occurring in the ecosystem.

Ex-situ conservation occurs outside the original ecosystem and may include relocating species to a new environment, breeding them in zoos, and re-releasing them into the wild.

Gene banks are a focus of *ex-situ conservation.*

Scientists maintain plant seeds, cuttings, and animal gametes, so these organisms may be reintroduced if the species become endangered or extinct.

Notes for active learning

Notes for active learning

REVIEW

Populations
&
Community Ecology

Ecology of Populations

Population Growth Models

Population Diagrams

Population Size Constraints

Community Ecology

Predation–Prey Interactions

Symbiosis

Community Dynamics

Succession and Biodiversity

Page intentionally left blank

Ecology of Populations

Ecological hierarchy

Humans have been studying the natural world for hundreds of years, but the term *ecology* was coined in the 19th century by the German zoologist Ernst Haeckel (1834-1919).

Ecology studies organisms' distribution, abundance, and interactions with one another and the environment.

Widespread acceptance of the theory of evolution significantly advanced the field.

Evolution allowed scientists to understand how ecological pressures such as natural selection shape the environment.

Ecology has modernized with rigorous, comprehensive studies and sophisticated statistics.

Modern ecology includes several fields (e.g., conservation, agriculture, and social science).

Ecology is hierarchical, studied at many levels from cellular to the *biosphere,* the entire region of Earth in which organisms reside.

Most ecologists begin their study at the *organismal level.*

Habitats and community

Habitat is an organism's physical and biological surroundings, including nearby organisms.

Species members live in groups called *populations,* which occupy the same region.

Community includes the populations of all species in each locale.

For example, a freshwater lake is a community of algae, plants, fish, and microorganisms.

Organisms and their interactions are *biotic factors.*

Ecosystems and biosphere

Ecosystem includes all biotic factors as well as the physical environment.

For example, in a lake, the ecosystem includes the populations, water salinity, temperature, pH, density, light level, soil composition, and other *abiotic factors.*

Ecosystems with similar *abiotic factors* make a *biome,* usually defined by its climate.

For example, a tropical rainforest is a biome that includes all hot, humid ecosystems supporting a high diversity of life.

Collectively, biomes comprise the *biosphere.*

Population ecology and dispersal

Population ecology studies growth, abundance, and distribution.

Population size is denoted as N, the total number of individuals.

Population size concerns *population density* or the number of individuals per given area unit.

Population dispersal is how density is patterned over a range.

Populations may be spread uniformly, randomly, or clumped.

Ecologists often study the changes in population distribution across space or time.

Physiological stress

Population is densest near the center of its range and sparse at the edge.

Zone of physiological stress is the edge because it has suboptimal conditions for the species.

Physiological stressors may include extreme temperatures, inadequate water, or pollution.

Species' theoretical range is the multitude of physiological stressors it can tolerate.

Species may restrict this range due to *biological stressors* like *competition* and *predation*.

Zone of intolerance is beyond this, where no species can survive.

Environmental resistance

Biotic and *abiotic resources* are often in limited supply, and the environment can only support some organisms in *carrying capacity* (K).

Populations approaching carrying capacity and depleted resources encounter *environmental resistance,* and growth slows.

Environmental resistance is density-dependent, becoming *restricted as growth increases.*

Stable populations do not maximize biotic potential but remain under carrying capacity.

Carrying capacity

Carrying capacity is determined by the available water, space, food, light, and other factors.

However, overshooting carrying capacity can be valuable, provided the population can introduce new individuals before crashing.

Carrying capacity is an essential regulator of *population size* and a powerful driver of *evolution.*

Populations respond to carrying capacity by *expanding their range* or *evolving adaptations,* which relieves some carrying capacity restrictions.

Populations cannot evade carrying capacity indefinitely, and *high mortality* results if overshot.

Limiting factors

Stressors are *limiting factors*, conditions that limit the growth or abundance of a population.

Density-independent limiting factors are independent of population density (e.g., light availability and precipitation).

Density-dependent limiting factors become severe as population density increases.

Density-dependent factors include competition, disease, parasites, and food scarcity.

Population cycle

Factors typically fluctuate and drive a *population cycle,* a cyclic change in the population size.

Population size (N) over time can be predicted by:

> *natality* (birth rate) and

> *mortality* (death rate).

Together, natality and mortality calculate the *intrinsic rate of natural increase* (r).

$$r = \frac{(\text{birth rate} - \text{death rate})}{N}$$

However, population increase is usually subject to many factors.

For example, population ecologists must consider the *immigration* of individuals into or the *emigration* of others out of the population.

Notes for active learning

Notes for active learning

Population Growth Models

Discrete growth

Population growth typically exhibits one of two patterns.

Discrete growth (*discrete breeding* or *discrete reproduction*) is when organisms breed at a particular time.

They may breed once as *semelparous* or reproduce as *iteroparous* yearly.

Discrete growth produces *discrete generations,* in which the adult generation reproduces and soon dies, leaving behind the next generation.

Discrete generations result in a population with *one generation* at any given time.

Iteroparity (i.e., multiple reproductive cycles) produces *overlapping generations*; an elderly generation lives simultaneously as a reproductive generation and a sexually immature generation. At least two generations can be observed at any time.

Continuous growth

Continuous growth is when organisms reproduce without regard for a specific breeding season.

Iteroparous populations exhibit continuous growth and have overlapping generations.

Most organisms do not fit into one pattern and instead exhibit a combination of the two.

For example, plants reproduce sexually each year but asexually at any time.

Exponential growth

Exponential growth often occurs in iteroparous (i.e., multiple reproductive cycles) populations with overlapping generations and is represented by a J-shaped *exponential growth curve*.

Populations enter exponential growth at a critical size when *growth accelerates rapidly*.

Lag phase is the first phase when growth is slow because the population is small.

Biotic potential

Biotic potential considers the number of offspring produced by each reproductive event (clutch size), the frequency and the total number of reproductive events, offspring survival rate, and the age at which an individual reaches sexual maturity.

Maximum growth populations fulfill biotic potential with *no limiting factors hindrance*.

Populations reach biotic potential with ample *space, resources,* and the absence of *predation*.

Logistic growth curves

S-shaped (*sigmoidal-shaped*) *logistic growth curve* is growth under environmental resistance.

Logistic growth (*S*-shaped) curve: $\frac{\Delta N}{\Delta t} = rN\left(\frac{K-N}{K}\right)$

The first portion of the curve is *exponential*, with *lag* and *exponential phases*.

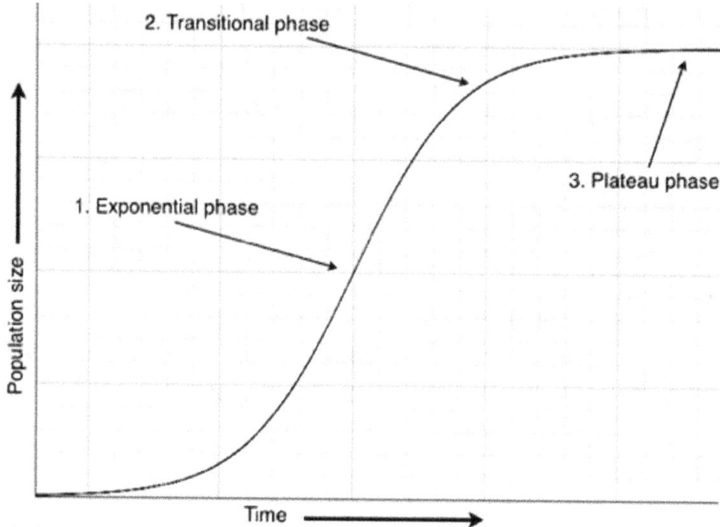

S-shaped logistic growth curve of population growth with environmental resistance

Stable equilibrium

Populations enter a *stable equilibrium* phase with *minimal growth at carrying capacity*.

During stable equilibrium, *natality and mortality* are roughly *equal*.

Deceleration phase

Populations eventually reach a *transitional* or *deceleration phase* when the *birth rate falls below the death rate* due to resource competition, predation, disease, and other density-dependent factors. At this point, growth slows.

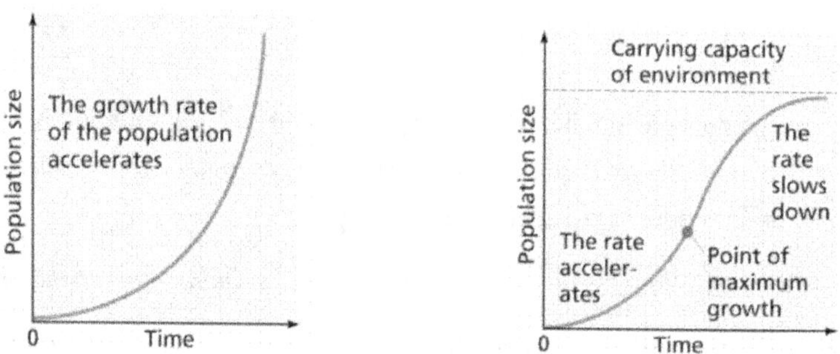

Exponential (unrestricted) growth (left) and logistic (restricted) growth (right)

Population Diagrams

Age structure diagrams

Age structure diagrams represent the abundance of each gender and age group of a population.

Horizontal bars represent the number of individuals in each age group.

A population with overlapping generations typically exhibits pre-reproductive, reproductive, and post-reproductive generations.

Expanding population diagrams

Pyramid shape diagrams show expanding populations with high birth rates and exponential growth.

Pre-reproductive generation is the largest because offspring are rapidly reproduced, while the reproductive generation is intermediate.

Post-reproductive generation is the smallest as the elderly die.

Stable and declining population diagrams

Bell-shaped diagrams represent a relatively *stable population* in which the pre-reproductive and reproductive generations are roughly equal, and the post-reproductive generation is smaller by a narrow margin.

Urn-shaped diagrams indicate a *declining population.*

Individuals from the reproductive generation enter the post-reproductive generation and continually die, while the pre-reproductive generation is too small to sustain growth.

The post-reproductive generation is the largest because of few new individuals.

Population diagrams

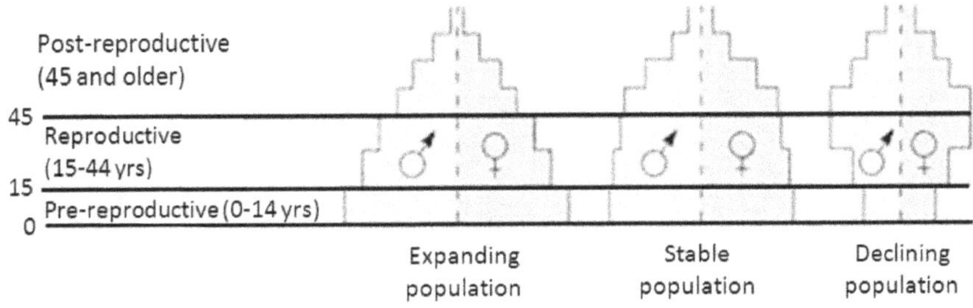

Age structure diagrams: pyramid (left), bell-shaped (center), urn-shaped (right).

Mortality patterns

Predictions in demography ascertain the probability, based on age, that an individual will die before their upcoming birthday.

This information signifies the survivorship of specific age-based populations.

A life table (*mortality* or *actuarial tables*) is used to make these predictions.

Life tables

Actuarial science uses two varieties of life tables.

Period table calculates mortality rates during a set period for a specified population.

Cohort life table (or *generation life table*) represents a population's overall mortality rates.

Cohort is a group born at the same time and aging together.

Life tables track cohorts over their lifetime.

Region	1990	1995	2000	2005	2010	2012	MDG target 2015	Decline (percent) 1990–2012	Annual rate of reduction (percent)		
									1990–2012	1990–2000	2000–2012
Developed regions	15	11	10	8	7	6	5	57	3.8	3.9	3.8
Developing regions	99	93	83	69	57	53	33	47	2.9	1.8	3.8
Northern Africa	73	57	43	31	24	22	24	69	5.4	5.3	5.5
Sub-Saharan Africa	177	170	155	130	106	98	59	45	2.7	1.4	3.8
Latin America and the Caribbean	54	43	32	25	23	19	18	65	4.7	5.1	4.4
Caucasus and Central Asia	73	73	62	49	39	36	24	50	3.2	1.6	4.5
Eastern Asia	53	46	37	24	16	14	18	74	6.1	3.7	8.0
Excluding China	27	33	31	20	17	15	9	45	2.7	−1.2	5.9
Southern Asia	126	109	92	76	63	58	42	54	3.5	3.1	3.9
Excluding India	125	109	93	78	66	61	42	51	3.3	3.0	3.5
South-eastern Asia	71	58	48	38	33	30	24	57	3.9	3.9	3.8
Western Asia	65	54	42	34	26	25	22	62	4.4	4.4	4.5
Oceania	74	70	67	64	58	55	25	26	1.4	1.0	1.7
World	90	85	75	63	52	48	30	47	2.9	1.7	3.8

UN life table indicates mortality levels and trends for children under five years

Survivorship curves

Survivorship is how many individuals remain alive at a given time.

Three general survivorship curves are:

> ***Type I survivorship curve*** shows a long curve with a relatively short drop-off near the end, in which most individuals survive until old age. For example, the human population.

> ***Type II survivorship curve***, which is negative and linear, shows individuals dying at a constant lifespan rate. For example, some birds and lizards.

> ***Type III survivorship curve*** is when most individuals die at an early age. However, those who survive tend to live for a relatively long time.

It is opposite a Type I curve and seen in many invertebrates, plants, and fish.

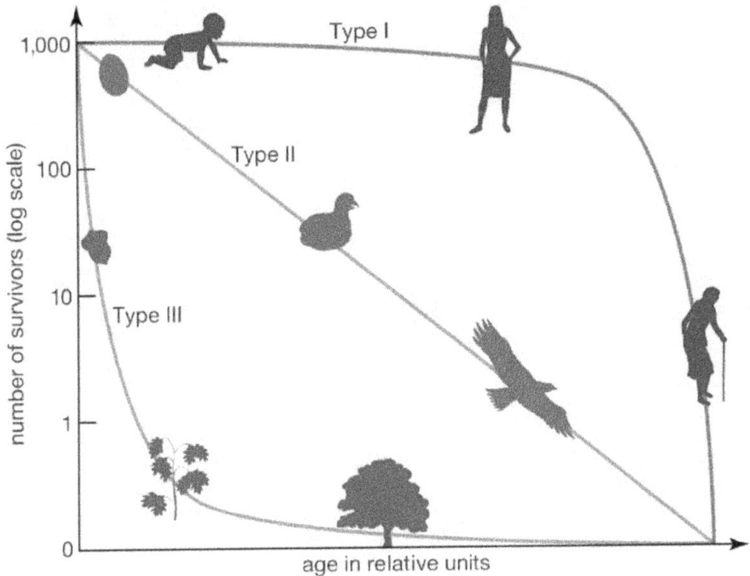

Survivorship curves comparing type I, type II, and type III organisms

Notes for active learning

Population Size Constraints

Intrinsic and extrinsic factors

Density-dependent and *density-independent* factors regulate population*s*.

Factors may be *intrinsic* (i.e., within the population) or *extrinsic.*

Intrinsic factors include the behavior and anatomy of the species.

Extrinsic factors include climate, habitat, and other organisms.

Exponential and *logistic* growth curve models are a straightforward view of population growth that only considers *classic limiting factors.*

Natural populations may be affected by hundreds of complex and interrelated factors.

These are usually *intrinsic factors,* such as social behavior, influencing how competition proceeds and individuals immigrating or emigrating.

For example, populations may actively recruit or exclude members due to territoriality.

Straightforward models have *difficulty predicting randomness.* Populations deviate from expectations by chance or unpredictable events, like natural disasters.

Life history patterns

Ecologists divide organisms into two major life-history patterns: *r-selection* and *K-selection.*

Most species are not strictly r-strategists or K-strategists; it is typical for a species to exhibit both characteristics.

Organisms may be able to shift strategy in response to environmental factors.

r-selection growth

r-selected species attempt to *maximize* their *rate of natural increase.*

They typically overshoot carrying capacity, causing the population to crash suddenly.

Therefore, population growth may show *severe fluctuations.*

Opportunistic species, typically r-strategists, rapidly seize the opportunity to proliferate.

r-selected species are often the *first to colonize* a habitat and do well in *unstable environments* subject to *density-independent factors.*

They reach sexual maturity early and reproduce quickly, maximizing reproduction before death.

r-selected species may reproduce once; semelparity (single reproductive event), a common characteristic of r-strategists.

They produce many offspring simultaneously because infant mortality rates are high.

r-selected organisms have *short lifespans* and must *quickly adapt* to new environments.

K-selection growth

K-selected species attempt to *maintain* their *rate of natural increase*.

Equilibrium species exist near the carrying capacity at a state of equilibrium.

Unlike r-strategists, K-strategists are specialists uniquely suited to their environment.

K-strategists typically enter a new habitat after r-strategists colonize it; making them successful but vulnerable to disturbances.

K-strategists reach sexual maturity slowly, but they can live long.

They can reproduce several times throughout their lifespan, making them *iteroparous* (*multiple reproductive cycles during their lifetime*).

K-selected species are typically large and invest considerable energy in caring for offspring, which they rear one at a time.

Human population growth

Human population is in the *exponential phase of a J-shaped* growth curve.

Global population is currently increasing by about 80 million people per year.

Technological advances, increased food supply, disease reduction, and habitat expansion have fueled this tremendous growth.

Estimates predict that the world population will level off this century at 8 and 10 billion.

Some claim this is a vast underestimate, and that the human population may reach 14 billion by the end of the 21st century.

In the mid-20th century, developed countries had a significant decline in mortality rates, followed by a decline in birth rates.

Currently, the growth rate in developed nations is about 0.1%.

Their age structures are relatively stable, with some countries exhibiting declining populations.

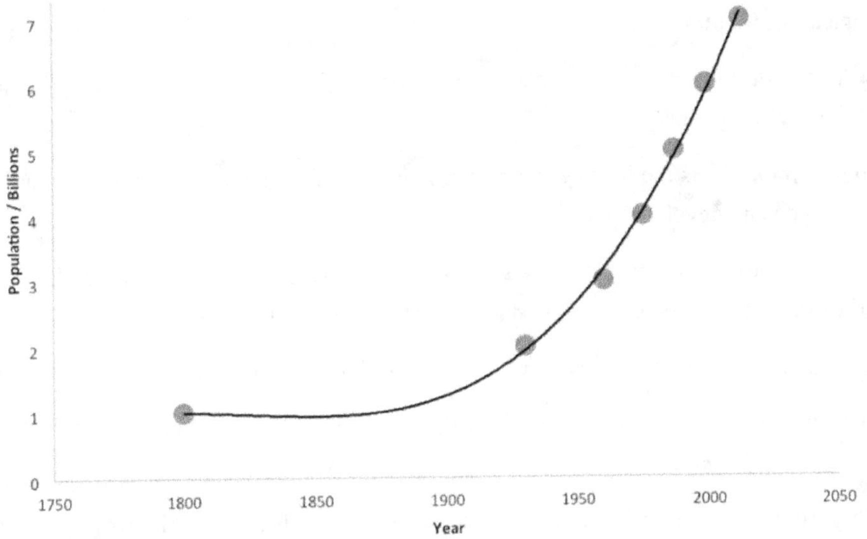

Human population growth with exponential population growth between 1800 and 2020

Developing countries' growth

In the coming years, nearly all population growth will be seen in less developed countries, especially in Africa, Asia, and Latin America.

Growth rate in these countries is lower than at its peak of 2.5% in the 1960s.

Population growth includes family planning, birth control, and producing fewer children.

However, due to cultural attitudes and a high infant mortality rate in underdeveloped nations, convincing people to have fewer children or delay childbearing is difficult.

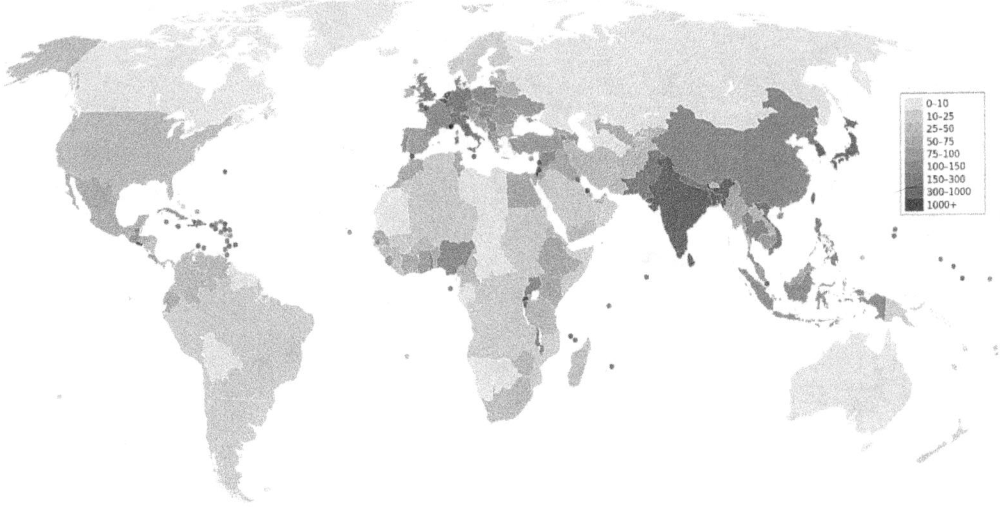

This world map indicates the average population density per km²

Ecological footprints

Growing populations of less developed countries and *high consumption* by developed countries stress the environment.

Ecological footprint is the land required to sustain an individual's lifestyle; it is unsustainable for developed and developing nations.

Ecological footprint includes the area where people live, farmland for food, factories for material goods, and distances that products travel to reach consumers.

For example, an American family consumes and produces waste for thirty people in India.

Developed countries account for *one-fourth of the world population* but provide 90% of the hazardous waste production.

Intense resource consumption affects the cycling of chemicals and contributes to pollution and species extinction.

Without drastic reductions in the collective ecological footprint, humans may overshoot carrying capacity and experience catastrophic disease, famine, and density-dependent factors.

Community Ecology

Communities

Community ecology studies the composition, diversity, interactions, and relationships between populations and how these characteristics change.

Community includes all interacting populations within an environment.

Community may be large (*entire forest*) or small (*bacterial community in an animal's gut*).

Because of this variability in scale, it is not easy to delineate the boundaries of a community.

Community composition

Community composition is constantly in flux due to natural selection, migration, environmental changes, and random chance.

Many communities fluctuate regularly with the seasons.

For example, tundra is inhospitable in winter but supports plant and animal life in the summer.

Communities may be transient, like an animal corpse, which supports a community until decay is complete.

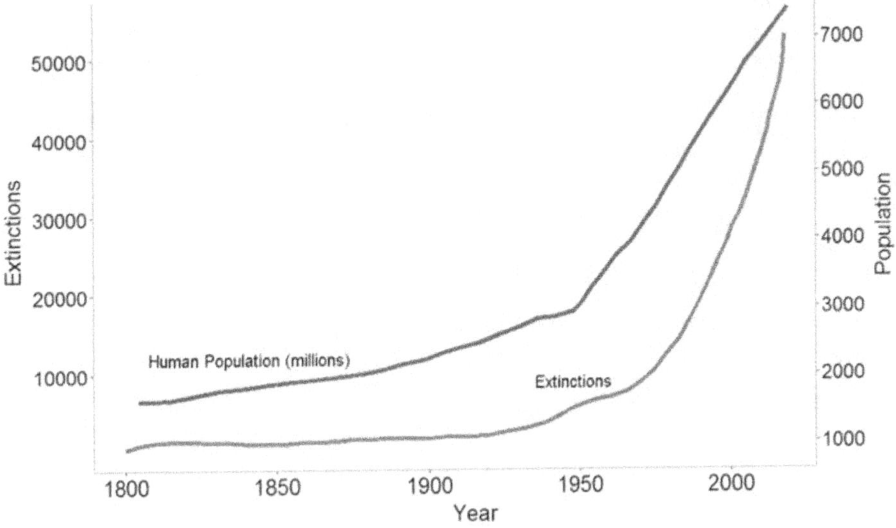

Correlation between human population levels and the number of species lost to extinction

Community models

Models were proposed in the 20th century to articulate the concept of a community.

Frederic Clements (1874-1945) described a *holistic theory* in which the community acts together as a *superorganism*.

Henry Gleason (1882-1975) proposed the *individualistic theory,* which states that each population can inhabit a community due to its unique adaptations.

Individualistic theory proposes that a species' range is due to its tolerance to physiological stressors and is independent of the species' distribution.

Biodiversity is a product of chance and not of inherent characteristics of the species.

Stephen Hubbell (b. 1942) proposes a *neutral theory* that species adapt, grow, and disperse.

Differences are negligible, and variation seen in communities is due to *randomness*.

Likely, none of these models are precisely correct.

Communities are affected by biotic and abiotic factors, as well as by random chance.

Community structure

Species composition (or *species richness*) is the number of species within a community without information about their relative abundances.

Relative abundance is a species' evenness relative to the size of the community.

For example, a forest with 40 yellow poplars and 40 American elms has more species evenness than a forest with 70 poplars and 10 elms.

Together, evenness and richness describe the *species diversity* of a community.

The most diverse communities have a high level of richness and evenness.

Community structure depends on abiotic factors and complex interactions between populations.

Niche theory

Niche theory describes how organisms and populations fit into the community.

Ecological niche is an organism's role in its community, including habitat, resources consumed, and interactions with other organisms.

For example, two deer species may occupy the same geographic range but inhabit different niches because they feed on distinct species of plants.

Fundamental niche is the place an organism occupies without competition from other species.

Organisms are usually limited to a *realized niche* (or *restricted niche*) to avoid overlapping with other organisms.

Species typically have niche overlap in the middle region where intense competition occurs.

For example, one barnacle species may live on rocks exposed to the full range of tides, making their fundamental niche the entire tidal area.

However, a second barnacle species may be capable of out-competing the first but can live in the lower tidal region where desiccation is minimal.

This forces the first species into a niche that only includes the higher tidal region.

Generalists *vs.* specialists

Generalists, such as humans, can occupy a variety of niches.

They quickly adapt to a new niche if the current one is threatened.

Organisms have developed strategies to maximize success under niche theory constraints.

Specialists become highly adapted to a single niche.

Population interactions are complex, including resource competition, predation, coevolution, and symbiotic relationships.

Competition between populations

Interspecific competition is when species utilize a limited resource.

Competitive exclusion principle is that no two species simultaneously occupy the same niche.

Over time, one population replaces the other or evolves to occupy different niches.

Natural selection favors adaptations that minimize competition.

Resource partitioning

Resource partitioning is when two species occupy the same habitat but pursue slightly different resources or secure resources differently, minimizing competition and maximizing success.

For example, birds inhabit the same tree in different tree zones to avoid competition.

When bird species are separated, they have intermediate beak sizes, but when forced together, they diversify and develop beaks of many sizes.

Character displacement, or a *niche shift*, is a powerful form of evolution.

For example, flocks of swallows, swifts, and martins fly and eat the same insects but use different nesting sites.

Predator–Prey Interactions

Predation

Predation is a community interaction when one organism feeds on another.

Predation includes carnivores killing prey and filter feeders that strain microorganisms from the water, parasites that feed on a host, and herbivores that eat plants.

Herbivores are *grazers* (grass eaters) and *browsers* (leaf eaters), animals that eat part of their prey, weakening it, similar to *parasitic relationships*.

Predator-prey relationships in the food web may fluctuate.

Predator-prey cycling

Predator-prey population densities show *peaks and valleys*, with the predator population often lagging slightly behind prey.

Population densities fluctuate because the predator can overconsume the prey, which causes the prey population to decline, closely followed by the predator population.

It may be the opposite, in which the prey cannot keep pace with the prey population, causing the prey to *overshoot carrying capacity* and *crash*.

In many cases, several scenarios affect predator-prey cycling.

For example, the snowshoe hare and the Canadian lynx exhibit cycling, affected by predation and the hare's food supply.

Grouse populations cycle, perhaps because the lynx switches to grouse when hare populations decline, evidence that predators and prey do not usually exist as simple two-species systems.

Coevolution

Predator-prey interactions drive *coevolution,* in which one species evolves in response to the adaptation of another. Prey has evolved several predator defenses.

Crypsis is a common adaptation that allows an organism to escape predator detection. It may include camouflage, hiding behavior, or *mimicry* (imitation of another species).

Batesian mimicry is when one vulnerable species (the mimic) imitates another (the model) with successful antipredator defenses.

For example, the harmless corn snake exhibits similar coloration to the venomous copperhead.

Mullerian mimicry is when several species, with some defense mechanism, coevolved to have similar coloration serving as a universal warning.

This warning is *aposematic coloration.*

Prey may have passive defenses that make prey difficult, unpalatable, or fatal.

This may include large body size, sharp spines, tough skin or shells, and a foul odor.

Predation defenses

Defenses against predation may be active, such as fleeing, frightening, or fighting a predator.

Active defenses are more costly in energy but can quickly adapt to a situation and are effective.

Coevolution need not be competitive, as many beneficial relationships result.

For example, pollination used millions of years of evolution between flowers and pollinators.

Flowers have evolved energy-rich nectar and coloration and pheromones, attracting pollinators.

Pollinators have evolved anatomy well adapted for nectar consumption and pollen transfer.

This coevolution is an example of a *symbiotic relationship.*

Symbiosis

Symbiotic relationships

Symbiosis is a relationship between species involving:

> *parasitism*

> *commensalism*

> *mutualism*

Symbiosis is an intimate, often permanent, association between members of two populations that may (or may not) be beneficial or *obligatory*.

One or both organisms cannot survive without the other.

Parasitism

Parasitism is when an organism (the parasite) derives benefits to another's (the host) detriment.

This relationship benefits the parasite at the host's expense and allows the parasite to live with minimal energy expenditure.

For example, tapeworms live in the intestines of animals, causing illness.

Parasites may be *ectoparasites*, which cling to the exterior of hosts using special appendages, or *endoparasites,* which live in the host.

Parasites occur in all kingdoms of life. Pathogenic bacteria and viruses are parasites.

Many parasites have several hosts.

Primary host is the main source of nutrition, while the *secondary host* may serve as a vector to transport the parasite to other hosts.

Parasitoids invariably kill their host, unlike parasites, which usually permit the host to live.

Commensalism

Commensalism is when one species benefits and the other is neither benefitted nor harmed.

It is challenging to determine commensalism because classification must determine that one organism is unaffected.

For example, barnacles on a whale could be considered commensalism, but this may be parasitism because they slow the whale.

Commensalism is when plants disperse seeds by sticking to an animal's fur. The animal is neither harmed nor benefited, but the plant has the advantage of broader seed distribution.

Ecologists argue that any relationship between species has subtle parasitism or commensalism.

Some relationships are so loose that it is difficult to classify them as true commensalism.

However, relationships that may be defined as commensalism include insects on animals for transport and crustaceans inhabiting the discarded shells of organisms.

Mutualism

Mutualism is a cooperative relationship that benefits each, provided the relationship is balanced.

The imbalance is commonly seen in mutualistic relationships, whereby one individual violates the terms of the relationship to gain an unfair advantage.

A classic mutualistic relationship is between fungi and algae.

For example, mycorrhizae of plant roots and fungi are common mutualists, in which the fungus provides inorganic minerals to the plant in exchange for organic nutrients.

Fungus provides anchorage and absorption for the alga, while the alga provides photosynthesis; together, they form a *lichen.*

Essential mutualism

Plant–fungus mutualism is often not obligatory because each organism can survive without the relationship.

By contrast, the relationship between ant colonies and the bullhorn acacia tree is necessary for the acacia's survival.

The ants are protected within the tree and receive nutrients, while the ants defend against herbivores and plants that might block light to the tree.

If the ants are killed, the tree is quickly overrun and dies.

Cleaning symbiosis is another common mutualism.

For example, crustaceans, fish, and birds clean ectoparasites from other animals, improving the client's health while providing the cleaner with food.

However, cleaners may feed on the client's tissues, turning this into a case of parasitism.

Mutualistic relationships may involve:

exchange of resources (e.g., *mycorrhizae*),

service for a resource (e.g., cleaning symbiosis, pollination), or

exchange of services (e.g., sea anemones and clownfish protecting one another from their respective predators).

Community Dynamics

Community development

Ecological succession is experienced by changing communities.

This process can be observed over years or vast periods of geologic time.

Primary succession occurs after an event exposes a substrate that never supported life.

This may be bare rock left after a glacier moves or a lava flow after volcanic activity.

Pioneer species are the organisms first to colonize a newly exposed habitat.

They are opportunistic, r-selected species that can tolerate harsh conditions.

In primary succession, moss and lichens are the pioneer species, which die and leave behind organic matter that accumulates into the soil.

After the soil is deposited, grass grows, followed by shrubs and then trees.

Herbivores enter the community, closely followed by their predators.

As succession progresses, many K-selected species out-compete the pioneers.

If an existing community is disturbed, life is destroyed, and the habitat reverts to a barren state.

For example, everyday events are forest fires or abandonment of farmland.

The habitat undergoes *secondary succession.*

Unlike primary succession, secondary succession is strongly influenced by the previous conditions of the habitat; the soil is present and does not need to be built.

Climax communities

Frederic Clements (1874-1945) popularized that species diversity and total biomass increase until a final equilibrium, or *climax community,* is reached.

Climax community is the stable state of the community, which remains unchanged until perturbed by a catastrophic event.

Stability of communities is:

> *persistence through time,*

> *resistance to change,* and

> *recovery after disturbance.*

However, modern ecologists recognize that true climax communities are rare.

Dynamic steady state

Realistically, disturbances are so frequent that most communities are in succession and never truly reach a climax community.

The *steady state* of a community is dynamic.

Many ecologists refer to the steady-state as the *mature* or *old-growth communities*.

Climatic climax theory

The transitional state is a *seral community* or *sere*.

Clements' ideas are summarized under the *climatic climax theory*, where each region has one climax community determined by the climate.

Other factors are negligible compared to climate.

Polyclimax theory states that a region has multiple climax communities depending on climate plus environments such as topography and the nature of the disturbance.

Climax pattern theory proposes multiple climax communities but is influenced by the environment *and* the species present.

Climax pattern theory emphasizes how organisms respond to the *changing environment* and how *succession proceeds*.

Finally, many ecologists believe succession is cyclical, with a habitat passing through several alternating climax communities.

Succession and Biodiversity

Succession models

Three main models describe succession.

Facilitation model applies to species that alter the environment to make it hospitable to the following species. Soil building is a crucial example.

Inhibition model describes species that attempt to hold on to their place in the community, making it more difficult for new species to succeed.

It assumes that each successional stage has a dominant species, which must be outcompeted or destroyed by a disturbance to allow the next species to establish itself.

Tolerance model describes species that neither help nor hurt succeeding species; this model assumes that the climax community comprises species that can co-exist.

Three models are manifest, but predicting what an environment will experience is difficult.

Community biodiversity

Intermediate disturbance hypothesis states that a moderate level of disturbance yields the highest community diversity.

Frequent disturbances may cause extinction, while few allow one species to grow dominant and out-compete others.

Occasional disturbances periodically inhibit dominant species and dampen competition to allow new species to enter, maximizing biodiversity.

Disturbances may alter the physical environment to favor different species than before.

Many communities rely on disturbances to keep them healthy, so forest management personnel set controlled forest fires.

Competition must be at moderate levels to maintain diverse communities.

r-strategists dominate communities that experience widespread, frequent disturbances are dominated by r-strategists,

K-strategists dominate undisturbed communities, which out-compete others.

The jaguar is an example of a keystone species that regulates competition

Keystone predators

Keystone predators are essential species that regulate competition by controlling the population of species that would otherwise overrun a community.

For example, the starfish *Pisaster* is a keystone predator that keeps the mussel *Mytilus* from out-competing invertebrates and algae for space.

Intermediate migration best serves biodiversity when emigration is sufficient to offset mortality and immigration.

Island communities

Island communities may be islands or isolated regions, a lake, or forest surrounded by cropland.

Isolated communities have difficulty sustaining migration and may experience extinction. Insular biogeography studies how isolation affects community structure.

Insular biogeography proposes that larger islands support high diversity, mainly because they include keystone predators.

Islands distant from other communities have the lowest migration rates and exhibit low diversity.

Islands may experience extinction since individuals cannot easily emigrate and replenish their population.

Heterogeneity

Spatial heterogeneity model in biogeography has heterogeneous habitats with higher diversity.

The best habitats are patchy or heterogeneous, creating various niches.

Heterogeneity may be seen in the topography, soil, and climate.

Forests usually have vertical heterogeneity, or *stratification,* creating different habitats.

Spatial heterogeneity is self-reinforcing since greater heterogeneity leads to more biodiversity, and diversity is a form of heterogeneity.

Global biodiversity has been on the decline because of humans.

For example, pollution, habitat destruction, and hunting cause extinctions, which have a domino effect that can collapse entire communities.

Invasive species

Invasive species are rampant, which is a grave threat to diversity.

Invasive species often have *no natural predators* in the environment they are introduced to, allowing them to *out-compete* other species rapidly.

Many communities have become overrun by invasive species (within decades) and are barren.

The problem has been compounded by misguided human efforts to introduce a more invasive species to cull the original invader.

In many cases, the new invaders replace the old ones.

However, some efforts have successfully suppressed invasive species.

Ecologists continue to research methods to minimize the effects of human disturbances and interventions and preserve biodiversity.

Notes for active learning

Notes for active learning

Notes for active learning

Notes for active learning

PRACTICE QUESTIONS
&
DETAILED EXPLANATIONS

Page intentionally left blank

Practice Questions: Ecosystems, Biosphere & Conservation Biology

1. The lowest level of environmental complexity that includes living and nonliving factors is:

    A. ecosystem

    B. biosphere

    C. biome

    D. community

    E. population

2. How does an area's weather differ from the area's climate?

    A. Weather does not change very much, and an area's climate may change many times

    B. Weather is the area's daily conditions, while climate is the area's average conditions

    C. Weather involves temperature and precipitation, while climate involves only temperature

    D. Weather depends on where it is on Earth, while the area's climate does not

    E. Weather involves temperature and precipitation, while climate involves only precipitation

3. One type of symbiosis is:

    A. parasitism

    B. predation

    C. competition

    D. succession

    E. none of the above

4. Climate zones are the result of differences in:

    A. thickness of the ozone layer

    B. greenhouse gases

    C. angle of the sun's rays

    D. heat transport

    E. altitude of the observer

5. The greenhouse effect is:

    A. an unnatural phenomenon that causes heat energy to be radiated back into the atmosphere

    B. the result of the differences in the angle of the sun's rays

    C. primarily related to the levels of ozone in the atmosphere

    D. a phenomenon that has only occurred in the last 50 years

    E. a natural phenomenon that maintains Earth's temperature range

6. The tendency for warm air to rise and cool air to sink results in:

A. regional precipitation

B. the seasons

C. ocean upwelling

D. global wind patterns

E. regional temperature

7. An ecosystem with water covering the soil or near the surface of the soil for part of the year is a(n):

A. estuary

B. salt marsh

C. mangrove swamp

D. pond

E. wetland

8. What is the biological aspect of an organism's niche?

A. composition of soil

B. amount of sunlight

C. predators

D. the water in the area

E. availability of minerals

9. An organism's niche is:

A. the range of temperatures that the organism needs to survive

B. a complete description of the place an organism lives

C. the range of physical and biological conditions in which an organism lives and the way it obtains what it needs to survive and reproduce

D. all the physical factors in the organism's environment

E. all the biological factors in the organism's environment

10. No two species can occupy the same niche in the same habitat at the same time:

A. unless the species require different biotic factors

B. because of the competitive exclusion principle

C. unless the species requires different abiotic factors

D. because of the interactions that shape the ecosystem

E. unless the species require different biotic and the same abiotic factors

11. Plants are:

A. omnivores

B. herbivores

C. primary consumers

D. primary producers

E. detritivores

12. How do most primary producers make their food?

A. By breaking down remains into carbon dioxide
B. By converting water into carbon dioxide
C. By using chemical energy to make carbohydrates
D. By using heat energy to make nutrients
E. By using light energy to make carbohydrates

13. Compared to land, the open oceans:

A. are nutrient-poor environments
B. are rich in silica and iron
C. have less zooplankton
D. contain abundant oxygen
E. are nutrient-rich environments

14. Several species of warblers can live in the same spruce tree ONLY because they:

A. can find different temperatures within the tree
B. occupy different niches within the tree
C. have different habitats within the tree
D. do not eat food from the tree
E. can find different amounts of direct sunlight within the tree

15. All the interconnected feeding relationships in an ecosystem make up the food:

A. web
B. network
C. chain
D. framework
E. scheme

16. A symbiotic relationship in which both species benefit is:

A. predation
B. parasitism
C. commensalism
D. omnivorism
E. mutualism

17. A wolf pack hunts, kills, and feeds on a moose. In this interaction, the wolves are:

A. predators
B. mutualists
C. prey
D. hosts
E. symbionts

18. The total amount of living tissue within a given trophic level is:

A. energy mass

B. biomass

C. organic mass

D. trophic mass

E. abiotic

19. An interaction in which an animal feeds on plants is:

A. symbiosis

B. predation

C. herbivory

D. carnivory

E. parasitism

20. A symbiotic relationship in which one organism is harmed, and another benefits is:

A. synnecrosis

B. predation

C. mutualism

D. parasitism

E. commensalism

21. Which animals eat, both producers and consumers?

A. autotrophs

B. chemotrophs

C. omnivores

D. herbivores

E. heterotrophs

22. Ecosystem services include:

A. food production

B. production of oxygen

C. solar energy

D. all the above

E. none of the above

23. Organisms that can capture energy and produce food are:

A. omnivores

B. heterotrophs

C. herbivores

D. consumers

E. autotrophs

24. What is one difference between primary and secondary succession?

   A. Secondary succession begins with lichens, and primary succession begins with trees

   B. Primary succession modifies the environment, while secondary succession does not

   C. Secondary succession begins on the soil, while primary succession begins on newly exposed surfaces

   D. Primary succession is rapid and secondary succession is slow

   E. Both primary succession and secondary succession are rapid

25. A term that means the same thing as a *consumer* is:

   A. carbohydrate

   B. heterotroph

   C. autotroph

   D. producer

   E. detritivore

26. Primary succession would likely occur after:

   A. severe storm

   B. farmland is abandoned

   C. earthquake

   D. forest fire

   E. lava flow

27. Which organism is a detritivore?

   A. fungus

   B. snail

   C. crow

   D. caterpillar

   E. mouse

28. Matter can be recycled through the biosphere because:

   A. biological systems do not deplete matter but transform it

   B. biological systems use only carbon, oxygen, hydrogen, and nitrogen

   C. matter does not change into new compounds

   D. matter is assembled into chemical compounds

   E. biological systems do not change matter into new compounds

29. A tropical rainforest may not return to its original climax community after which type of disturbances?

   A. volcanic eruption

   B. flooding after hurricane

   C. burning of a forest fire

   D. clearing and farming

   E. earthquake

30. A collection of the organisms living in a place, together with their nonliving environment, is a(n):

A. ecosystem

B. biome

C. population

D. community

E. biomass

31. Which biome is characterized by very low temperatures, little precipitation, and permafrost?

A. tropical dry forest

B. tundra

C. temperate forest

D. desert

E. savannah

32. A bird stalks, kills and eats an insect. Based on its behavior, which ecological terms describe the bird?

A. herbivore ↔ decomposer

B. autotroph ↔ herbivore

C. carnivore ↔ consumer

D. producer ↔ heterotroph

E. herbivore ↔ consumer

33. Which two biomes have the least precipitation?

A. boreal forest and temperate woodland

B. tundra and desert

C. tropical savanna and tropical dry forest

D. tundra and temperate shrubland

E. tropical rainforest and temperate grassland

34. Which represents box 5 of the food web in the figure?

A. decomposers

B. carnivores

C. scavengers

D. herbivores

E. omnivores

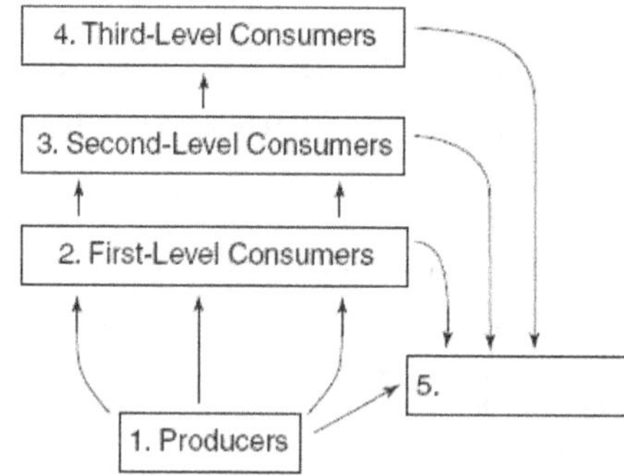

35. The average, year-after-year conditions of temperature and precipitation in a region are:

A. zonation

B. microclimate

C. weather

D. climate

E. weather and climate

36. Nitrogen fixation is carried out primarily by:

A. producers

B. consumers

C. humans

D. plants

E. bacteria

37. The rate at which producers create organic matter is:

A. primary succession

B. nitrogen fixation

C. primary productivity

D. nutrient limit

E. secondary succession

38. Which landforms are NOT classified into a major biome?

A. coastlines

B. islands

C. prairies

D. mountain ranges

E. deserts

39. The North Pole and the South Poles are:

A. not classified into major biomes

B. part of aquatic ecosystems

C. classified as tundra biomes

D. not home to any animals

E. classified as temperate biomes

40. The interaction in which one organism captures and feeds on another is:

A. mutualism

B. symbiosis

C. competition

D. parasitism

E. predation

41. Are zooplankton in the aphotic, benthic zone of an ocean?

    A. No, zooplankton cannot undergo chemosynthesis in the dark without oxygen in the water

    B. No, zooplankton feed on phytoplankton that cannot photosynthesize without light

    C. No, zooplankton cannot photosynthesize in the dark without oxygen in the water

    D. Yes, zooplankton is a chemosynthetic autotroph

    E. Yes, zooplankton can photosynthesize in the dark

42. Carbon cycles through the biosphere in the following processes EXCEPT:

    A. decomposition of plants

    B. burning of fossil fuels

    C. transpiration

    D. photosynthesis

    E. decomposition of animals

43. The nutrient availability of aquatic ecosystems is the:

    A. number of different animal species living in the water

    B. amount of rainfall the water receives

    C. number of other organisms present in the water

    D. amount of nitrogen, oxygen, and other elements dissolved in the water

    E. amount of salinity of the water

44. What organism forms the base of many aquatic food webs?

    A. phytoplankton

    B. mangrove trees

    C. secondary consumers

    D. plants

    E. zooplankton

45. The movements of energy and nutrients through living systems are different because:

    A. nutrients flow in two directions, while energy recycles

    B. energy forms chemical compounds while nutrients are lost as heat

    C. energy flows in one direction while nutrients are recycled

    D. energy is limited in the biosphere while nutrients are always available

    E. nutrients are lost as heat while energy is limited in the biosphere

46. Boreal Forest biomes are:

A. near the equator
B. known as taiga
C. home to more species than all other biomes combined
D. hot and wet year-round
E. made up of mostly hardwood

47. Freshwater ecosystems that often originate from underground sources in mountains or hills are:

A. lakes
B. wetlands
C. estuaries
D. ponds
E. rivers and streams

48. Which is how a wetland differs from a lake or pond?

A. Water does not always cover a wetland as it does a lake or pond
B. Wetlands are salty, while lakes and ponds are freshwaters
C. Water flows in a lake or pond but never flows in a wetland
D. Wetlands are nesting areas for birds, while lakes and ponds are not nesting areas
E. None of the above are differences

49. A wetland that contains a mixture of fresh water and saltwater is:

A. pond
B. river
C. stream
D. estuary
E. wetland

50. The permanently dark zone of the ocean is the:

A. aphotic zone
B. intertidal zone
C. photic zone
D. coastal zone
E. intercoastal zone

51. Each is an abiotic factor in the environment, EXCEPT:

A. temperature
B. rainfall
C. plant life
D. soil type
E. pH

52. Estuaries are commercially important because:

    A. fossil fuels are found in estuaries

    B. lumber trees grow in estuaries

    C. hotels are often built in estuaries

    D. abundant fish species live in estuaries

    E. the shoreline of estuaries attracts tourists

53. Animals that get energy by eating the carcasses of animals killed by predators or died by natural causes are:

    A. detritivores

    B. heterotrophs

    C. omnivores

    D. autotrophs

    E. scavengers

54. Which statement is NOT true about the open ocean?

    A. Open ocean begins at the low-tide mark and extends to the end of the continental shelf

    B. Most of the photosynthetic activity on Earth occurs in the open ocean within the photic zone

    C. The open ocean has low levels of nutrients

    D. Organisms in the deep ocean are exposed to frigid temperatures

    E. Organisms in the deep ocean are exposed to total darkness

55. The branch of biology focusing on interactions among organisms and between organisms and their environment is:

    A. paleontology

    B. ecology

    C. microbiology

    D. entomology

    E. zoology

56. Which description of the organization of an ecosystem is correct?

    A. Species make up communities that comprise populations

    B. Species make up populations that comprise communities

    C. Communities make up species that comprise populations

    D. Populations make up species that comprise communities

    E. Communities make up populations that comprise species

57. The photic zone:

    A. is deep, cold, and permanently dark

    B. extends to where the light intensity is reduced to 50% compared to the surface

    C. extends to the bottom of the open ocean

    D. extends to a depth of about 600 feet

    E. extends to where chemosynthetic bacteria are the producers

58. Which is an example of mutualism?

    A. nematodes   **C.** tapeworms

    B. bread mold   **D.** lichens

                            E. epiphytes

59. Organisms that must obtain nutrients and energy by eating other organisms are:

    A. heterotrophic   **C.** herbivores

    B. eukaryotic   **D.** autotrophic

                            E. multicellular

60. Complex animals break down food through the process of:

    A. cephalization   **C.** complete metamorphosis

    B. intracellular digestion   **D.** extracellular digestion

                            E. all the above

61. Genetically modified (GM) crops produce a higher yield per plant by:

    A. less food but with higher nutritional content

    B. the same amount of food but with higher nutritional content

    C. more food per acre

    D. less food per acre

    E. none of the above

Notes or active learning

Notes or active learning

Notes or active learning

Detailed Explanations: Ecosystems, Biosphere & Conservation Biology

Answer Key

1: A	11: D	21: C	31: B	41: B	51: C	61: C
2: B	12: E	22: D	32: C	42: C	52: D	
3: A	13: A	23: E	33: B	43: D	53: E	
4: C	14: B	24: C	34: A	44: A	54: A	
5: E	15: A	25: B	35: D	45: C	55: B	
6: D	16: E	26: E	36: E	46: B	56: B	
7: E	17: A	27: B	37: C	47: E	57: D	
8: C	18: B	28: A	38: B	48: A	58: D	
9: C	19: C	29: D	39: A	49: D	59: A	
10: B	20: D	30: A	40: E	50: A	60: D	

1. A is correct.

Ecosystem is a community of organisms (e.g., plants, animals, microbes) with nonliving (i.e., *abiotic*) components of their environment (e.g., air, water, minerals). It is the network of interactions among organisms and between organisms and their environment.

Nutrient cycles and *energy flows* link *biotic* (living) and *abiotic* (nonliving) components.

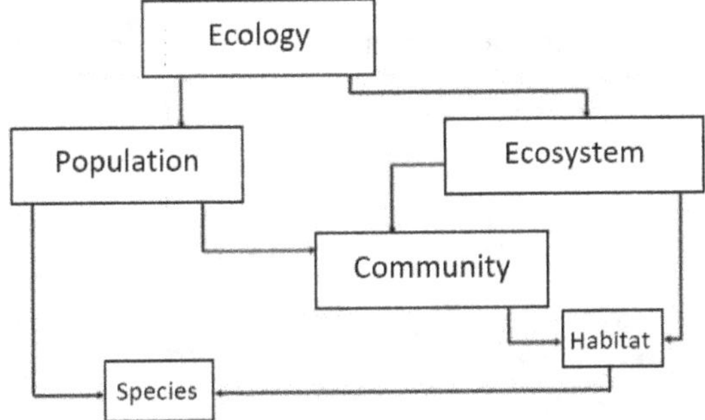

Relationship between organisms and their environment. Population, ecosystem, community, habitat, and species relationship are highlighted.

Ecology is the relationships between living organisms and between their environments.

Population is a group of organisms of the same species living in the same area.

Community is a group of populations living and interacting in an area.

Habitat is the environment in which a species lives.

Species are a group of organisms that can breed and produce fertile offspring.

2. B is correct.

Weather is the immediate conditions (e.g., hourly, daily, weekly), while *climate* is the average conditions.

3. A is correct.

Symbiosis is the close and often long-term interaction between species.

Historically, some biologists proposed symbiosis as *persistent mutualisms* (i.e., all organisms benefit).

Biologists and ecologists now propose symbiosis as *persistent biological interactions*; mutualistic (+/+), commensalism (+/0), or parasitic (+/−).

4. C is correct.

Climate zones are distinct in an east-west direction around Earth and are classified by climate parameters.

Climate zones are primarily determined by *variations in temperature* related to *latitude* and *altitude*.

Angle of the sun's rays contributes to differences in climate zones.

5. E is correct.

Greenhouse effect is a natural phenomenon that maintains Earth's temperature range.

Greenhouse gases on Earth are water vapor (36–70%), CO_2 (9–26%), methane (4–9%), and ozone (3–7%).

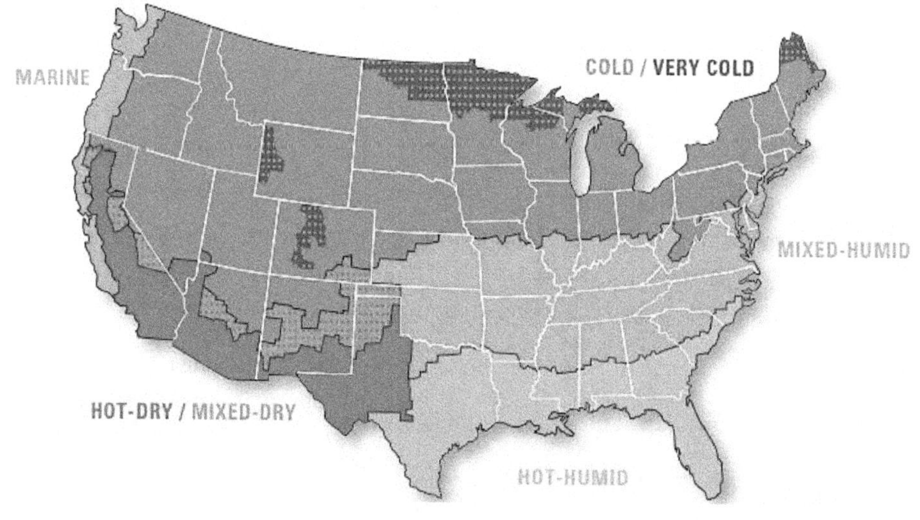

U.S. climate zones

6. D is correct.

Convection is movement caused by hotter (i.e., less dense) air rising and colder (i.e., denser) air sinking under the influence of gravity, resulting in heat transfer.

Global wind patterns in the atmosphere are created by *convection* (i.e., air movement based on density).

When *warm air rises* and cools in a low-pressure zone, it may not hold water as vapor.

Some water vapor condenses to form clouds or precipitation.

When *cool air descends*, it warms.

7. E is correct.

Wetlands ecosystems have saturated ground surfaces either permanently or temporarily.

8. C is correct.

Niche describes when each species has separate, unique physical and environmental conditions.

Biological aspects of an organism's niche are *biotic factors* (i.e., living) required for survival.

Abiotic factors (i.e., nonliving) include soil, sunlight, water, and minerals.

Ecological niche is how organisms (or populations) respond to the distribution of resources and competitors (e.g., growing with abundant resources while predators are scarce) and how it alters those factors (e.g., limiting access by other organisms, being a food source for predators and a consumer of prey).

9. C is correct.

Niche is when each species has separate, unique physical and environmental conditions.

Niche is the range of *physical and biological conditions* in which an organism lives and how it obtains resources for survival and reproduction.

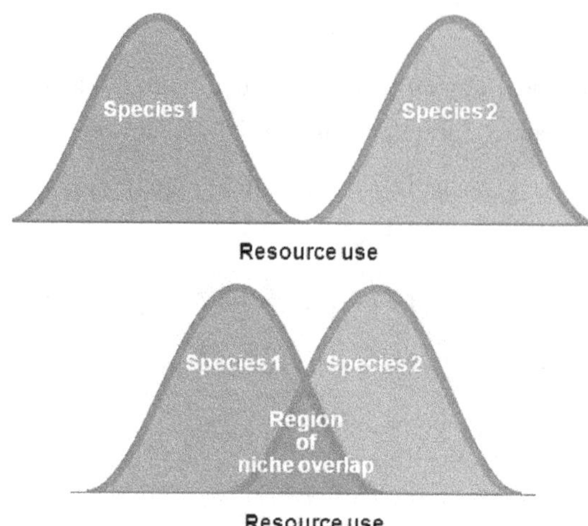

Resource partitioning results in competition for scarce resources when niche regions overlap

10. B is correct.

Competitive exclusion principle (*Gause's law of competitive exclusion* or *Gause's law*) states that two species competing for resources cannot coexist when ecological factors are constant.

Domination occurs when one species has even a slight advantage.

One competitor overcomes another, leading to extinction or a behavioral shift toward a different ecological niche.

11. D is correct.

Primary producers (i.e., *autotrophs*) produce energy from inorganic compounds.

Primary producers often use *photosynthesis* (e.g., plants and cyanobacteria).

Autotrophs (e.g., plants) support the ecosystem and feed heterotrophs.

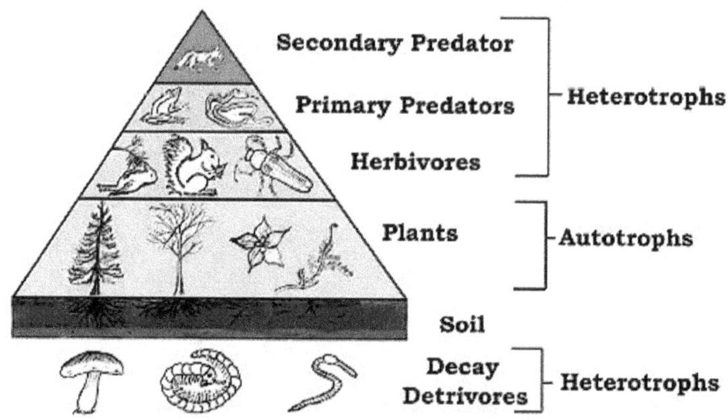

Trophic levels as positions on a food web.
Autotrophs support the ecosystem and feed heterotrophs.

12. E is correct.

Primary producers (i.e., *autotrophs*) produce energy from inorganic compounds in an ecosystem.

Primary producers often use *photosynthesis* (e.g., plants and cyanobacteria).

Plants are primary producers.

Autotrophs support the ecosystem and feed heterotrophs.

Autotrophs create organic compounds using energy from the sun or inorganic compounds.

Autotrophs divide into *photoautotrophs* and *chemoautotrophs*.

Photoautotrophs (e.g., algae, plants, cyanobacteria) use photosynthesis, converting solar energy into organic compounds.

Chemoautotrophs are bacteria that oxidize inorganic compounds such as ammonia, nitrite, and sulfide to generate organic compounds.

They are rare and typically found in caves, hydrothermal ocean vents, and other environments lacking light.

Archaea (single-cell prokaryotes) may produce biomass from oxidizing inorganic compounds (i.e., chemoautotrophs).

For example, *archaea* produce biomass in *deep ocean hydrothermal vents*.

Decomposers are fungi and other organisms that produce biomass from oxidizing organic materials.

Decomposers absorb and metabolize nutrients (i.e., saprotrophic nutrition from dead or decaying material).

13. A is correct.

Open ocean waters are separated from cold, nutrient-rich interior water by *density differences* restricting water mixing and reducing nutrient supply, which becomes the limiting factor for productivity.

Open oceans have negligible nutrients from land and little upwelling to supply nutrients from deep oceans.

14. B is correct.

Habitat is an ecological area inhabited by a species.

Habitat is the natural environment where an organism lives or the physical environment encompassing a population.

Niche describes when each species has separate, unique physical and environmental conditions.

Niche is the range of *physical and biological conditions* in which an organism lives and how it obtains resources for survival and reproduction.

Niche breadth is the range of habitat by an organism.

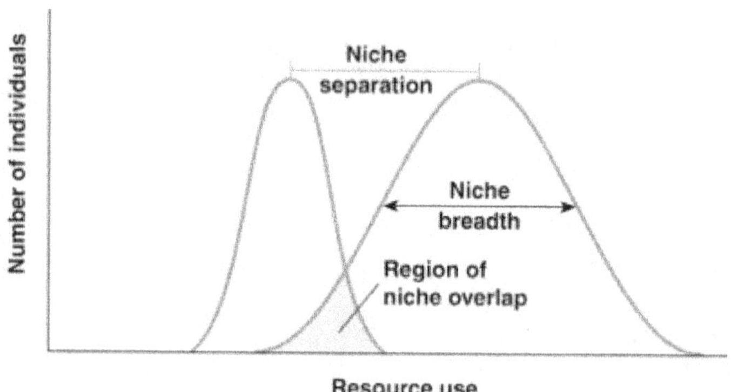

Niches may overlap and introduce competition for scarce resources

15. A is correct.

Food web is a graphical model depicting linked *food chains by* feeding relationships in an ecosystem.

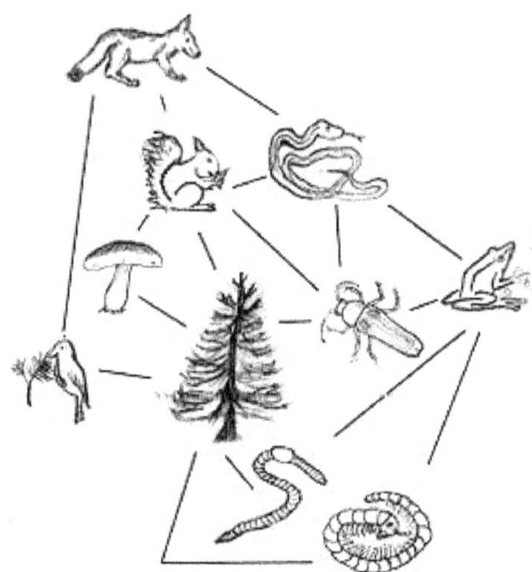

Food web and energy flow relationship examples

Food chain is a *linear succession* whereby another eats each species.

16. E is correct.

Mutualism is when two organisms of distinct species exist in a relationship, each benefit.

B: *parasitism* is a non-mutual symbiotic relationship between species, where one species (i.e., the parasite) benefits at the expense of the other (i.e., the host).

C: *commensalism* is when two organisms of distinct species exist in a relationship, each benefit.

D: *omnivorism* is a human diet consuming meat, eggs, dairy, and produce from organic farms.

17. A is correct.

Predation is a biological interaction when a predator (i.e., a hunting organism) feeds on prey.

A predator may (or *may not*) kill its prey before feeding, but predation often results in the prey's death and the eventual absorption of the prey's tissue through consumption.

Given an alternative, *predators* (e.g., lions, tigers, wolves) may engage in *scavenging* feeding.

Mutualism (+/+) is a symbiosis of *persistent biological interactions.*

18. B is correct.

Biomass is the mass (i.e., a body of matter without a defined shape) of living organisms in an area (or ecosystem).

Biomass can include microorganisms, plants, or animals.

Mass can be expressed as the average mass per unit area or the total mass in the community.

How biomass is measured depends on why it is being measured.

Species biomass is the mass of one or more species.

Community biomass is the mass of the species in the community.

Trophic levels show a succession of the flow of *food energy* and *feeding relationships.*

It is a food chain or ecological pyramid occupied by groups with similar feeding modes.

Trophic level 1	Producers
Trophic level 2	Primary consumers
Trophic level 3	Secondary consumers
Trophic level 4	Tertiary consumers

continued...

Food chain is the hierarchy in which organisms in an ecosystem are grouped into trophic (nutritional) levels.

Ecological pyramid represents the biomass or the energy flow in an ecosystem.

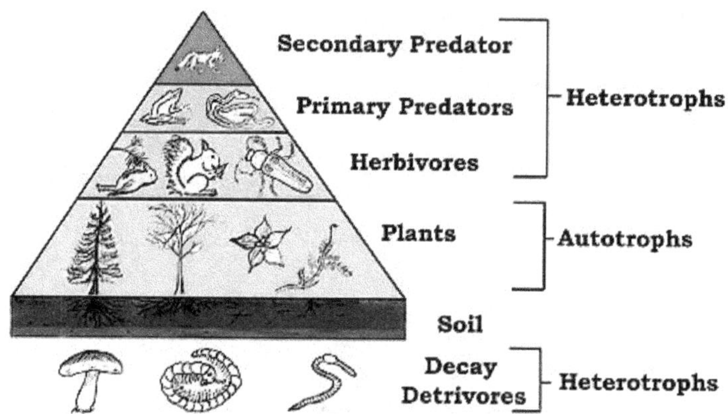

Trophic levels as positions on a food web.
Autotrophs support the ecosystem and feed heterotrophs.

19. C is correct.

Herbivory is an animal anatomically and physiologically adapted to eating plants.

As a result of their plant diet, herbivorous animals typically have mouthparts adapted to rasping or grinding.

For example, foliage or marine algae are the main components of herbivores.

20. D is correct.

Parasitism (+/−) is a non-mutual symbiotic relationship between species, where one species (i.e., the parasite) benefits at the expense of the other (i.e., the host).

A: *synnecrosis* is a rare symbiosis when the interaction between species is detrimental to both.

It is short-lived because the interaction eventually causes death.

Evolution selects against synnecrosis and is uncommon.

B: *predation* is a biological interaction when a predator (i.e., hunting organism) feeds on prey.

Predators may not kill their prey before feeding, but predation often results in the prey's death and eventual absorption of their tissue through consumption.

The remains of prey may become a food source for scavengers.

Scavengers feed on dead organisms that they did not kill.

continued...

Organisms (e.g., lions, tigers, wolves) considered predators may engage in scavenging feeding behavior when given the alternative.

C: *mutualism* (+/+) is when two different species exist in a relationship, each benefit.

E: *commensalism* is a relationship between organisms where an organism benefits without affecting the other.

21. C is correct.

Omnivores consume meat, eggs, dairy, and produce.

Autotrophs support the ecosystem and feed heterotrophs.

Autotrophs create organic compounds using energy from the sun or inorganic compounds.

Autotrophs divide into photoautotrophs and chemoautotrophs.

Photoautotrophs (e.g., algae, plants, cyanobacteria) use photosynthesis to convert solar energy into organic compounds.

Chemotrophs are organisms that obtain energy by oxidation of electron donors in their environments.

These molecules can be organic or inorganic.

Chemotrophs can be either *autotrophic* or *heterotrophic*.

Herbivores are animals anatomically and physiologically adapted to eating plants.

As a result of their plant diet, herbivorous animals typically have mouthparts adapted to rasping or grinding.

22. D is correct.

Ecosystems include food production, solar energy (photosynthesis), and O_2 production (e.g., photosynthesis).

They are the network of interactions among organisms and between organisms and their environment.

23. E is correct.

Autotrophs support the ecosystem and feed heterotrophs.

Autotrophs create organic compounds using energy from the sun or inorganic compounds; they are divided into *photoautotrophs* and *chemoautotrophs*.

Photoautotrophs (e.g., algae, plants, cyanobacteria) use photosynthesis, converting solar energy into organic compounds.

Heterotrophs obtain nutrients and energy by consuming organic substances.

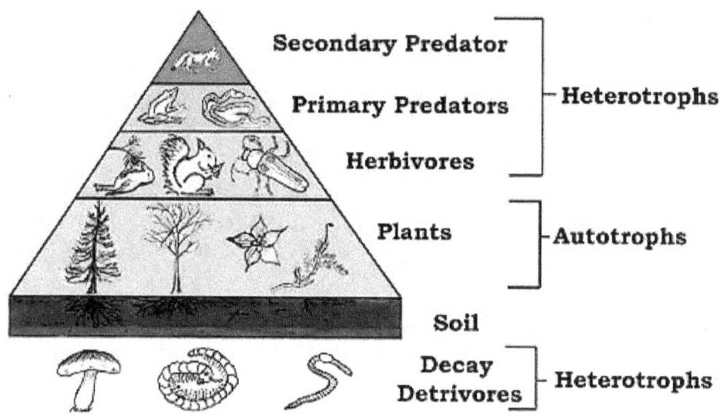

Trophic levels as positions on a food web.
Autotrophs support the ecosystem and feed heterotrophs.

24. C is correct.

Primary succession is one of two biological and ecological successions of plant life, occurring in an environment devoid of vegetation and usually lacking soil (e.g., lava flow).

It is the gradual growth of an ecosystem over a longer period.

Secondary succession occurs on a substrate that supports vegetation before an ecological disturbance from less cataclysmic events (e.g., floods, hurricanes, tornadoes), which destroy plant life.

25. B is correct.

Heterotrophs obtain nutrients and energy by consuming organic substances.

Autotrophs are *producers*.

Heterotrophs are *consumers* and rely on producers.

26. E is correct.

Primary succession is one of two biological and ecological successions of plant life, occurring in an environment devoid of vegetation and usually lacking soil (e.g., lava flow).

Primary succession is the gradual growth of an ecosystem over a more extended period.

Secondary succession occurs on a substrate that supports vegetation before an ecological disturbance from less cataclysmic events (e.g., floods, hurricanes, tornadoes), which destroy plant life.

27. B is correct.

The snail is a typical detritivore.

Detritivores are heterotrophs that obtain nutrition from decomposing (waste or detritus) plants, dead organisms, and feces and contribute to decomposition and the nutrient cycles.

Detritivores are not to be confused with other decomposers, such as bacteria, fungi, and protists, which cannot ingest minute lumps of matter.

Decomposers absorb and metabolize nutrients (i.e., saprotrophic nutrition from dead or decaying material).

28. A is correct.

Matter recycles through the biosphere because biological systems do not deplete it but transform it.

29. D is correct.

Clearing and farming are physical disturbances to the ecosystem.

Climax community is a biological community of plants, animals, and fungi that has reached a *steady-state* through ecological succession (i.e., vegetation in an area over time).

Equilibrium occurs because the climax community has species best adapted to average conditions in that area.

30. A is correct.

Ecosystems include food production, solar energy (photosynthesis), and O_2 production (e.g., photosynthesis).

Ecosystems are the network of interactions among organisms and between organisms and their environment.

Biomes are geographically and climatically defined as contiguous with similar conditions, such as communities of plants, animals, and soil organisms.

31. B is correct.

Tundra is a biome where low temperatures and short growing seasons hinder tree growth.

Vegetation includes dwarf shrubs, grasses, mosses, and lichens.

Desert is a barren land where little precipitation occurs, and consequently, living conditions are hostile to plant and animal life.

32. C is correct.

The bird is the carnivore, while the insect is the consumer (heterotroph).

33. B is correct.

Tundra is a biome where low temperatures and short growing seasons hinder tree growth. The vegetation includes dwarf shrubs, grasses, mosses, and lichens.

Desert is a barren land where little precipitation occurs, and consequently, living conditions are hostile to plant and animal life.

Boreal forest (or *taiga*) is a biome characterized by coniferous (i.e., softwood) forests mainly consisting of pines, spruces, and larches, and is the world's largest terrestrial biome.

34. A is correct.

Decomposers are fungi and other organisms that produce biomass from oxidizing organic materials. They absorb and metabolize nutrients (i.e., saprotrophic nutrition from dead or decaying material).

Scavengers feed on dead organisms that they did *not* kill.

Often, the remains of the prey become a food source for scavengers.

35. D is correct.

Climate is the average conditions, *while the weather* is the immediate conditions (e.g., hourly, daily, weekly).

36. E is correct.

Nitrogen fixation is when atmospheric nitrogen (N_2) is converted into ammonium (NH_4).

Nitrogen fixation is necessary for life because nitrogen is required for nucleotides of DNA and RNA and amino acids of proteins.

Diazotrophs are prokaryotic (i.e., bacteria and archaea) microorganisms that can fix nitrogen.

Some higher plants and animals (e.g., termites) have symbiotic relationships with diazotrophs.

37. C is correct.

Primary productivity is the rate at which producers (autotrophs) produce organic matter.

38. B is correct.

Biomes are climatically and geographically defined as *contiguous areas* with *similar climatic conditions,* such as communities of animals, plants, and soil organisms, and are often called ecosystems.

Factors such as plant structures define biomes (e.g., shrubs, trees, and grasses), leaf types (e.g., broadleaf and needle leaf), plant spacing (e.g., forest, woodland, savanna), and climate.

Biomes, unlike ecozones, are not defined by genetic, taxonomic, or historical similarities.

Patterns of ecological succession and climax vegetation often identify biomes.

39. A is correct.

North Pole and the South Pole are not classified into major biomes.

40. E is correct.

Predation is a biological interaction when a predator (i.e., a hunting organism) feeds on prey.

A predator may (or may not kill) its prey before feeding on them, but predation often results in the prey's death and the eventual absorption of the prey's tissue through consumption.

Scavengers feed on dead organisms that they did not kill. Often, the remains of the prey become a food source for scavengers.

Organisms (e.g., lions, tigers, wolves) considered predators may engage in scavenging feeding behavior when given the alternative.

41. B is correct.

Aphotic zone is the area of a lake or ocean with little or no sunlight, the depths beyond which less than 1 percent of sunlight penetrates.

Below the photic zone is the dark aphotic zone, where photosynthesis cannot occur.

Benthic zone is the lowest ecological zone in water bodies and usually involves sediments on the seafloor.

These sediments are essential in providing nutrients for living organisms in the benthic zone.

continued...

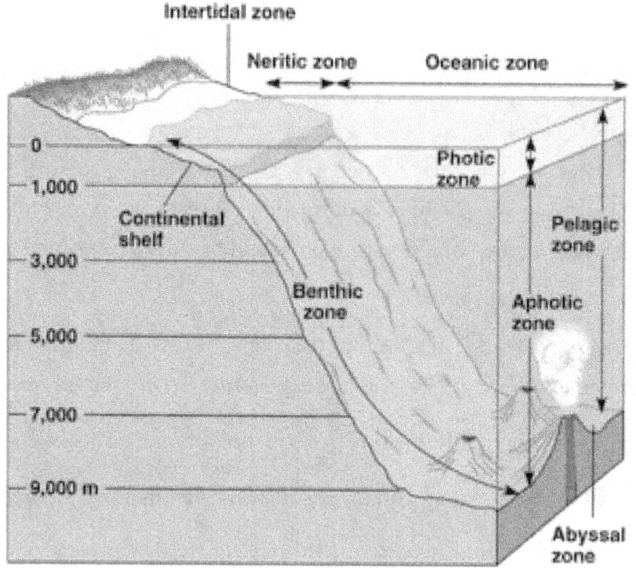

Deep ocean zones include photic, pelagic, aphotic, and abyssal zones

Phytoplankton (microalgae), like terrestrial plants, contain chlorophyll and require sunlight to live and grow.

Most phytoplankton is buoyant and floats in the ocean's upper layers, where sunlight penetrates the water.

Phytoplankton is the base of many aquatic food webs whereby shrimp, jellyfish, and whales feed on them.

Zooplankton is heterotrophic (sometimes detritivores) plankton – organisms drifting in oceans, seas, and freshwater bodies.

Individual zooplankton is usually microscopic but may (e.g., jellyfish) be larger and visible to the unaided eye.

42. C is correct.

Transpiration is when water moves in a plant and evaporates from aerial parts, such as leaves, stems, and flowers.

43. D is correct.

In aquatic ecosystems, *nitrogen* and *phosphorus* are the most important, often in short supply relative to the needs of plants, algae, and microbes.

Elements like iron, manganese, and copper are needed in lesser amounts.

44. A is correct.

Phytoplankton (microalgae), like terrestrial plants, contain chlorophyll and require sunlight to live and grow.

Most phytoplankton is buoyant and floats in the ocean's upper layers, where sunlight penetrates the water.

Phytoplankton is the base of many aquatic food webs whereby shrimp, jellyfish, and whales feed on them.

Zooplankton is heterotrophic (sometimes detritivores) plankton – organisms drifting in oceans, seas, and freshwater bodies.

Individual zooplankton is usually microscopic but may (e.g., jellyfish) be larger and visible to the unaided eye.

45. C is correct.

Energy flows in one direction while nutrients are recycled.

Nutrient cycles and *energy flows* link *biotic* (i.e., living) and *abiotic* (i.e., nonliving) components.

46. B is correct.

Boreal forest (or *taiga*) is a biome characterized by coniferous (i.e., softwood) forests mainly consisting of pines, spruces, and larches, and is the world's largest terrestrial biome.

47. E is correct.

Freshwater ecosystems naturally share resources between habitats.

At lower elevations, rivers and streams bring salt and nutrients from the mountains to lakes, ponds, and wetlands. Eventually, they bring those nutrients to the ocean.

48. A is correct.

Wetlands are areas filled with water most of the year. It might not always be wet.

Ponds and *lakes* are usually kept filled with water from many sources. They receive more water than they give off through evaporation.

Lakes and ponds are distinguished by their *depth* and *surface area.*

Lakes usually are much deeper than ponds and have a larger surface area.

Ponds have water in the photic zone, meaning ponds are shallow enough to allow sunlight to reach the bottom.

49. D is correct.

Estuaries are partly enclosed coastal bodies of brackish water (i.e., saline levels of 0.05 to 3% between fresh and saltwater).

Estuaries form when rivers or streams flow in and connect freely to the open sea.

Estuaries form a transition zone between the river and maritime environments and have marine influences (e.g., tides, waves, and saline water) and river influences (e.g., freshwater and sediment).

Inflows of seawater and freshwater provide nutrients in the water column and sediment, making *estuaries* among the most *productive natural habitats*.

50. A is correct.

Aphotic zone is the area of a lake or ocean with little or no sunlight, the depths beyond which less than 1 percent of sunlight penetrates.

Below the photic zone is the dark aphotic zone, where photosynthesis cannot occur.

51. C is correct.

Abiotic factors (i.e., nonliving) include soil, sunlight, water, and minerals.

Biotic factors are living components affecting other organisms. Biotic factors need food and metabolic energy for proper growth.

52. D is correct.

Estuaries are partly enclosed coastal bodies of brackish water (i.e., saline levels of 0.05 to 3% between fresh and saltwater).

Estuaries form when rivers or streams flow in and connect freely to the open sea.

Estuaries form a *transition zone* between rivers and maritime environments and have marine influences (e.g., tides, waves, and saline water) and river influences (e.g., freshwater and sediment).

Inflows of seawater and freshwater provide nutrients in the water column and sediment, making estuaries among the most *productive natural habitats*.

53. E is correct.

Scavengers feed on dead organisms that they did not kill.

Often, the remains of the prey become a food source for scavengers.

Detritivores are heterotrophs that obtain nutrition from decomposing (waste or detritus) plants, dead organisms, and feces and contribute to decomposition and the nutrient cycles.

Detritivores are not to be confused with other decomposers, such as bacteria, fungi, and protists, which cannot ingest minute lumps of matter.

Decomposers absorb and metabolize nutrients (i.e., saprotrophic nutrition from dead or decaying material).

54. A is correct.

Open ocean (or *pelagic zone*) is the area of the ocean outside of coastal areas.

The open ocean lies beyond the continental shelf: extending from the Arctic to the Antarctic.

It is from the surface to the deepest ocean parts and encompasses the entire water column.

Open ocean accounts for 64% of the ocean and 45% of Earth.

55. B is correct.

A: *paleontology* studies prehistoric life and includes the study of fossils to determine organisms' evolution.

C: *microbiology* is the scientific study of microscopic organisms, unicellular (i.e., single cell), multicellular (i.e., cell colony), or acellular (i.e., lacking cells).

Microbiology encompasses sub-disciplines of *mycology* (i.e., fungi), *virology, parasitology,* and *bacteriology*.

D: *entomology* is the study of insects (a branch of arthropodology), a branch of zoology.

E: *zoology* is the branch of biology that studies the animal kingdom, including the structure, embryology, evolution, habits, classification, and distribution of living and extinct animals.

56. B is correct.

Species make up *populations* that comprise *communities*.

57. D is correct.

Photic zone (sunlight zone) is the depth of the water in a lake or ocean exposed to sufficient sunlight for photosynthesis. It extends from the surface to a depth where light intensity falls to one percent.

Thickness of the photic zone depends on the extent of intensity loss in the water column. It can vary from a few inches in highly turbid lakes (i.e., seasonal effects) to around 600 feet in the ocean.

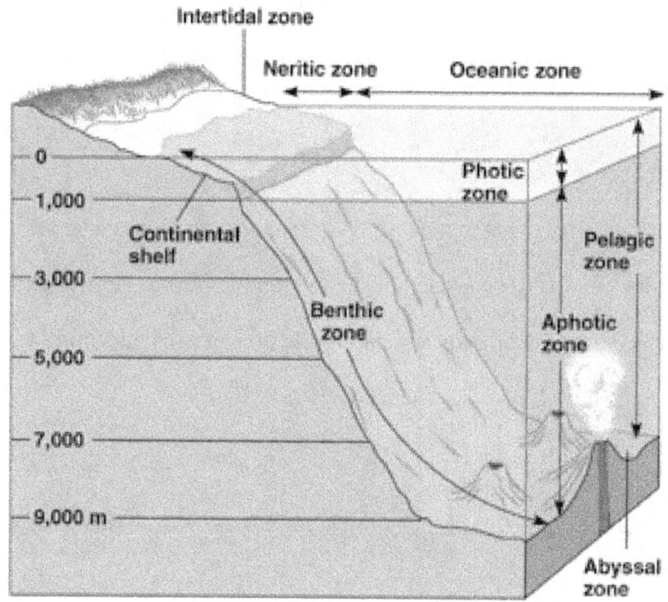

58. D is correct.

Mutualism is when organisms of different species exist in a relationship where each benefit (+/+ relationship).

Symbiosis includes *mutualistic, parasitic,* or *commensal* relationships.

Mutualism is one *type* of symbiosis.

Most lichens' bodies differ from those of either fungus or alga growing separately.

The fungus surrounds the algal cells, often enclosing them within complex fungal tissues.

Algal cells are photosynthetic and reduce atmospheric CO_2 into organic carbon sugars to feed both symbionts.

Both partners gain water and mineral nutrients from the atmosphere through rain and dust.

continued...

The fungal partner protects the alga by retaining water, serving as a larger capture area for mineral nutrients and, in some cases, providing minerals obtained from the substrate.

If a cyanobacterium is another symbiont in addition to green alga (tripartite lichens), they can fix atmospheric nitrogen, complementing the activities of the green alga.

A: *nematodes* (i.e., roundworms) are unlike cnidarians or flatworms because nematodes have tubular digestive systems with openings at each end.

Nematodes are obligate aquatic organisms consisting of cylindrical unsegmented worms.

Nematodes are free-living saprophytes or parasites.

B: *bread mold* is a *saprophyte* that feeds on dead and decaying material.

C: *tapeworms* are *parasites* extracting nutrition (they benefit) from the host while the host is depleted (host harmed) of nutrients.

This is a +/− relationship.

E: *epiphytes* are plants that live on the branches of other plants and receive greater exposure to sunlight than they would typically be able to.

This is an example of commensalism and a +/0 relationship.

59. A is correct.

Heterotrophic organisms obtain nutrients and energy by consuming organic substances.

Autotrophic organisms synthesize food from inorganic environmental substances (e.g., light, chemical energy).

Autotrophs are the basis of the ecosystem and feed heterotrophs.

Autotrophs create organic compounds using energy from the sun or inorganic compounds.

Autotrophs divide into photoautotrophs and chemoautotrophs.

Photoautotrophs (e.g., algae, plants, cyanobacteria) use photosynthesis to convert solar energy into organic compounds.

Chemoautotrophs are bacteria that oxidize inorganic compounds such as ammonia, nitrite, and sulfide to generate organic compounds.

Chemoautotrophs are rare and typically in caves, hydrothermal ocean vents, and other environments lacking light.

60. D is correct.

Extracellular digestion allows for the digestion of food outside of the cell, permitting the ingestion of large pieces of food.

Intracellular digestion is limited to small particles to be taken into individual cells.

Complex animals typically have digestive tract enzymes that act on the food material.

61. C is correct.

Disease- and *drought-resistant plants* require fewer environmental resources (e.g., water, fertilizer) and fewer pesticides. This results in an increased supply of food with reduced cost and longer shelf life.

Potential development of *allergens and toxicity* in GM-related crops is a risk for humans.

However, studies show GM crops have *increased yield and nutritional value.*

Notes for active learning

Notes for active learning

Practice Questions: Populations & Community Ecology

1. A developer wants to build a new housing development in or around a large city. Which plans would be LEAST harmful to the environment?

  A. Building a neighborhood in a meadow at the edge of the city

  B. Filling a wetland area and building oceanfront condominiums

  C. Clearing a forested area outside of the city to build houses

  D. Building apartments at the site of an abandoned factory in the city

  E. Building apartments on an abandoned farm

2. Assemblages of different populations that live together in a defined area are:

  A. communities

  B. species

  C. ecosystems

  D. habitats

  E. biodiversity

3. There are over 165 Saguaro cactus plants per square kilometer in an area of the Arizona desert. To which population characteristic does this information refer?

  A. age structure

  B. population density

  C. growth rate

  D. geographic range

  E. death rate

4. Using resources in a way that does not cause long-term environmental harm is:

  A. subsistence hunting

  B. biological magnification

  C. monoculture

  D. sustainable development

  E. none of the above

5. What does the range of a population teach the observer that density does not?

  A. The deaths per unit area

  B. The births per unit area

  C. The areas inhabited by a population

  D. The number that lives in an area

  E. The migrations per unit area

6. Which ecological inquiry method is an ecologist using when she enters an area periodically to count the population numbers of a particular species?

A. modeling

B. experimenting

C. hypothesizing

D. questioning

E. observing

7. Which is NOT a factor for population growth rates?

A. demography

B. emigration

C. death rate

D. Immigration

E. birth rate

8. What is an example of population density?

A. number of deaths per year

B. number of bacteria per square millimeter

C. number of births per year

D. number of frogs in a pond

E. immigration rate per year

9. An example of a biotic factor is:

A. sunlight

B. soil type

C. competing species

D. average temperature

E. average monthly rainfall

10. An example of a non-renewable resource is:

A. wood

B. fish

C. sunlight

D. wind

E. coal

11. A mathematical formula designed to predict population fluctuations in a community is:

A. ecological model

B. ecological observation

C. biological experiment

D. biological system

E. population experiment

12. The 1930s Dust Bowl in the Great Plains was caused by:

A. using renewable resources

B. poor farming practices

C. deforestation

D. contour plowing

E. using non-renewable resources

13. The movement of organisms into a range is:

A. population shift

B. carrying capacity

C. immigration

D. emigration

E. bottleneck effect

14. Which is NOT a basic method ecologists use to study the living world?

A. modeling

B. observing

C. experimenting

D. animal training

E. hypothesizing

15. If immigration and emigration numbers remain equal, which is the most important contributing factor to a slowed growth rate?

A. decreased death rate

B. constant birth rate

C. increased birth rate

D. constant death rate

E. decreased birth rate

16. When farming, overgrazing, climate change, or seasonal drought change farmland into land that cannot support plant life, it is:

A. deforestation

B. monoculture

C. extinction

D. depletion

E. desertification

17. Which factor might NOT contribute to an exponential growth rate in a given population?

A. reduced resources

B. less competition

C. higher birth rates

D. lower death rates

E. increased longevity

18. Which is NOT a sustainable development strategy for managing Earth's resources?

A. selective harvesting of trees

B. crop rotation

C. desertification

D. contour plowing

E. none of the above

19. Which are two ways a population can decrease in size?

A. Emigration and increased birth rate

B. Decreased birth rate and emigration

C. Increased death rate and immigration

D. Immigration and emigration

E. Increased birth rate and death rate

20. Farmers can reduce soil erosion by:

A. plowing up roots

B. grazing cattle on the land

C. contour plowing

D. increasing irrigation

E. planting monocultures

21. Which age structure is likely for a population that has not completed the demographic transition?

A. 10 percent of people aged 50–54

B. 5 percent of people aged 10–14

C. 15 percent of people under age 15

D. 50 percent of people under age 15

E. 20 percent of people above age 60

22. Which two factors increase population size?

A. births and immigration

B. deaths and emigration

C. births and emigration

D. deaths and immigration

E. none of the above

23. In a logistic growth curve, exponential growth is the phase in which the population:

A. growth begins to slow down

B. growth stops

C. reaches carrying capacity

D. death rate exceeds the growth rate

E. grows quickly

24. An example of sustainable resource use is the use of predators and parasites to:

A. control pest insects

B. eat unwanted plants

C. harm natural resources

D. pollinate plants

E. feed livestock

25. The graph shows the growth of a bacterial population. Which describes the growth curve?

A. demographic

B. exponential

C. logistic

D. limiting

E. linear

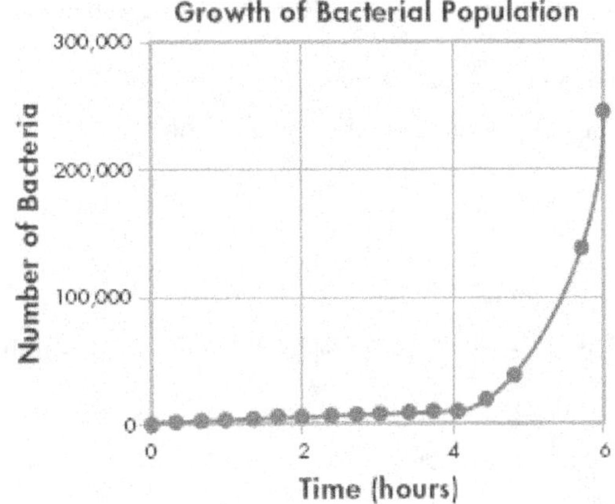

26. DDT was used to:

A. form ozone

B. feed animals

C. kill insects

D. fertilize the soil

E. form greenhouse gases

27. All renewable resources:

A. are living

B. can be recycled or reused

C. are unlimited in supply

D. can regenerate or be replenished

E. once were living

28. Density-dependent limiting factors include:

A. blizzards

B. damming of rivers

C. disease

D. earthquakes

E. average temperature

29. If a population grows larger than the carrying capacity of the environment:

A. birth rate must fall

B. death rate must fall

C. birth rate may rise

D. birth rate and death rate may rise

E. death rate may rise

30. One property that makes dichlorodiphenyltrichloroethane (DDT) hazardous is that it is:

A. deadly to herbivores

B. subject to biological magnification

C. volatile pesticide

D. insecticide

E. organic pesticide

31. As the population gets larger, it grows more quickly because the size of each generation of offspring is larger than the generation before, resulting in:

A. multiple growth

B. exponential growth

C. growth density

D. logistic growth

E. linear growth

32. The gray-brown haze often observed over large cities is:

A. vapor

B. particulates

C. greenhouse gases

D. ozone layer

E. smog

33. Compounds that contribute to the formation of acid rain contain:

A. nitrogen and sulfur

B. ammonia and nitrates

C. carbon dioxide and oxygen

D. calcium and phosphorus

E. carbon dioxide and ammonia

34. The various growth phases through which most populations go are represented on:

A. normal curve

B. population curve

C. logistic growth curve

D. exponential growth curve

E. linear growth curve

35. Water lilies do not grow in desert sand because water availability to these plants in a desert is:

A. competition factor

B. logistic growth curve

C. limiting factor

D. carrying capacity

E. none of the above

36. The sulfur and nitrogen compounds in smog combine with water to form:

A. acid rain

B. chlorofluorocarbons

C. ozone

D. ammonia

E. greenhouse gases

37. Air and water pollution have been reduced by:

A. raising more cattle for food

B. increasing biological magnification

C. using fossil fuels in factories

D. using only unleaded gasoline

E. using more effective pesticides

38. Which would be least likely affected by a density-dependent limiting factor?

A. population with a high immigration rate

B. large, dense population

C. population with a high birth rate

D. small, scattered population

E. population with a low death rate

39. Raising cattle and farming rice contribute to air pollution by:

A. releasing ozone into the atmosphere

B. producing smog which reacts to form dangerous ozone gas

C. producing particulates into the air

D. releasing sulfur compounds that form acid rain

E. releasing the greenhouse gas methane into the atmosphere

40. For most populations that are growing, as resources become less available, the population:

A. enters a phase of exponential growth

B. reaches carrying capacity

C. increases more rapidly

D. declines rapidly

E. enters a phase of linear growth

41. Which best describes the number of distinct species in the biosphere or a particular area?

A. species diversity

B. genetic diversity

C. ecosystem diversity

D. biodiversity

E. homogeneity

42. Which density-dependent factors other than the predator/prey relationship affect the populations of moose and wolves on an island?

A. A hurricane for both moose and wolves

B. Food availability for the moose and disease for the wolf

C. Extreme temperatures for the moose and flooding for the wolves

D. Parasitic wasps for the wolves and clear-cut forest for the moose

E. A drought for both moose and wolves

43. How are species diversity and genetic diversity different?

A. Species diversity measures the number of individuals of a species, while genetic diversity measures the total variety of species

B. Conservation biology is concerned with species diversity but not with genetic diversity

C. Species diversity is evaluated in ecosystems, while genetic diversity is evaluated in the entire biosphere

D. Species diversity measures the number of species in the biosphere, while genetic diversity measures the variety of genes in the biosphere, including genetic variation within species

E. Species diversity results from natural selection, while genetic diversity results from genetic engineering

44. Which is NOT likely to be a limiting factor on the sea otter population living in the ocean?

A. prey availability

B. predation

C. disease

D. competition

E. drought

45. Introduced species can threaten biodiversity because they can:

A. crowd out native species

B. reduce the fertility of native species

C. cause desertification of land

D. cause biological magnification

E. mate with native species

46. Which is a density-independent limiting factor?

A. parasitism and disease

B. eruption of a volcano

C. predator/prey relationships

D. struggle for food

E. available water or sunlight

47. Which would reduce competition within a species' population?

A. higher population density

B. fewer resources

C. higher birth rate

D. fewer individuals

E. lower death rate

48. A significant factor that negatively affects biodiversity is:

A. non-renewable resources

B. contour plowing

C. habitat fragmentation

D. biological magnification

E. preservation of ecosystems

49. All are threats to biodiversity EXCEPT:

A. habitat fragmentation

B. desertification

C. habitat preservation

D. biological magnification of toxic compounds

E. all the above are threats

50. The graph shows the changes in the mosquito population. What caused the changes in the graph?

A. increase in resources

B. density-dependent limiting factor

C. reduction in resources

D. increase in predation

E. density-independent limiting factor

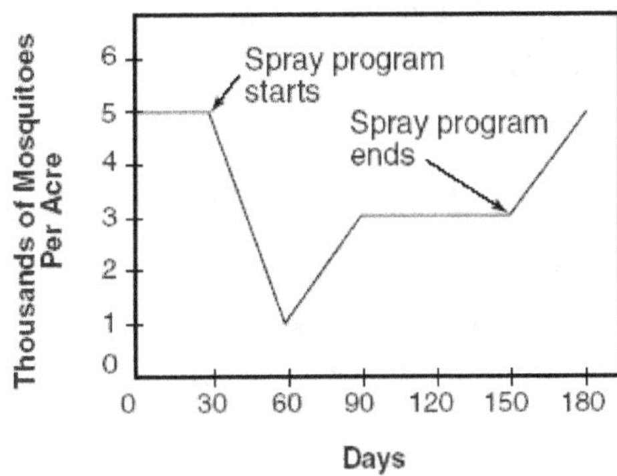

51. Each is a density-dependent limiting factor, EXCEPT:

A. crowding

B. disease

C. competition

D. temperature

E. predation

52. The "hot spot" strategy seeks to protect species in danger of extinction due to the following:

A. human activity

B. biological magnification

C. captive breeding programs

D. expanding national parks

E. preservation of ecosystems

53. About 500 years ago, the world's population started to:

A. level off

B. grow more rapidly

C. reach carrying capacity

D. decrease

E. grow sporadically

54. Protecting an entire ecosystem ensures that:

A. interactions among many species are preserved

B. governments will set aside land

C. existing parks and reserves will expand

D. captive breeding programs will succeed

E. wetlands will not be disturbed

55. The goals of biodiversity conservation include all the following EXCEPT:

A. Ensuring that local people benefit from conservation efforts

B. Preserving habitats and ecosystems

C. Introducing exotic species into new environments

D. Protecting individual species

E. Protecting populations

56. Countries in the first stage of demographic transition have:

A. slowly growing population

B. more older adults than young people

C. low death rate and a low birth rate

D. high death rate and a low birth rate

E. high death rate and a high birth rate

57. Demography is the scientific study of:

A. disease

B. human populations

C. parasitism

D. modernized countries

E. urban development

58. The amount of land and water necessary to provide the resources for a person's living and to neutralize that person's waste is that person's:

A. habitat

B. ecological sustainability

C. biodiversity

D. ecological footprint

E. environmental sustainability

59. Population density refers to the:

A. number of people in each age group

B. carrying capacity

C. number of individuals in a community

D. area inhabited by a population

E. number of individuals per unit area

60. The anticipated human population by the year 2050 is about:

A. 780 million

B. 11 trillion

C. 9.8 billion

D. 3.6 billion

E. 980 million

61. The demographic transition changes from high birth rates and high death rates to:

A. indefinite growth

B. low birth rates and high death rates

C. low birth rates and low death rates

D. exponential growth

E. high birth rates and low death rates

62. Imported plants and animals in Hawaii have:

A. increased crop yields

B. improved soil fertility

C. increased the native bird species

D. caused native species to die out

E. caused habitat fragmentation

63. A benefit of monoculture farming practices is:

A. pest resistance of crops

B. the ability to grow a lot of food

C. the ability to spend less money on fertilizer

D. the use of less water for irrigation

E. disease resistance of crops

64. An example of a density-independent limiting factor is:

A. disease

B. predation

C. mutualism

D. competition

E. unusual weather

65. In countries like India, the human population is growing:

A. logistically

B. linearly

C. exponentially

D. transitionally

E. demographically

66. Most of the worldwide human population is growing exponentially because:

A. human population does not conform to the logistic model

B. the food supply is limitless

C. human populations have not reached their exponential curve

D. most countries have not yet completed the demographic transition

E. competition for resources is absent

67. Success at solving an environmental problem is more likely when researchers follow the basic principles of ecology because:

A. ecology uses scientific research to identify the cause of problems and the best practices to solve them

B. ecologists are good at influencing government officials to change laws to improve the environment

C. ecological solutions to problems are usually straightforward to implement and can be done quickly

D. most people worldwide are more interested in saving the environment than comfort and convenience

E. ecology is concerned with the preservation of natural resources

68. Which problem can be identified by ecologists through graphical data?

A. habitat fragmentation
B. desertification
C. the hole in the ozone layer
D. ecological diversity
E. global warming

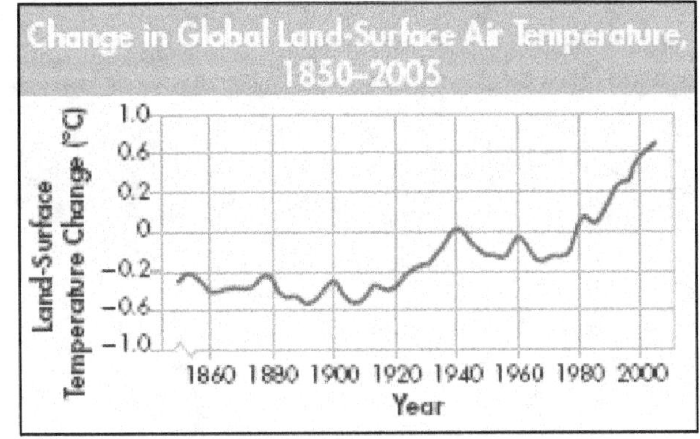

69. The total genetically based variety of organisms in the biosphere is:

A. ecosystem diversity
B. biodiversity
C. genetic diversity
D. species diversity
E. none of the above

70. An ecological hot spot is an area where:

A. many habitats and species are at substantial risk of extinction
B. species diversity is too high
C. habitats show a high amount of biodiversity
D. hunting is encouraged
E. species show a high amount of biodiversity

71. In a climax community, which would be a dominant species?

A. shrubs
B. annual grasses
C. mosses
D. deciduous trees
E. evergreens

72. Which statement is TRUE for a climax community?

A. It is relatively stable within a given climate
B. It is independent of the environment
C. It consists of only one species of life
D. It is populated mainly by so-called pioneer organisms
E. It consists of only dead and decaying organic matter

Notes or active learning

Notes or active learning

Notes or active learning

Detailed Explanations: Populations & Community Ecology

Answer Key

1: D	11: A	21: D	31: B	41: A	51: D	61: C	71: D
2: A	12: B	22: A	32: E	42: B	52: A	62: D	72: A
3: B	13: C	23: E	33: A	43: D	53: B	63: B	
4: D	14: D	24: A	34: C	44: E	54: A	64: E	
5: C	15: E	25: B	35: C	45: A	55: C	65: C	
6: E	16: E	26: C	36: A	46: B	56: E	66: D	
7: A	17: A	27: D	37: D	47: D	57: B	67: A	
8: B	18: C	28: C	38: D	48: C	58: D	68: E	
9: C	19: B	29: E	39: E	49: C	59: E	69: B	
10: E	20: D	30: B	40: B	50: E	60: C	70: A	

1. D is correct.

Sustainable development minimizes environmental impact. Sustainable buildings preserve precious natural resources and improve the quality of life.

Buildings should consider design, construction, or operation, reducing or eliminating negative impacts and positively impacting climate and the natural environment.

Features can make a development *green*, including:

Efficient use of energy, water, and other resources; renewable energy (e.g., solar energy)

Pollution and waste reduction measures and enabling re-use and recycling

Good indoor environmental air quality

Use of materials that are non-toxic, ethical, and sustainable

Consideration of the environment in design, construction, and operation

Design enables adaptation to a changing environment

2. A is correct.

Community is a population of species occupying the same geographical area.

In ecology, a community is an association of populations of two or more species simultaneously occupying the same geographical area.

continued...

Ecosystem is a community of organisms (e.g., plants, animals, microbes) with nonliving (i.e., *abiotic*) components of their environment (e.g., air, water, minerals).

Ecosystems are the network of interactions among and between organisms and their environment.

Habitat is an *ecological area* inhabited by a species. It is the natural environment in which an organism lives or the physical environment encompassing a population.

3. B is correct.

Population density measures population per unit area.

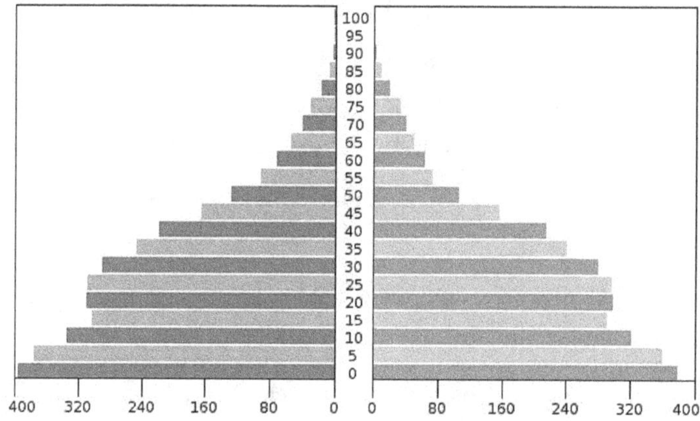

Population density plots age vs. population (in thousands) with males (left) and females

4. D is correct.

Sustainable development meets people's needs without compromising future generations' ability to meet their natural resources and environmental quality needs.

Preventing long-term environmental harm ensures that people can benefit from its use in the future.

5. C is correct.

Range (or *distribution*) of a population is the geographical area.

Dispersion is the variation in local *density* within a range.

continued...

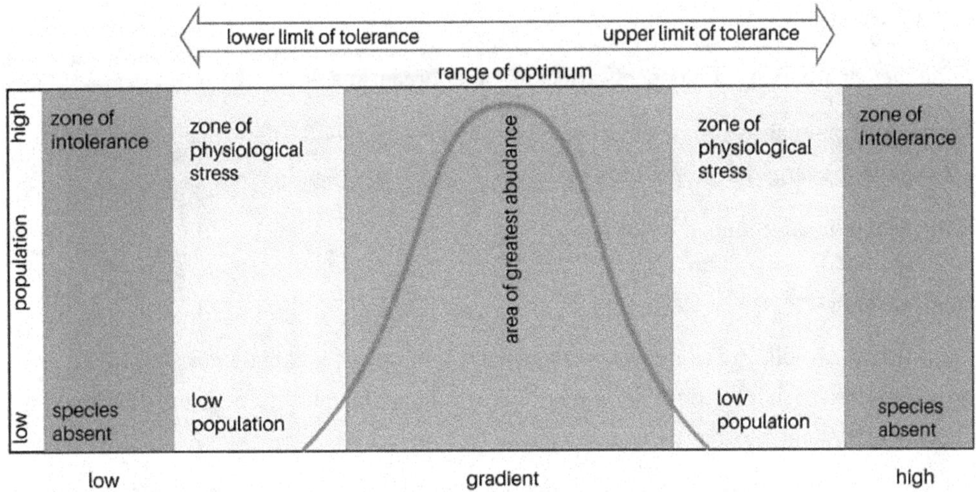

Range of tolerance plots population vs. bifurcated range of optimum stress

6. E is correct.

Observation notes characteristics *without* engagement or intervention by the researcher.

7. A is correct.

Demography uses statistics such as births, deaths, income, the incidence of disease, and education, illustrating the changing structure of human populations.

Population growth rate is how the number of people changes in a given period; the flow of people in and out, births, and deaths affect the number of individuals within a population.

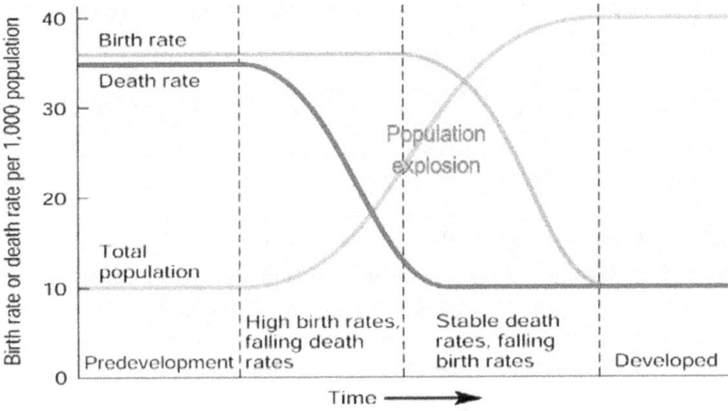

Birth rate and death rate affect population size transitioning from high to low rates with increasing population

8. B is correct.

Population density measures population per unit area (e.g., people per square mile).

9. C is correct.

Biotic factors are living components affecting other organisms.

For example, animals consume other organisms and organic food. Biotic factors need food and metabolic energy for proper growth.

Biotic factors include human influence.

10. E is correct.

Coal, natural gas, oil, and energy are derived from fossil fuels, including minerals (e.g., copper and magnesium). Non-renewable resources are not replenished at a sufficient rate for sustainable economic extraction.

Non-renewable resources require tens of thousands to millions of years and specific conditions to form.

Renewable resources are replenished over time through biological reproduction or other naturally recurring processes. They are integral to Earth's natural environment and its largest ecosphere components.

Renewable resources may be the source of power for renewable energy.

However, renewal and sustainability will not be sustainable when resource consumption exceeds the renewal rate.

11. A is correct.

Ecological models trace the interaction between and interdependence of factors within and across all population levels.

Ecological models highlight people's interactions with physical and environmental factors.

12. B is correct.

The Dust Bowl was a period of severe dust storms that significantly damaged the ecology and agriculture of the American and Canadian prairies during the 1930s; severe drought and a failure to apply dryland farming methods to prevent the aeolian processes (wind erosion) caused the phenomenon.

Crops began to fail with the onset of drought in 1931, exposing the bare, over-plowed farmland. It began to blow away without deep-rooted prairie grasses to hold the soil in place.

The eroding soil led to massive dust storms and economic devastation—especially in the Southern Plains.

13. C is correct.

Immigration is moving *into* an area.

Carrying capacity is the maximum population size the environment can sustain based on resources. If a population grows larger than the carrying capacity, species may die due to a lack of environmental resources.

Emigration is moving *out* of an area.

14. D is correct.

Animal training is not a method used by ecologists to study the environment.

15. E is correct.

Slower growth rate means fewer new individuals in a population. Increased birth rate and decreased death rates lead to a rise in growth rate, whereas decreased birth rate slows down the population growth rate.

	High stationary	Early expanding	Late expanding	Low stationary	Declining
	Stage 1	Stage 2	Stage 3	Stage 4	Stage 5
Birth rate	High	High	Falling	Low	Rising again
Death rate	High	Falls rapidly	Falls slowly	Low	Low
Natural output	Stable or slow increase	Very rapid increase	Increase slows down	Falling and then stable	Stable or slow increase

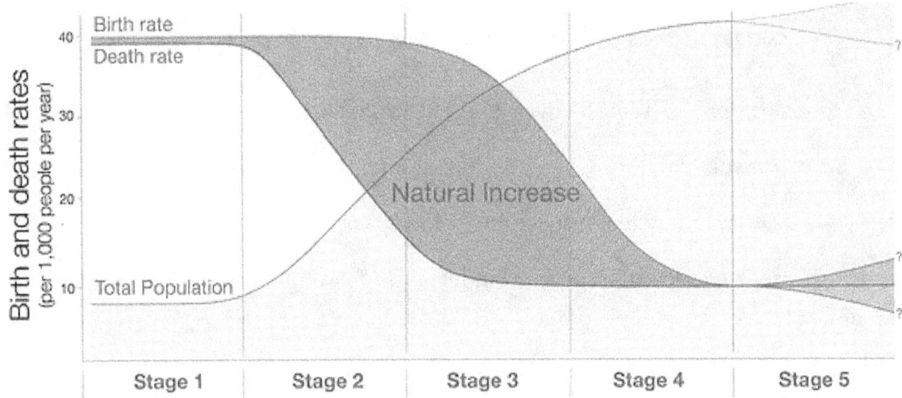

Five stages of demographic transition transitioning from high to low rates with increasing population

16. E is correct.

Desertification is land degradation when a relatively dry land region becomes increasingly arid, typically losing its bodies of water, vegetation, and wildlife.

Desertification is caused by factors such as climate change and human activities.

Removal of most vegetation is the immediate cause of desertification.

Desertification is driven by drought, climatic shifts, agriculture tillage, overgrazing, fuel deforestation, and construction materials harvesting.

Desertification is a global ecological and environmental problem.

B: *monoculture* is the practice of growing a single crop for many consecutive years.

Monocultures are widely used in industrial agriculture, and their implementation has allowed for large harvests from minimal labor.

However, monocultures quickly spread pests and diseases, making a uniform crop susceptible to a pathogen.

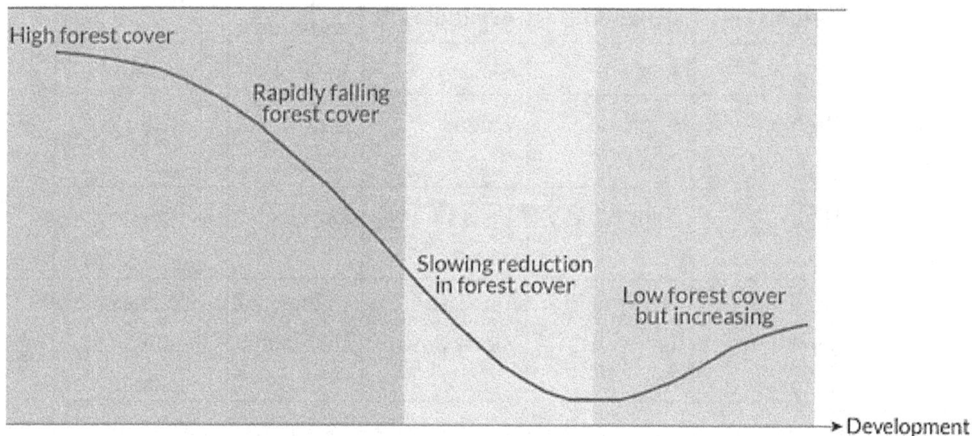

Four stages of forest transition model plotting forest cover vs. development

Stage 1 *Pre-transition*: high forest cover. No or slow loss of forest. (left panel on the graph)

Stage 2 *Early transition*: deforestation rates increasing.

Stage 3 *Late transition*: low forest cover but a slowing rate of deforestation

Stage 4 *Post-transition*: low forest cover but increasing through reforestation. (right panel on the graph)

17. A is correct.

Exponential growth is a process that increases quantity over time.

Exponential growth graphs exhibit *a steep curve up*.

Animals require resources (e.g., food, water, biotic factors) for survival.

Number of microorganisms in the culture increases *exponentially* until an essential nutrient is exhausted, which impedes the organisms' growth.

Typically, the first organism divides into two, which split to form four, eight, etc.

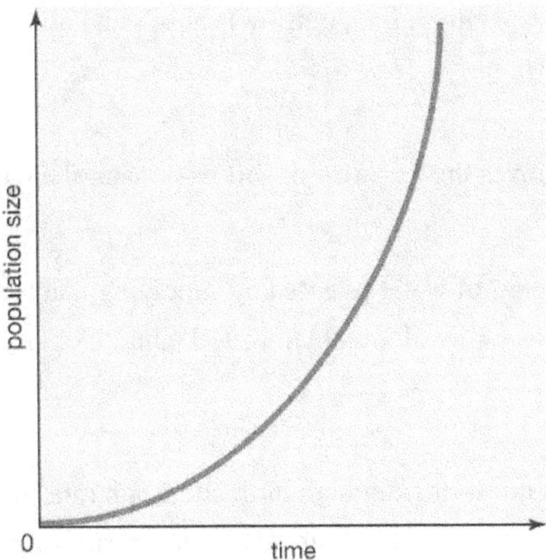

Exponential growth plotting population size vs. time with a steep positive slope indicating increasing numbers

18. C is correct.

Desertification is land degradation when a relatively dry land region becomes increasingly arid, typically losing its bodies of water, vegetation, and wildlife.

Desertification is caused by factors such as climate change and human activities. The immediate cause of desertification is the removal of most vegetation.

Desertification is driven by factors (alone or in combination) such as drought, climatic shifts, tillage for agriculture, overgrazing, deforestation for fuel, and harvesting of construction materials.

Desertification is a significant global ecological and environmental problem.

B: *monoculture* is the agricultural practice of growing a *single crop* for many consecutive years. It is widely used in industrial agriculture, and its implementation has allowed for large harvests from minimal labor.

continued...

However, monocultures quickly *spread pests and diseases*, making a uniform crop susceptible to a pathogen.

Stage 1 Pre-transition: high forest cover. No or slow loss of forest.

Stage 2 Early transition: deforestation rates increasing.

Stage 3 Late transition: low forest cover but a slowing rate of deforestation

Stage 4 Post-transition: low forest cover but increasing through reforestation.

19. B is correct.

Decreased birth rate and *emigration* (i.e., outflow) cause population size to *decrease*.

20. D is correct.

Soil erosion gradually removes the top layer of soil from natural elements such as water, wind, and farming.

Irrigation controls the amount of water released by supplying it at regular intervals for farming, which is an effective way of maintaining soil quality.

21. D is correct.

Demographic transition is the shift from high birth and death rates to low birth and death rates as a country develops from a pre-industrial to an industrialized economic system.

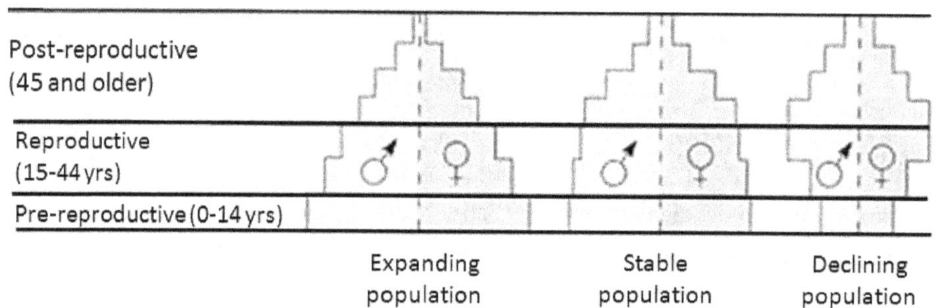

Age structure diagrams: pyramid (left) for expanding, bell-shaped (center) for stable, urn-shaped (right) for declining population profiles

continued...

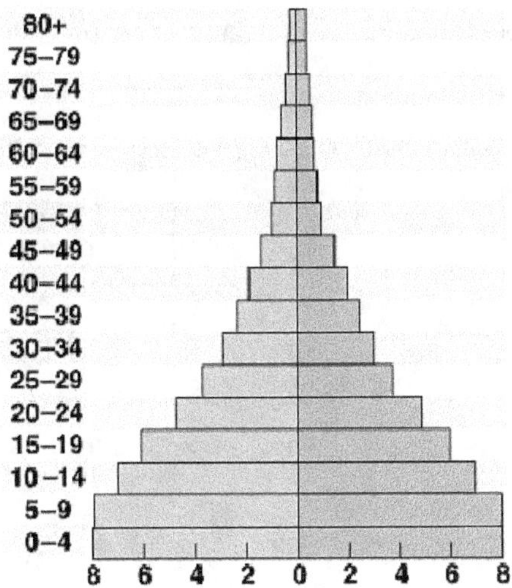

An expansive population pyramid plots age vs. percent. Males on the left. The graph is skewed towards younger members when the demographic transition is incomplete

22. A is correct.

Births and *immigration* (inflows) *increase* population size.

23. E is correct.

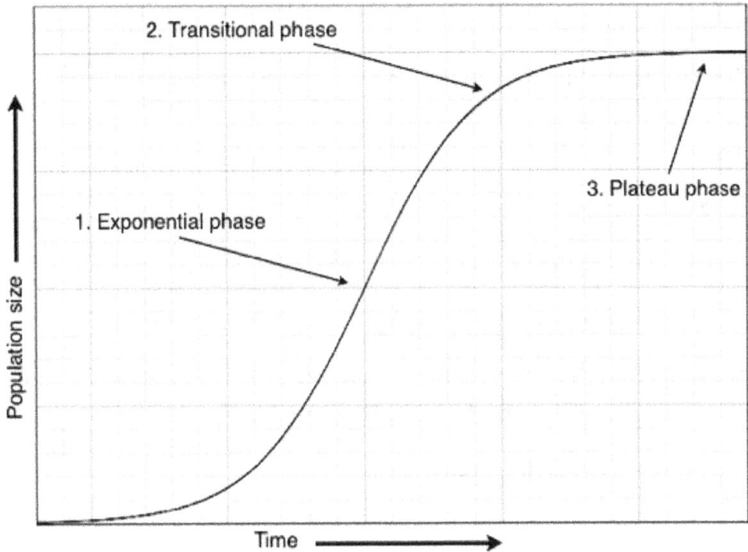

Sigmoidal (S)-shaped logistic growth curve of population growth with environmental resistance. The exponential phase has an accelerating growth rate. Exponential phase is marked by a steep positive slope, the transitional phase with a slightly positive slope, and the plateau phase with flat curve profiles

Exponential growth is a process that increases quantity over time; the graph exhibits a steep curve upward.

Logistic curve (or *function*) is a *sigmoid function* (S-shape) concerning population growth.

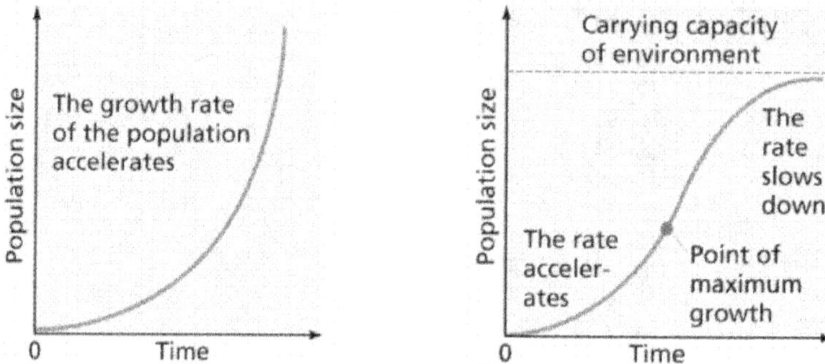

Exponential (unrestricted) growth (left) has accelerating growth patterns and logistic (restricted) growth (right) where the rate decreases as environmental carrying capacity is achieved

Animals require resources (e.g., food, water, biotic factors) for survival.

Number of microorganisms in the culture increases exponentially until an essential nutrient is exhausted, which impedes the organisms' growth.

24. A is correct.

Using predators and parasites for pest management is a sustainable resource in ecology.

25. B is correct.

Exponential growth is a process that increases quantity over time.

Exponential growth graph exhibits a steep curve upward.

Animals require resources (e.g., food, water, biotic factors) for survival.

The number of microorganisms in the culture increases exponentially until an essential nutrient is exhausted, which impedes the organisms' growth.

Typically, the first organism divides into two, forming four, eight, etc.

continued…

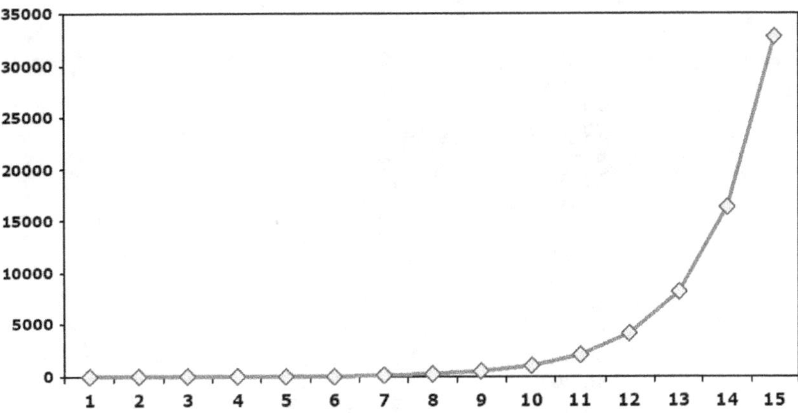

Exponential growth with population vs. generation plotted shows accelerated growth rates

26. C is correct.

DDT (or d*ichlorodiphenyltrichloroethane*) was a modern synthetic pesticide used in the United States (beginning in the 1940s) to control insects on food crops and in buildings for pest control.

DDT was discontinued in 1972 because of its harmful effects on humans and wildlife.

27. D is correct.

Renewable resources can be regenerated or replenished.

A renewable resource is a natural resource that can replenish over time through biological reproduction or other naturally recurring processes.

Renewable resources are a part of Earth's natural environment and the largest component of its ecosphere.

They may be the source of power for renewable energy.

Renewal and sustainability are not ensured if the renewable resource consumption exceeds its renewal rate.

28. C is correct.

Density-dependent limiting factors affect the size or growth due to variations in population density.

Dense populations are more strongly affected than less crowded ones.

Density-dependent limiting factors include food availability, disease, living space, predation, and migration.

continued...

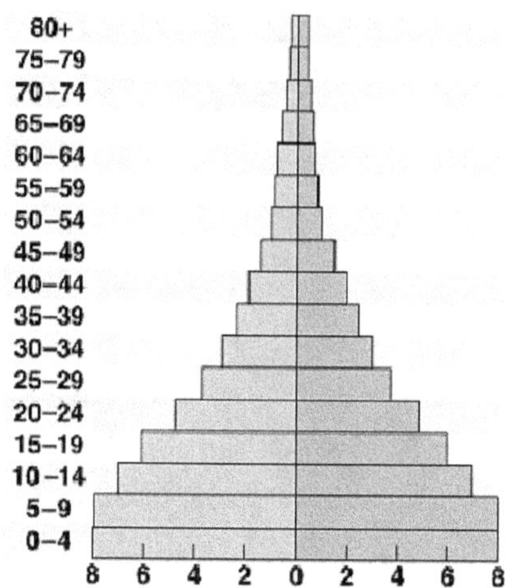

An expansive population pyramid plots age vs. percent. Males on the left. The graph is skewed towards younger members when the demographic transition is incomplete

29. E is correct.

Carrying capacity is the maximum population size the environment can sustain indefinitely based on the available resources.

If a population grows larger than the carrying capacity, species may die due to a lack of environmental resources.

30. B is correct.

Biological magnification is any concentration of a toxin, such as pesticides, in the tissues of tolerant organisms at successively higher levels in a food chain.

Biomagnification is when an organism's chemical concentration exceeds its food concentration when the primary exposure route occurs from the diet.

Higher-level predators (e.g., fish, birds, marine mammals) build up greater dangerous amounts of toxic materials than animals lower on the food chain.

DDT was banned in 1972 as a suspected carginogen (i.e., cancer causing agent).

31. B is correct.

Exponential growth is a process that increases quantity over time.

Graph of exponential growth exhibits a steep curve upward.

continued...

Animals require resources (e.g., food, water, biotic factors) for survival.

Number of microorganisms in culture increases exponentially until an essential nutrient is exhausted, which impedes the organisms' growth.

Typically, the first organism divides into two, who split to form four, eight, etc.

32. E is correct.

Photochemical smog is air pollution from the interaction of sunlight with certain atmospheric chemicals.

*Ozone i*s one of the primary components of photochemical smog.

Smog is air pollution that reduces visibility, labeled in the early 1900s to describe a mix of smoke and fog.

Smoke usually came from burning coal, while smog was common in industrial areas and remains a familiar sight in cities today.

Atmospheric pollutants or gases that form smog are released into the air when fuels are burnt.

Smog is formed when sunlight and its heat react with these gases and fine particles in the atmosphere.

Particulate matter is a mixture of tiny particles and liquid droplets.

Particle pollution comprises several components: acids (nitrates and sulfates), organic chemicals, metals, and soil or dust particles.

Greenhouse gas absorbs infrared radiation (net heat energy) emitted from Earth's surface and reradiates it back to Earth's surface, thus contributing to the greenhouse effect.

Carbon dioxide, methane, and water vapor are the most important greenhouse gases.

Ozone layer is a region in the Earth's stratosphere that contains high ozone (O_3) concentrations and protects the Earth from the sun's harmful ultraviolet (UV) radiation.

33. A is correct.

Acid rain is any form of precipitation when acidic components (e.g., sulfur dioxide, nitrogen oxides) fall to the ground from the atmosphere.

These compounds rise into the atmosphere, reacting with water and oxygen and falling to the ground as precipitation.

34. C is correct.

Logistic curve (or *function*) is a *sigmoid function* (S-shape) concerning population growth.

Initial growth stage is exponential.

As saturation begins, growth slows, and at maturity, growth stops.

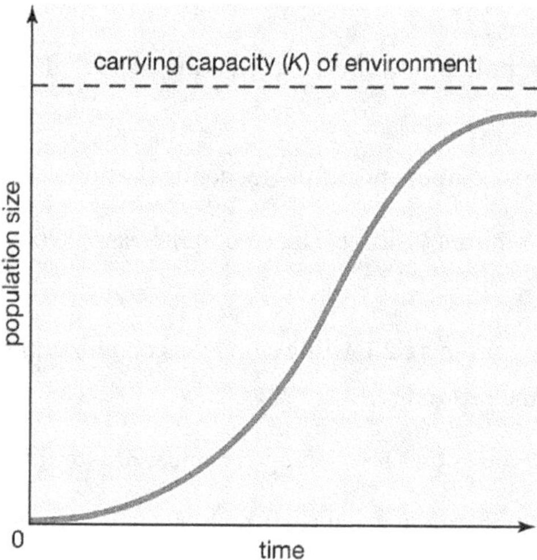

Logistic growth plotting population size vs. time where rate decreases at carrying capacity

Exponential growth is a process that increases quantity over time; the graph exhibits a *steep curve upward.*

35. C is correct.

Limiting factors in an ecosystem are typically food, water, habitat, and mate. The availability factors will affect the carrying capacity of an environment.

As the population increases, food demand increases. Since food is a limited resource, organisms will begin competing for it.

36. A is correct.

Acid rain is a chemical reaction with sulfur dioxide, and nitrogen oxides are released into the air. These compounds rise into the atmosphere, reacting with water and oxygen and falling to the ground as precipitation.

37. D is correct.

The vapors given off when gasoline evaporates and the substances produced when gasoline is burned (carbon monoxide, nitrogen oxides, particulates, and unburned hydrocarbons) contribute to air pollution.

Burning gasoline produces carbon dioxide (CO_2), a greenhouse gas.

Lead gasoline (prohibited in 1996) releases suspended particles into the air. Motor-vehicle emissions have been reduced by banning lead gasoline for motor vehicles.

However, lead is used in general-aviation gasoline for piston-engine aircraft.

Lead poisoning causes brain damage, chronic illness, lowered IQ, and elevated mortality.

38. D is correct.

Density-dependent limiting factors affect the size or growth due to variations in population density.

Dense populations are more strongly affected than less crowded ones.

Density-dependent limiting factors include food availability, disease, living space, predation, and migration.

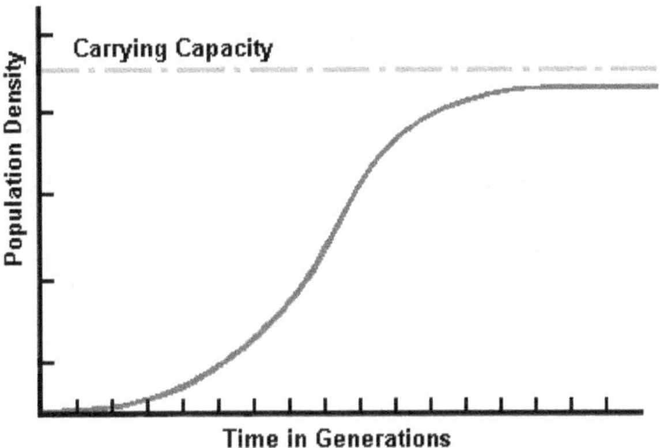

Logistic growth plotting population size vs. time where rate decreases at carrying capacity

39. E is correct.

Particulate matter is a mixture of tiny particles and liquid droplets.

Particle pollution comprises several components: acids (nitrates and sulfates), organic chemicals, metals, and soil or dust particles.

40. B is correct.

Carrying capacity is the maximum population size the environment can sustain indefinitely based on the available resources.

If a population grows larger than the carrying capacity, species may die due to a lack of environmental resources.

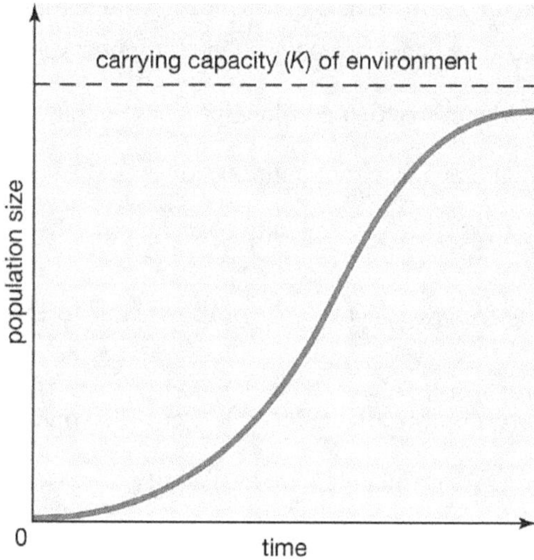

Logistic growth plotting population size vs. time where rate decreases at carrying capacity

41. A is correct.

Species diversity is the adequate number of species represented in a collection of individuals.

B: *genetic diversity* refers to the total number of genetic characteristics in the genetic makeup of a species.

It is distinguished from genetic variability, which describes the tendency of genetic characteristics to vary.

Genetic diversity serves as a way for populations to adapt to changing environments.

C: *ecosystem diversity* refers to the diversity of a place at the level of ecosystems (i.e., biotic and abiotic factors).

D: *biodiversity* refers to variation in species rather than ecosystems.

42. B is correct.

Density-dependent limiting factors affect the size or growth due to variations in population density.

Dense populations are more strongly affected than less crowded ones.

Density-dependent limiting factors include food availability, disease, living space, predation, and migration.

43. D is correct.

Species diversity is the adequate number of species represented in a collection of individuals.

B: *genetic diversity* refers to the total number of genetic characteristics in the genetic makeup of a species.

Genetic diversity is distinguished from *genetic variability*, which describes the tendency of genetic characteristics to vary. It serves as a way for populations to adapt to changing environments.

44. E is correct.

Drought is a prolonged period of abnormally low rainfall, leading to a water shortage. This limiting factor does not apply to marine animals.

45. A is correct.

Introduced species (or exotic species) is an organism not native to the place or area that has been accidentally or deliberately transported to the new location by human activity.

Introduced species may be predators or ecological consumers and crowd out native species.

46. B is correct.

Density-independent limiting factors are *not* influenced by population size.

Factors include weather, climate, and natural disasters. All species populations in the ecosystem will be similarly affected, regardless of population size.

Density-dependent limiting factors affect the size or growth due to variations in population density.

Dense populations are more strongly affected than less crowded ones.

Density-dependent limiting factors include food availability, disease, living space, predation, and migration.

47. D is correct.

Higher birth and lower death rates increase the number of individuals, thus increasing competition.

Fewer resources and higher population density lead to increased competition.

A decrease in population size can reduce competition.

48. C is correct.

Habitat is the natural environment in which an organism lives or the physical environment encompassing a population.

Habitat is an ecological area inhabited by a species.

Habitat fragmentation divides large habitats into smaller, isolated patches due to *habitat loss* by human activity and natural causes. This negatively affects biodiversity and reduces the suitable habitat for certain species.

49. C is correct.

Habitat is an ecological area inhabited by a species. It is the natural environment in which an organism lives or the physical environment encompassing a population.

50. E is correct.

Density-independent limiting factors are *not* influenced by population size.

Density-independent factors include weather, climate, and natural disasters.

Species populations in the ecosystem are similarly affected, regardless of population size.

The spray program affected the mosquito population as a density-independent limiting factor.

51. D is correct.

Density-dependent limiting factors affect the size or growth due to variations in population density.

Dense populations are more strongly affected than less crowded ones.

Density-dependent limiting factors include food availability, disease, living space, predation, and migration.

Density-independent limiting factors are *not* influenced by population size. Factors include weather, climate, and natural disasters.

All species populations in the ecosystem will be similarly affected, regardless of population size.

52. A is correct.

Hot spots are regions of species in a single geographic region (i.e., endemism).

Ecological hot spots tend to occur in tropical environments where species richness and biodiversity are higher than in ecosystems closer to the poles.

For example, biodiversity hotspots are forest habitats, as they constantly face destruction and degradation due to illegal logging, pollution, and deforestation.

53. B is correct.

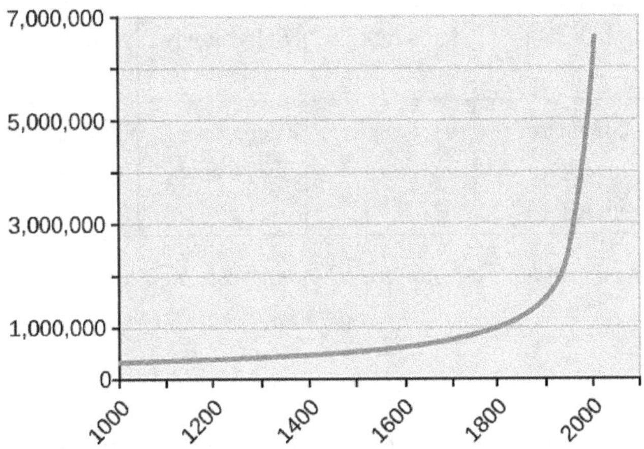

World population from 1000 AD. Graph plots population (in thousands) vs. year

54. A is correct.

Ecosystems include interactions between species. Protecting the entire ecosystem preserves this equilibrium.

55. C is correct.

Biodiversity conservation protects and preserves the wealth and variety of species, habitats, ecosystems, and genetic diversity.

Introduced species (or exotic species) is an organism not native to the place or area it is introduced.

Instead, it has been accidentally or deliberately transported to a new location by human activity.

Introduced species may be predators or ecological consumers and crowd out native species.

56. E is correct.

Demographic transition is the shift from high birth and high death rates to low birth and low death rates as a country develops from a pre-industrial to an industrialized economic system.

	High stationary	**Early expanding**	**Late expanding**	**Low stationary**	**Declining**
	Stage 1	Stage 2	Stage 3	Stage 4	Stage 5
Birth rate	High	High	Falling	Low	Rising again
Death rate	High	Falls rapidly	Falls slowly	Low	Low
Natural output	Stable or slow increase	Very rapid increase	Increase slows down	Falling and then stable	Stable or slow increase

Five stages of demographic transition transitioning from high to low rates with increasing population

57. B is correct.

Demography is the statistical study of human populations. Demographers use census data, surveys, and statistical models to analyze populations' size, movement, and structure.

58. D is correct.

Ecological footprint is environmental impact expressed as the amount of land required to sustain the use of natural resources.

59. E is correct.

Population density measures population per unit area (e.g., people per square mile).

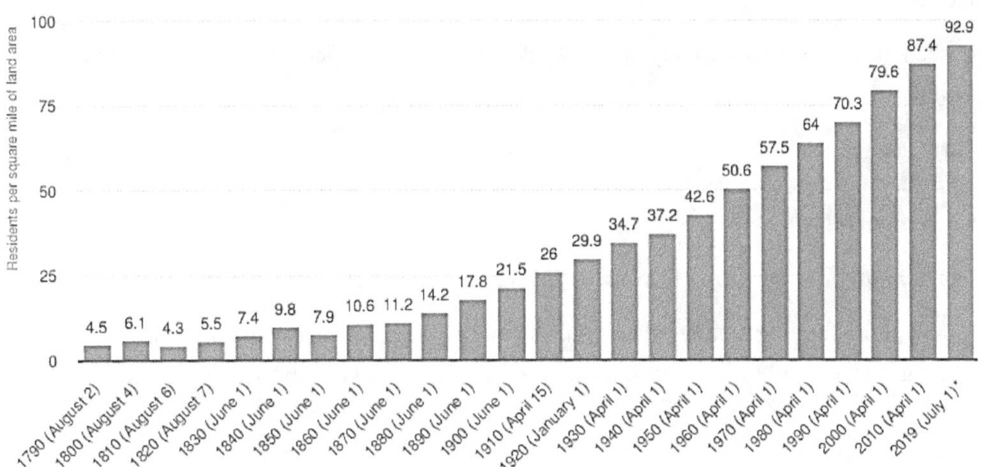

Population density of the United States from 1790 to 2019 in residents per square mile of land area

60. C is correct.

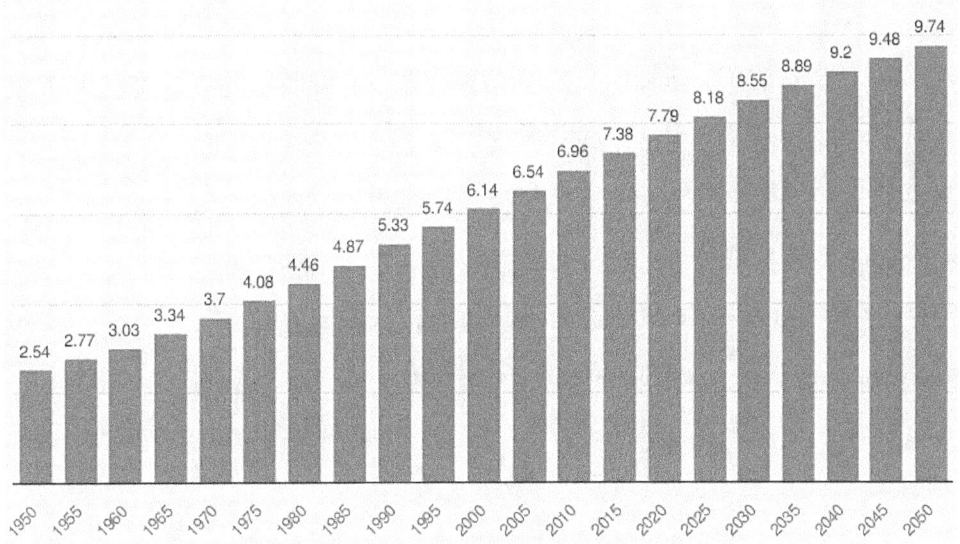

World population from 1950 to 2020 in billion

61. C is correct.

Demographic transition is the shift from high birth and high death rates to low birth and low death rates as a country develops from a pre-industrial to an industrialized economic system.

62. D is correct.

Introduced species (or exotic species) is an organism not native to the place or area it is introduced.

Instead, it has been accidentally or deliberately transported to the new location by human activity.

Introduced species may be predators or ecological consumers and crowd out native species.

63. B is correct.

Monoculture farming grows the same crop or plant yearly in a field.

Monoculture farming requires standardized planting, maintenance, and harvesting, resulting in greater yields and lower costs but can lead to quicker buildup and *spread of pests and diseases.*

64. E is correct.

Density-independent limiting factors are *not* influenced by population size.

Density-independent factors include weather, climate, and natural disasters.

All species populations in the ecosystem will be similarly affected, regardless of population size.

Predation is a biological interaction when a predator (i.e., a hunting organism) feeds on prey.

Exponential growth is a process that increases quantity over time.

Graph of *exponential growth* exhibits a steep curve upward.

65. C is correct.

Exponential growth is a process that increases quantity over time.

Exponential growth graph exhibits a *steep curve upward.*

66. D is correct.

Demographic transition is the shift from high birth and high death rates to low birth and low death rates as a country develops from a pre-industrial to an industrialized economic system.

	High stationary	**Early expanding**	**Late expanding**	**Low stationary**	**Declining**
	Stage 1	Stage 2	Stage 3	Stage 4	Stage 5
Birth rate	High	High	Falling	Low	Rising again
Death rate	High	Falls rapidly	Falls slowly	Low	Low
Natural output	Stable or slow increase	Very rapid increase	Increase slows down	Falling and then stable	Stable or slow increase

Five stages of demographic transition transitioning from high to low rates with increasing population

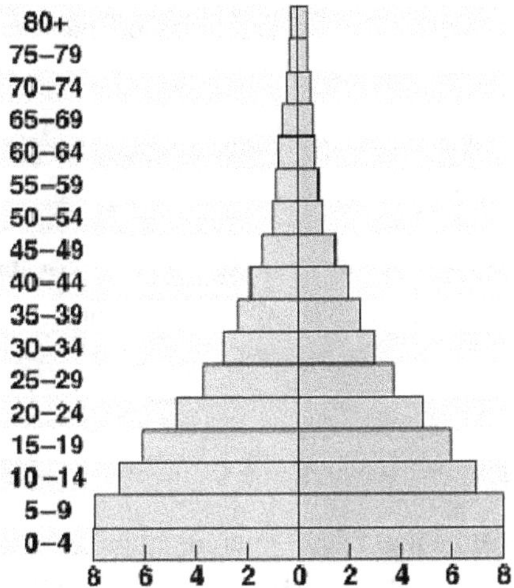

An expansive population pyramid plots age vs. percent. Males on the left. The graph is skewed towards younger members when the demographic transition is incomplete

67. A is correct.

Ecology uses scientific research to identify the cause and best practices to solve problems.

68. E is correct.

Global warming refers to the rise in the average temperature of the Earth's climate system.

The graph shows that the land-surface air temperature has increased over the last century.

69. B is correct.

Biodiversity is the biological variety and variability of life on Earth—biodiversity measures variation at the genetic, species, and ecosystem levels.

Terrestrial biodiversity is greater near the equator because of the warm climate and high primary productivity.

Genetic diversity refers to the total number of genetic characteristics in the genetic makeup of a species.

Genetic variability is the tendency of genetic characteristics to vary. It serves as a way for populations to adapt to changing environments.

70. A is correct.

Hot spots are regions of species in a single geographic region (i.e., endemism).

Hot spots are sensitive to human intervention, and many habitats and species are at a high risk of extinction.

Ecological hot spots tend to occur in tropical environments where species richness and biodiversity are higher than in ecosystems closer to the poles.

For example, biodiversity hotspots are forest habitats, as they constantly face destruction and degradation due to illegal logging, pollution, and deforestation.

71. D is correct.

Ecological succession in a rocky, barren area to a final climax community is:

> lichen → mosses → annual grasses → perennial grasses → shrubs → deciduous trees (e.g., thick shade trees such as oak and hemlock).

72. A is correct.

Climax community is when a biological community of plants, animals, and fungi reaches a steady-state through *ecological succession* (i.e., vegetation development in an area over time).

Equilibrium is when the climax community comprises species best adapted to average conditions.

For example, the climax community is grasslands in the Midwest, while deciduous forests are in the northeast.

B: *climax community* is mainly dependent on *environmental factors*.

Temperature, soil, and rainfall determine which organisms survive and thrive.

C: *biomes* are geographically and climatically defined as contiguous with similar conditions, such as communities of plants, animals, and soil organisms.

Many species live in a biome.

D: *pioneer species* are hardy species and the first to colonize previously disrupted ecosystems,

Pioneer species are the earliest species in a biome and initially colonize it (e.g., lichen on rocks). They begin a chain of ecological succession leading to a biodiverse steady-state ecosystem.

E: dead and decaying matter is a part of all communities but not the only aspect of them.

Notes for active learning

Notes for active learning

Notes for active learning

Notes for active learning

Annotated Glossary

1–in–100 flood – a flood with 1 in 100-year chance (used as a safety requirement for the construction industry).

100-year flood – a flood or storm with a 1% probability of occurring in any given year. The 100-year flood zone is the extent of the area of a flood with a 1% chance of occurring or being exceeded in a given year.

100,000-year problem – the discrepancy between climate response and forcing from incoming solar radiation.

20/30/10 standard – 20 mg/l Biochemical Oxygen Demand (BOD), 30 mg/l Suspended Solids (SS), 10 units of E. coli: the *water quality standard for greywater* use in toilets, laundry, and surface irrigation.

5Rs (*sustainability*) – reduce, remanufacture, reuse, recycle, recover.

A

A1B emissions scenario – a medium emissions scenario in which greenhouse gas emissions increase, with reductions in the rate of increase in emissions after 2070.

A2 emissions scenario – a high emissions scenario assuming continued increases in greenhouse gas emissions.

Abated – reduced by a degree or in intensity, elimination of pollution.

Abiotic – non-living chemical and physical factors of the environment. See *biotic*.

Abiotic component – non-living chemical and physical parts of the environment affecting living organisms and the functioning of ecosystems. *Abiotic factors and associated phenomena underpin biology.*

Abiotic factor – a nonliving environmental factor, such as water, soil, temperature, or sunlight.

Abrupt climate change – significant, sudden (on the order of decades) changes in some major climate system components, with rapid, widespread effects.

Absorption – one substance taking in another, either physically or chemically.

Absorption pit (or *soak away*) – a hole dug in the permeable ground filled with broken stones or granular material and usually covered with earth, allowing the collected water to soak into the ground.

Abundance – the number or amount of something.

Acclimation – the process of an organism adjusting to a chronic change in its environment.

Acids – substances that release hydrogen ions (H^+ or protons) in water.

Acid mine drainage – the outflow of acidic water from metal or coal mines.

Acid precipitation – acidic rain, snow, or dry particles deposited from the air due to increased acids released by anthropogenic or natural resources. See *acid rain*.

Acid rain – liquid, snow, fog, dust particles, etc.) containing acids that form in the atmosphere when sulfur dioxide and nitrogen oxide from industrial emissions and automobile exhaust combine with water.

Active solar system – a mechanical system to collect, concentrate, and store solar energy.

Acute – a short, short-term event. Contrast *chronic*.

Acute poverty – insufficient income or access to resources needed to provide the necessities for life, such as food, shelter, sanitation, clean water, medical care, and education.

Adapted – to become accustomed to the natural factors that are in each area and to be able to survive these factors; an organism can be either positively or negatively adapted.

Adaptation – 1. a characteristic of an organism favored by natural selection. 2. any adjustment in natural or human systems in response to a changed climate. *Adjustment or preparation of natural or human systems to a changing environment that moderates harm or exploits beneficial opportunities. Natural or human systems adjustment to a new or changing environment that exploits beneficial opportunities or moderates adverse effects.*

Adaptation science – integrated scientific research that directly contributes to enabling adjustments in natural or human systems to a new or changing environment in a way that exploits beneficial opportunities or moderates negative effects.

Adaptive behavior (*behavioral ecology*) – behavior that contributes to an individual's reproductive success and is thus subject to the forces of natural selection.

Adaptive capacity – the ability of a system to adjust to climate change (including climate variability and extremes) to moderate potential damages, exploit opportunities, or cope with consequences. *The potential of a system to adjust to climate change (including climate variability and extremes) to moderate potential damages, take advantage of opportunities, and cope with the consequences.*

Adaptive management – a plan designed from the outset to "learn by doing" and actively test hypotheses and adjust treatments as new information becomes available. *A structured process of flexible decision-making that incorporates learning from outcomes and new scientific information. The process facilitates decision-making by resource managers to manage and respond to climate change impacts.*

Adaptive radiation – closely related species that look very different due to having adapted to widely different ecological niches.

Additionality – in the context of a project funded by carbon offsets, the additionality is the reduction in greenhouse gas emissions in addition to what would have resulted in the absence of carbon offset funding.

Administrative courts – enforcement cases for agencies or consider appeals to agency rules.

Administrative law – executive orders, administrative rules and regulations, and enforcement decisions by administrative agencies and special administrative courts.

Adsorption – one substance taking up another at its surface.

Aerobic – requiring air or oxygen. *Decomposition processes in the presence of oxygen.*

Aerosol – solid or liquid particles suspended within the atmosphere. A suspension of solid or liquid particles within the air. Aerosols can cause cooling by scattering incoming radiation or by affecting cloud cover and cause warming by absorbing radiation. Some human-made aerosols (dust particles) in the atmosphere reflect solar radiation, therefore producing a cooling effect on global temperatures, while others can also absorb solar radiation (depending on the chemical's properties) to create a warming effect. *Depending on their composition, small particles or liquid droplets in the atmosphere can absorb or reflect sunlight.*

Aesthetic degradation – changes in environmental quality that offend our aesthetic senses.

Affluenza (*affluence and influenza*; defined in named book) – 1. the bloated, sluggish, and unfulfilled feeling resulting from efforts to keep up with the *Joneses*. 2. an epidemic of stress, overwork, waste, and indebtedness caused by the dogged pursuit of the Australian dream. 3. an unsustainable addiction to economic growth. *The traditional Western environmentally unfriendly high consumption lifestyle.* Compare *Froogle, freegan.*

Afforestation – planting new forests on lands not recently forested.

Agroforestry (*sustainability*) – an ecologically based farming system that, through the integration of trees in farms, increases social, environmental, and economic benefits to land users.

Air pollution – the modification of natural atmospheric characteristics by a chemical, particulate matter, or biological agent.

Alaska Pipeline – built from April 1974 to June 1977, this above-ground pipeline through Alaska brings oil from the oil wells in northern Alaska to shipping ports in southern Alaska.

Albedo (or reflectance) – an index of the "reflectiveness" of a surface; a way of quantifying how much radiation is reflected. The ratio of light from the Sun reflected by Earth's surface to the light it receives. Un-reflected light is converted to *infrared radiation* (i.e., heat), which causes atmospheric warming. Surfaces with a *high albedo* (e.g., snow and ice) generally contribute to *cooling*. Surfaces with a *low albedo* (e.g., forests) contribute to *warming. Land–use changes significantly alter land surface characteristics and can alter the albedo. Surfaces with low albedo (closer to 0) absorb most radiation directed toward them, and those with high albedo (closer to 1) reflect most of it.* See *radiative forcing.* Contrast *absorbed.*

Algae – any of the various chiefly aquatic, eukaryotic, photosynthetic organisms, ranging in size from single-celled forms to the giant kelp; once considered plants but now classified separately because they lack true roots, stems, leaves, and embryos.

Algal bloom – rapid and excessive algae growth, generally caused by high nutrient levels and other favorable conditions. *For example, warmer surface waters or increased nutrient levels. Some algal blooms may be toxic or harmful to humans and ecosystems. Blooms can deoxygenate the water leading to the loss of wildlife.*

Alien species (or *introduced species* and *exotic species*) – living outside its native distributional range, but which arrived there by human activity, directly or indirectly, and deliberately or accidentally.

Allee effect (*population ecology*) – the positive relationship between the size of a given population and its growth.

Alloy – a composite of materials made under conditions. Metal alloys like brass and bronze are well known, but many plastic alloys exist.

Alternative fuels – ethanol and compressed natural gas produce fewer emissions than traditional fossil fuels.

Alternative energy – derived from nontraditional sources (e.g., compressed natural gas, solar, hydroelectric, wind).

Alternative renewable energy – sources are replenished by natural processes at rates exceeding their use rate for human purposes, unlike fossil fuels that are not replenished at a useful rate, including solar, biomass, wind, geothermal, and hydropower.

Ambient air – the air immediately surrounding a location.

Amino acid –biological building blocks that make peptide and protein molecules; an organic compound containing amino and carboxyl groups.

Ammonia (NH_3) – a pungent, colorless, gaseous alkaline compound of nitrogen (N) and hydrogen (H) that is soluble in water and can be condensed to a liquid by cold and pressure.

Anaerobic – not requiring air or oxygen; used for decomposition processes occurring without oxygen. See *anaerobic digestion* and *anaerobic respiration.*

Anaerobic digestion – the biological degradation of organic materials in the absence of oxygen to yield methane (CH_4) gas (which may be combusted to produce energy) and stabilized organic residues (e.g., a soil additive).

Anaerobic respiration – the incomplete intracellular breakdown of sugar or other organic compounds without oxygen that releases some energy and produces organic acids or alcohol.

Ancient forest (or *old–growth forest*) – an area with great age and exhibits unique biological features.

Anemia – low levels of hemoglobin due to an iron deficiency or lack of red blood cells.

Animal behavior – the study of animal behavior. See *ethology.*

Annex I Countries (or *Annex I Parties*) – countries included in Annex I (as amended in 1998) to the U.N. Framework Convention on Climate Change, including all developed countries in the Organization of Economic Co-operation and Development and economies in transition. By default, the other countries are Non-Annex I countries. Under Articles 4.2 (a) and 4.2 (b) of the Convention, Annex I countries commit specifically to returning individually or jointly to their 1990 levels of greenhouse gas emissions by the year 2000.

Annual – a plant that lives for a single growing season.

Anomalies – deviation from the standard order or general rule.

Anoxic – with abnormally low levels of oxygen. See *euxinic.*

Anoxic event – when the Earth's oceans are free of oxygen below the surface layer.

Antarctic bottom water (ABW) – a type of water mass in the Southern Ocean surrounding Antarctica with temperatures ranging from −0.8 to 2 °C (35 °F) and salinities from 34.6 to 34.7 psu (i.e., *practical salinity units*). *As the densest water mass of the oceans, ABW is at depths below 4000 m of all ocean basins connected to the Southern Ocean at that level.*

Antarctic oscillation (AAO) – a low-frequency mode of atmospheric variability of the Southern Hemisphere.

Anthropocentric – 1. a belief that humans hold a special place in nature; 2. being centered primarily on humans and human affairs.

Anthropogenic – created, caused, or strongly influenced by humans or human activities; manufactured. *Originating from or due to human activity* (i.e., human-made, not natural).

Anthropogenic climate change – climate change with the presumption of human influence, usually warming.

Anthropogenic global warming (AGW) – global warming with presuming human influence.

Anthroposophy (*Rudolf Steiner*, 1861-1925) – spiritual philosophy and teachings which postulates the existence of an objective, intellectually comprehensible spiritual world accessible to direct experience through inner development – more specifically through cultivating a form of thinking independent of sensory experience conscientiously.

Anti-greenhouse effect – the cooling influence an atmosphere has on the ambient temperature of the planet.

Application efficiency (*sustainability*) – watering efficiency after losses due to runoff, leaching, evaporation, wind, and others.

Applied ecology – uses ecological principles and insights to solve environment-related problems. *Applied ecology includes agroecology and conservation biology.*

Aposematism (or *warning coloration*) – a warning signal consisting of brightly colored or starkly contrasting patterns used by a prey species to advertise its unprofitability to potential predator species.

Appropriate technology – made at an affordable price by ordinary people using local materials to do valuable work in ways that do the least possible harm to humans and the environment.

Appropriated carrying capacity (or *ecological footprint*) – the imported ecological capacity of overseas goods.

Aquaculture – the cultivation of aquatic organisms under controlled conditions.

Aquatic plant – a vascular plant adapted to living in saltwater or freshwater aquatic environments. They are referred to as hydrophytes or macrophytes to distinguish them from algae and other microphytes. A macrophyte is a plant that grows in or near water and is either emergent, submergent, or floating.

Aqueduct – a pipe or channel designed to transport water from a remote source, usually by gravity. *A bridge-like structure supporting a conduit or canal passing over a river or low ground.*

Aquifer – a bed or layer yielding water for wells and springs; an underground geological formation capable of receiving, storing, and transmitting large quantities of water. Aquifer types include *confined* (sealed and possibly containing "fossil" water), *unconfined* (capable of receiving inflow), and *artesian* (an aquifer in which the hydraulic pressure will cause the water to rise above the upper confining layer).

Arable land – land used for growing crops.

Arbitration – a formal dispute resolution process in which there are stringent rules of evidence, cross-examining witnesses, and a legally-binding decision the arbitrator makes that all parties must obey.

Area effect (*biogeographic*) – the hypothesis that larger islands can support more species than smaller ones.

Arctic amplification – a positive feedback loop triggered by melting sea ice replaces high-albedo ice with low-albedo sea capable of absorbing more solar radiation, trapping more heat near the Earth's surface, and contributing to more ice melting.

Arctic oscillation (AO) – the dominant pattern of non-seasonal sea-level pressure (SLP) variations north of 20 degrees N. It is characterized by SLP anomalies of one sign in the Arctic, and anomalies of the opposite sign centered about 37–45 degrees N. See *North Atlantic oscillation.*

Arctic shrinkage – the observed decrease in sea ice in the Arctic Ocean and Greenland Ice Sheet melting in recent years.

Arithmetical growth – a pattern of growth that increases at a constant amount per unit of time (e.g., 1, 2, 3, 4 or 1, 3, 5, 7).

Artesian well – the result of a pressurized aquifer intersecting the surface or being penetrated by a pipe or conduit, from which water gushes without being pumped; also called a "spring."

Asbestos – a fibrous incombustible mineral known to cause fibrosis and scarring in the lungs; a known carcinogenic material that causes lung cancer and mesothelioma.

Ash – the grayish white to black powdery residue left when something is burned.

Assisted migration – the intentional movement of individuals into areas assumed to be their future habitats.

Asthma – a distressing disease characterized by shortness of breath, wheezing, and bronchial muscle spasms.

Aswan High Dam – dam across the Nile River in Egypt, which impounds one of the largest reservoirs in the world; the artificial lake created by the dam Lake Nasser inundated many villages along the Nile and submerged some of the pyramids; hydroelectric installations were added in 1960 to the Aswan Dam.

Atlantic Multidecadal Oscillation (AMO) – a model of natural variability occurring in the North Atlantic Ocean with its principal expression in the sea surface temperature (SST) field.

Atmosphere – Earth's atmosphere is composed of gases and water retained by Earth's gravity and helps retain heat and reflect UV radiation from the Sun. The layer of gases around a material body. Earth's atmosphere consists, from the ground up, of the *troposphere* (including the planetary boundary layer or *peplosphere*, the lowest layer), *stratosphere, mesosphere, ionosphere* (or *thermosphere*), *exosphere,* and *magnetosphere. The dry atmosphere consists almost entirely of nitrogen (78.1% volume mixing ratio) and oxygen (20.9% volume mixing ratio), with trace gases, such as argon (0.93% volume mixing ratio), helium, radiatively active greenhouse gases such as carbon dioxide (0.035% volume mixing ratio), and ozone. In addition, the atmosphere contains water vapor, whose amount is highly variable but typically has a 1% volume mixing ratio. The atmosphere also contains clouds and aerosols.*

Atmospheric deposition – sedimentation of solids, liquids, or gaseous materials from the air.

Atmospheric lifetime – the average time a molecule resides in the atmosphere before it is removed by chemical reaction or deposition. In general, if a compound is emitted into the atmosphere at a particular time, about 35 percent of that quantity will remain at the end of the compound's lifetime. This fraction will continue to decrease exponentially so that about 15 percent of the quantity remains at the end of two times the atmospheric lifetime. *Some compounds, notably CO_2, have a simple exponential equation that does not define more complex lifecycles and their atmospheric lifetimes. Greenhouse gas lifetimes can range from a few years to a few thousand years.*

Atmospheric sciences – an umbrella term for studying the atmosphere, its processes, the effects other systems have, and the effects of the atmosphere on these other systems.

Atmospheric window – the parts of the electromagnetic spectrum not absorbed by Earth's atmosphere in its natural state.

Atom – the smallest unit of matter that has the characteristics of an element; consists of three main types of subatomic particles: protons, neutrons, and electrons.

Atomic number – the characteristic number of protons per atom of an element; used as an identifying attribute.

Attribution of recent climate change – the study of the causes of climate change.

Autecology (or *population ecology*) – a major sub-field of ecology that studies the dynamics of populations and how they interact with the environment.

Auto emissions standards – the standards that regulate how much pollution by one's vehicle is permissible.

Autotroph – an organism that produces complex organic compounds from simple inorganic molecules using energy from light (i.e., photosynthesis) or inorganic chemical reactions.

Available energy – energy with the potential to do work; also called "exergy."

Available water capacity – that proportion of soil water that plant roots can readily absorb.

Avoidance (*sustainability*) – the first step in the waste hierarchy where waste generation is prevented (avoided).

B

BOD: Biological oxygen demand

B1 emissions scenario – a lower emissions scenario in which emissions are reduced rapidly and substantially.

B2 emissions scenario – a low emissions scenario in which emissions are reduced substantially but not as rapidly as B1 scenario.

Baby Boom – a sudden large increase in the birthrate over a period, specifically the 15 years after World War II.

Backflow – the movement of water back to the source (e.g., contaminated water in a plumbing system).

Bacteria – any of a group (as kingdom *Prokaryotae*) of prokaryotic unicellular round, spiral, or rod-shaped single-celled microorganisms that are often aggregated into colonies or motile using flagella; live in soil, water, organic matter, or the bodies of plants and animals and are autotrophic, saprophytic, or parasitic in nutrition; important because of their biochemical effects and pathogenicity.

Baffle (*landscape design*) – an obstruction to trap debris in drainage water.

Ballast – anything that serves no purpose except to give bulk or weight to something or provide additional stability.

Bagasse – the fibrous residue of sugar cane milling used as a fuel to produce steam in sugar mills.

Barometric pressure – atmospheric pressure as indicated by a barometer.

Barrier islands – low, narrow, sandy islands that form offshore from a coastline.

Baseload – the steady and reliable supply of energy through the grid. This is punctuated by bursts of higher demand known as "peak–load." Supply companies must be able to respond instantly to extreme variations in demand and supply, especially during extreme conditions. *Gas generators react quickly, while coal is slow but provides a steady "baseload." Renewable energies are generally not available on demand.*

Bases – substances that bond readily with hydrogen ions.

Basin – a large, bowl-shaped depression on the surface of the land or on the ocean floor.

BAT – acronym for *Best available, economically achievable technology*.

Batesian mimicry – evolution by one species to resemble the coloration, body shape or behavior of another species that is protected from predators by a venomous stinger, being inedible or some other defensive adaptation.

Batters (*landscape design*) – the slope of earthworks such as drainage channels.

Behavioral ecology – studies the ecological and evolutionary basis of animal behavior, mainly at the level of individual animals.

Benthos – the bottom of a sea or lake.

Best available, economically achievable technology (BAT) – the least pollution-causing technological solution; also known as *best available techniques, best practicable means*, or *best practicable environmental option*.

Best practical control technology (BPT) – the best technology for pollution control available at a reasonable cost and operable under normal conditions.

Best practice – a process or innovative use of technology, equipment or resources, or other measurable factors with a proven record of success.

Beta particles – high-energy electrons released by radioactive decay.

Bhopal, India (December 3, 1984) – a noxious methylisocyanate gas blanketed the city when water mixed with a tank containing 40 tons of MIC, setting off a chemical reaction; 1,754 died, with over 200,000 injured.

Bill – legislation introduced in Congress and intended to become law.

Bioaccumulation – the accumulation of a substance, such as a toxic chemical, in the tissues of a living organism.

Biocapacity – a measure of the biological productivity of an area. *This may depend on natural conditions or human inputs like farming and forestry practices, the area needed to support the consumption of a defined population.*

Biocoenosis (or *biocoenose*) – all interacting organisms living in a habitat (or biotope).

Biocentric preservation – a philosophy that emphasizes living organisms' fundamental right to exist and pursue their goods.

Biocentrism – the belief that all creatures have rights and values, centered on nature rather than humans.

Biocide – a broad-spectrum poison that can kill a wide range of organisms.

Biodegradable – capable of decomposing through organisms' actions, especially bacteria.

Biodegradable plastics – plastics that microorganisms can decompose.

Biodiversity – the variety of life in all forms, levels, and combinations, including ecosystem, species, and genetic diversity. *Variety among and within plant and animal species in each environment.*

Bioelement – an element required by a living organism. *Atoms that make up all living things mainly consist of six chemical elements: carbon (C), oxygen (O), hydrogen (H), nitrogen (N), phosphorus (P), and sulfur (S). These elements constitute more than 99% of the matter found in living things.*

Bioenergy – 1. narrowly, a synonym for biofuel, fuel derived from biological sources. 2. broadly, it encompasses biomass, the biological material used as a biofuel, and the social, economic, scientific, and technical fields associated with using biological sources for energy. *For example, energy produced using plant or animal matter such as corn or manure.*

Biofuel – the fuel (or energy source) produced by the chemical or biological processing of biomass (i.e., organic mass). Biofuel is solid (e.g., charcoal), liquid (e.g., ethanol), or gas (e.g., methane). *Gas or liquid fuel made from plant material. Includes wood, wood waste, wood liquors, peat, railroad ties, wood sludge, spent sulfite liquors, agricultural waste, straw, tires, fish oils, tall oil, sludge waste, waste alcohol, municipal solid waste, landfill gases, other waste, and ethanol blended into motor gasoline.*

Biogas (or *biomass gas*) – landfill and sewage gas.

Biogeochemistry – studies the effects of biota on global chemistry and the cycles of matter and energy that transport Earth's chemical components in time and space.

Biogeochemical cycle – 1. a pathway by which a chemical element or molecule moves through biotic (*bio-*) and abiotic (*geo-*) parts of an ecosystem, the atmosphere, hydrosphere, lithosphere, and biosphere. 2. movement of matter within or between ecosystems; caused by living organisms, geological forces, or chemical reactions (e.g., the cycling of nitrogen, carbon, sulfur, oxygen, phosphorus, and water). *Movements through the Earth's system of key chemical constituents essential to life, including carbon, nitrogen, oxygen, and phosphorus.*

Biogeographic realm (or *ecozone*) – an area with characteristics of natural origin such as climate, terrain, and vegetation; the largest division of the Earth's surface, filled with living organisms.

Biogeographical area – an entire self-contained natural ecosystem and its associated land, water, air, and wildlife resources.

Biogeography – the study of the geographic distribution of species on Earth.

Bio-invader – a non-native species.

Biological community – the populations of plants, animals, and microorganisms living and interacting in a particular area at a given time.

Biological controls – use of natural predators, pathogens, or competitors to regulate pest populations.

Biological dispersal – the movement of organisms from birth to breeding sites or between breeding sites.

Biological factors (or *biotic factors*) – organisms and products of organisms that are part of the environment and potentially affect the lives of other organisms.

Biological magnification – the increase in the concentration of a chemical substance in the tissues of organisms comprising successively higher levels in a food chain.

Biological oxygen demand (BOD) – a chemical procedure for determining how fast biological organisms use oxygen in a body of water.

Biological pest control – a method of controlling pests (including insects, mites, weeds, and plant diseases) that relies on predation, parasitism, herbivory, or other natural mechanisms.

Biological pests – organisms that reduce the availability, quality, or value of resources useful to humans.

Biological productivity (or *bioproductivity*) – the capacity of a given area to produce biomass; different ecosystems (i.e., pasture, forest) will have different levels of bioproductivity. Biological productivity is determined by dividing the total biological production (how much is grown and living) by the total area available.

Biological resources – the plants and animals necessary for the services provided.

Biologically productive land – fertile soil to support forests, agriculture, or animal life. All the biologically productive lands of a country comprise its biological capacity. *Arable land is typically the most productive area.*

Biomagnification – an increase in the concentration of certain stable chemicals (e.g., heavy metals or fat-soluble pesticides) in a successively higher food chain or web trophic levels.

Biomass – 1. materials derived from photosynthesis (fossilized materials may be included) such as forest, crops, wood and wood wastes, animal wastes, livestock operation residues, aquatic plants, and municipal and industrial wastes; 2. the quantity of organic material present in a unit area at a particular time, mostly expressed as tons of dry matter per unit area; 3. organic matter that can be used as fuel. *Biological materials, including organic material (both living and dead) from above and below ground, for example, trees, crops, grasses, tree litter, roots, and animal and animal waste.*

Biomass fuel – organic material produced by plants, animals, or microorganisms that can be burned directly as a heat source or converted into a gaseous or liquid fuel.

Biomass gas (or *biogas*) – landfill gas and sewage gas.

Biomass pyramid (or *ecological pyramid*) – a graph that illustrates the productivity within a trophic level. *Diagram illustrating the relationship between biomass amounts at different trophic levels.*

Biome (or *ecosystems*) – the total complex of biotic communities occupying and characterizing a particular area. A climatic and geographically defined area of ecologically similar communities of plants, animals, and soil organisms, often called *ecosystems*.

Biophysical – the living and non-living components and processes of the ecosphere. *Biophysical measurements of nature quantify the ecosphere in physical units such as cubic meters, kilograms, or joules.*

Bioregion (*ecoregion*) – an area comprising a natural ecological community bounded by natural borders.

Bioremediation – using organisms to remove or neutralize contaminants (e.g., petroleum), mainly in soil or water.

Biosolids – nutrient-rich organic materials derived from *wastewater solids* (or *sewage sludge*) that have been stabilized through processing.

Biosphere – 1. the zone of air, land, and water at the surface of Earth occupied by living organisms; 2. the combination of all ecosystems on Earth maintained by the energy of the Sun; 3. the interface between the hydrosphere, the geosphere, and the atmosphere. *The global sum of all ecosystems on Earth. Part of the Earth system comprising all ecosystems and living organisms, in the atmosphere, on land (terrestrial biosphere), or in the oceans (marine biosphere), including derived dead organic matter, such as litter, soil organic matter, and oceanic detritus.*

Biosphere reserves – world heritage sites the *International Union for the Conservation of Nature* (IUCN) identified as worthy of national park or wildlife refuge status because of high biological diversity or unique ecological features.

Biota – the total of organisms belonging to a particular geographic region or extent during a particular time. *All organisms in a given area.*

Biotic – relating to, produced by, or caused by living organisms. Compare *abiotic.*

Biotic factors (or *biological factors*) – organisms and products of organisms that are part of the environment and potentially affect the lives of other organisms.

Biotic potential – the maximum reproductive capacity of a population under optimum environmental conditions. Compare *environmental resistance.*

Birth control – 1. any method used to reduce births, including celibacy, delayed marriage, and contraception; 2. devices or medication intended to prevent the implantation of fertilized zygotes.

Birth rate – the number of people born as a percentage of the total population in any given period, expressed in the number of live births per 1,000 people.

Black carbon – soot produced from coal burning, diesel engines, cooking fires, wildfires, and other combustion sources. These particles absorb solar energy and have a warming influence on the climate.

Black carbon (BC) aerosol – the most strongly light-absorbing *particulate matter* (PM) component and is formed by the incomplete combustion of fossil fuels, biofuels, and biomass. It is emitted directly into the atmosphere as fine particles ($PM_{2.5}$).

Black lung disease – inflammation and fibrosis caused by the accumulation of coal dust in the lungs or airways.

Blackwater – household wastewater that contains solid waste (i.e., toilet discharge) that cannot be reused without purification.

Blue-green algae (*Cyanobacteria* or *Cyanophyta*) – a phylum of bacteria obtaining energy through photosynthesis.

Blue revolution – new techniques of fish farming that may contribute as much to human nutrition as miracle cereal grains but also may create social and environmental problems.

Bluewater – collectible water from rainfall; the water that falls on roofs and hard surfaces usually flows into rivers and the sea and recharges the groundwater. The global average proportion of total rainfall in blue water is about 40%. Bluewater productivity in the garden can be increased by improving irrigation techniques, soil water storage, moderating the climate, using garden design and water–conserving plantings, and safe use of *grey water.*

Bog – an area of waterlogged soil that tends to be peaty, fed mainly by precipitation; low productivity; some bogs are acidic.

Boreal – 1. of the north or northern areas; 2. refers to the cold temperate Northern Hemisphere forests of birch, poplar, or conifers that grow where there is a mean annual temperature < 0 °C.

Boreal forest (or *taiga* in Siberia) – forest areas of the northern temperate zone, mainly consisting of conifers. *Broadband of mixed coniferous and deciduous trees that stretches across northern North America (and Europe and Asia)*; its northernmost edge, the taiga, intergrades with the arctic tundra.

Borehole – any exploratory hole drilled into the Earth or ice to gather geophysical data. *Climate researchers often take ice core samples, a type of borehole, to predict atmospheric composition in earlier years.* See *ice core*.

BPT (best practicable control technology) – the best technology available for pollution control at a reasonable cost and operable under normal conditions.

Brackish water – fresh and saltwater combined.

Breeder reactor – 1. a nuclear reactor that produces more fuel than it consumes; this type of reactor is used mainly to produce plutonium; 2. a nuclear reactor that produces fuel by bombarding isotopes of uranium and thorium with high-energy neutrons that convert inert atoms to fissionable ones.

Breeding – a group of organisms with common ancestors and certain distinguishable characteristics, especially a group within a species developed by artificial selection and maintained by controlled propagation.

Broad-acre farm – commercial farm covering a large area; usually a mixed farm in dryland conditions.

Brownfields – describes land previously used for industrial or commercial purposes with known or suspected pollution, including soil contamination due to hazardous waste. *Abandoned or underused urban areas in which redevelopment is blocked by liability or financing issues related to toxic contamination.*

Brundtland Commission Report (1987) – a UN report, *Our Common Future*, addressing sustainable development and the policies required to achieve it, which the report characterizes as "*development that meets the needs of the present without compromising the ability of future generations to meet their own needs.*"

C

C_2F_6 (hexafluoroethane) – the perfluorocarbon counterpart to the hydrocarbon ethane; a non-flammable gas negligibly soluble in water and slightly soluble in alcohol. It is an extremely potent and long-lived greenhouse gas. *Due to the high energy of C-F bonds, hexafluoroethane is inert and thus is an extremely stable greenhouse gas, with an atmospheric lifetime of 10,000 years. It has a global warming potential (GWP) of 9200 and an ozone depletion potential (ODP) of 0. Hexafluoroethane is included in the IPCC list of greenhouse gases.*

C3 plants – comprise 95% of all plants, photosynthesize to form 3 carbon molecules, and increase photosynthesis as CO_2 levels increase. Compare C4 plants.

C4 plants – comprise about 5% of all plants, are most abundant in hot and arid conditions, and include crops like sugar cane and soybeans. During photosynthesis, C4 plants form molecules with 4–carbon atoms and saturate at the given level of CO_2. Compare C3 plants.

Calendar effect (1938) – the theory linking rising atmospheric carbon dioxide (CO_2) concentrations to global temperatures. In 1938, Guy Calendar was among the first to show that the land temperature of Earth had risen over the previous 50 years. Svante Arrhenius earlier proposed this theory. *Calendar thought this warming was beneficial, delaying the return of deadly glaciers.*

Calorie – a basic measure of energy that the SI unit, the *joule*, has replaced; in physics, it approximates the energy needed to increase the temperature of 1 gram of water by 1 °C, which is about 4.184 joules. *Calories in food ratings (with capital C) and nutrition are 'capital C Calories or kcal.*

Calorific value – the energy content of a fuel measured as heat released on complete combustion.

Camouflage – an inconspicuous appearance adopted by an organism to deceive possible predators or prey.

Cancer – a group of diseases in which cells are aggressive (grow and divide without respect to normal limits), invasive (invade and destroy adjacent tissues) and sometimes metastatic (spread to other locations in the body).

Cap and trade – a system that limits aggregate emissions from a group of emitters by setting a "cap" on maximum emissions. It is a market-based policy to reduce emissions of pollutants and encourage business investment in fossil fuel alternatives and energy efficiency. See *emissions trading*.

Caprock – last layer of material on top of a geological formation such as Canadian Shield.

Capillary action (or *wicking*) – water drawn through a medium by surface tension.

Capillary water – droplets clinging in small pores, cracks, and spaces against the pull of gravity (e.g., the water retained in a sponge).

Capital – any form of wealth, resources, or knowledge available to produce more wealth.

Captive breeding – raising plants or animals in zoos or other controlled conditions to produce stock for subsequent release into the wild.

Carbohydrate – an organic compound consisting of a ring or chain of carbon atoms with hydrogen and oxygen attached (e.g., sugars, starches, cellulose, and glycogen).

Carbon budget – measures carbon inputs and outputs for a particular activity.

Carbon capture and sequestration (CCS) – technologies that can significantly reduce carbon dioxide (CO_2) emissions from new and existing coal- and gas-fired power plants, industrial processes, and other stationary sources of carbon dioxide. *It is a three-step process that includes the capture of carbon dioxide from power plants or industrial sources; transport of the captured and compressed carbon dioxide (usually in pipelines); and underground injection and geologic sequestration, or permanent storage, of that carbon dioxide in rock formations that contain tiny openings or pores that trap and hold the carbon dioxide.*

Carbon capture and storage – the process of capturing carbon dioxide and injecting it into geologic formations underground for long-term storage.

Carbon credit – a market–driven way of reducing the impact of greenhouse gas emissions; it allows an agent to benefit financially from an emission reduction. Two forms of carbon credit are part of national and international trade and those that individuals purchase.

Kyoto Protocol sets *caps* (or *limits*) on participating countries' emissions are established. Countries set 'caps' (credits: 1 convertible and transferable credit = 1 metric ton of CO_2 emissions) for operators. Operators who meet the agreed *caps* can sell unused credits to operators who exceed 'caps.' *Operators can choose the most cost–effective way of reducing emissions. Individual carbon credits would operate similarly.*

Carbon cycle (*biogeochemical cycle*) – the biogeochemical cycle exchanging carbon between Earth's biosphere, geosphere, hydrosphere, and atmosphere Carbon is exchanged between the biosphere, the geosphere, the hydrosphere, and the atmosphere of Earth. Circulation of carbon atoms through Earth's systems because of the photosynthetic conversion of carbon dioxide into complex organic compounds by plants, which are consumed by other organisms, and return of the carbon to the atmosphere as carbon dioxide (CO_2) because of respiration, decay of organisms, and combustion of fossil fuels. *Includes photosynthesis, decomposition, and respiration (e.g., carbon dioxide is taken from the atmosphere by photosynthesizing plants and returned by the respiration of plants and animals and by the combustion of fossil fuels).*

Carbon diet – the act of reducing the output of CO_2 to reduce environmental impact.

Carbon dioxide (CO_2) – the most abundant *greenhouse gas* emitted from fossil fuels. A naturally occurring gas and by-product of burning fossil fuels and biomass, land-use changes, and other industrial processes. *Carbon dioxide is the principal human-caused greenhouse gas affecting Earth's radiative balance. It is the reference gas against which other greenhouse gases are measured and has a Global Warming Potential of 1.* See *climate change* and *global warming.*

Carbon dioxide equivalent (CO_2e) – the unit used to measure the impacts of releasing (or avoiding the release of) the seven different greenhouse gases; it is obtained by multiplying the mass of the greenhouse gas by its global warming potential. *For example, this would be 21 for methane and 310 for nitrous oxide.* A metric measure comparing the emissions from various greenhouse gases based on their *global warming potential* (GWP). Carbon dioxide equivalents are "million metric tons of *carbon dioxide equivalents* (MMTCO2Eq)." The carbon dioxide equivalent for a gas is derived by multiplying the tons of the gas by the associated GWP. MMTCO2Eq = (million metric tons of a gas) * (GWP of the gas). See *greenhouse gas, global warming potential,* and *metric tons.*

Carbon dioxide fertilization – the enhancement of the growth of plants because of increased atmospheric CO_2 concentration. *Depending on their photosynthesis mechanism, certain plants are more sensitive to changes in atmospheric CO_2 concentration.*

Carbon dioxide removal (**CDR**; or *carbon removal, greenhouse gas removal* (GGR) or *negative emissions*) – a process in which carbon dioxide gas (CO_2) is removed from the atmosphere by deliberate human activities and durably stored in geological, terrestrial, or ocean reservoirs, or in products. CDR is increasingly integrated into climate policy, as a climate change mitigation strategy. CDR methods include afforestation, reforestation, agricultural practices that sequester carbon in soils (carbon farming), wetland restoration and blue carbon approaches, bioenergy with carbon capture and storage (BECCS), ocean fertilization, ocean alkalinity enhancement, and direct air capture combined with storage.

Carbon equivalent (C-e) – obtained by multiplying the CO_2-e by the factor 12/44.

Carbon footprint – the total greenhouse gas emissions caused by an organization, event, or product. *A measure of the carbon emissions emitted over the entire lifecycle of a product or service, usually expressed as grams of CO_2-e. A person's carbon footprint includes greenhouse gas emissions from fuel that an individual burns directly, such as by heating a home or riding in a car. It also includes greenhouse gases from producing the goods or services that the individual uses, including emissions from power plants that make electricity, factories that make products, and landfills where trash gets sent.*

Carbon labeling – product labels displaying greenhouse emissions associated with goods.

Carbon management – storing CO_2 or using it to prevent its release into the air.

Carbon monoxide (CO) – colorless, odorless, nonirritating, but highly toxic gas produced by incomplete combustion of fuel, incineration of biomass or solid waste, or partially anaerobic decomposition of organic material.

Carbon neutral – activities where net carbon inputs and outputs are the same. *For example, assuming a constant amount of vegetation on the planet, burning wood will add carbon to the atmosphere in the short term, but this carbon will cycle back into new plant growth.*

Carbon offset – a mechanism for individuals and businesses to neutralize rather than reduce their greenhouse gas emissions by purchasing the right to claim someone else's reductions as their own.

Carbon pool – a storage reservoir of carbon.

Carbon sequestration – storage of carbon through natural or technological processes in biomass or in deep geological formations. Proposals for removing CO_2 from the atmosphere or preventing CO_2 from fossil fuel combustion from reaching the atmosphere. *Terrestrial or biological carbon sequestration is how trees and plants absorb carbon dioxide, release oxygen, and store carbon. Geologic sequestration is one step in carbon capture and sequestration (CCS) and involves injecting carbon dioxide deep underground, where it stays permanently.*

Carbon sinks – a natural or artificial reservoir accumulating and storing carbon-containing chemical compounds. Any carbon storage system that causes a net removal of greenhouse gases from the atmosphere. Places of carbon accumulation, such as large forests (*organic compounds*) or ocean sediments (*calcium carbonate*); carbon is removed from the carbon cycle for moderately long to very long periods. Contrast *carbon source.*

Carbon source – opposite of carbon sink; a net carbon source for the atmosphere. *The originating point of carbon that reenters the carbon cycle; cellular respiration and combustion.* Contrast *carbon sink.*

Carbon stocks – the quantity of carbon held within a carbon pool at a specified time.

Carbon tax – a governmental charge on energy sources emitting carbon dioxide (CO_2).

Carbon taxes – a surcharge on fossil fuels to reduce carbon dioxide emissions.

Carbon tetrafluoride (or *tetrafluoromethane*) – the perfluorinated counterpart to the hydrocarbon methane. It can be classified as a haloalkane or halomethane. *Tetrafluoromethane is a useful refrigerant but also a potent greenhouse gas. It has a very high bond strength due to the nature of the carbon–fluorine bond.*

Carbon trading (or *emissions trading*) – a system by which states and institutions receive permits to produce a specified amount of carbon dioxide (CO_2) and other greenhouse gases, which they may trade with others.

Carcinogen – a substance, radionuclide, or radiation that is an agent directly involved in promoting cancer or facilitating its propagation.

Carnivores – an organism that eats only or primarily the meat of other organisms.

Carpooling – when people ride in cars together to help reduce emissions and traffic.

Carrying capacity – the maximum number of individuals a given environment's resources can support, including the food and water available for that environment. *The maximum population that an ecosystem can sustain.*

Case law – precedents from both civil and criminal court cases.

Cash crops – crops that are sold rather than consumed or bartered.

Casks – barrels that are used to store spent fuels.

Catalytic converter – a reaction chamber typically containing a finely-divided platinum-iridium catalyst into which exhaust gases from an automotive engine are passed together with excess air to oxidize carbon monoxide and hydrocarbon pollutants to carbon dioxide and water.

Catastrophic systems – 1. dynamic systems that jump abruptly from one seemingly steady state to another without any immediate changes; 2. the detrimental effect that something, perhaps a natural disaster, has on the environment, destroying the ecosystem and surrounding living conditions.

Catchment area – the source of water for a water supply, whether a dam or rainwater tank.

CDM (Clean Development Mechanism) – an arrangement under the *Kyoto Protocol* allowing industrialized countries with a greenhouse gas reduction commitment (called *Annex 1 countries*) to invest in projects that reduce emissions in developing countries as an alternative to more expensive emission reductions in their own countries.

Cell (*biology*) – the structural and functional unit of all known living organisms and is the smallest unit of an organism classified as living.

Cellular respiration – the process by which a cell breaks down sugar or other organic compounds to release energy used for cellular work; it may be anaerobic or aerobic, depending on oxygen availability.

CERCLA (Comprehensive Environmental Response, Compensation, and Liability Act of 1980; Superfund) – established fund to clean up abandoned hazardous waste sites; establishes strict liability, which means that any individual or corporation associated with the site can be held liable for the entire cost of the cleanup, regardless of their contribution to the pollution at the site; sets guidelines on how to clean up sites.

CFC (chlorofluorocarbons) – a series of hydrocarbons containing both chlorine and fluorine; have been used as refrigerants, blowing agents, cleaning fluids, solvents, and fire extinguishing agents. These gases cause stratospheric ozone depletion and have been banned for many uses. Potent greenhouse gases which the Kyoto Protocol does not regulate since the *Montreal Protocol* covers them.

CH₄ (or *methane*) – a gas emitted while producing and transporting coal, natural gas, and oil. Methane emissions also result from livestock and other agricultural practices and the decay of organic waste in municipal solid waste landfills.

Chain reaction – a self-sustaining reaction in which the fission of nuclei produces subatomic particles that cause the fission of other nuclei.

Channelization – to straighten using a channel.

Chaotic systems – systems that exhibit variability, which may not necessarily be "random," but whose complex patterns are not discernible over a typical human timescale.

Charismatic megafauna – a large animal species with widespread popular appeal that environmental activists use to achieve conservation goals beyond just those species. Examples include the giant panda, the Bengal tiger, and the blue whale. Compare *flagship species*.

Chemical bond – the force that holds atoms together in molecules and compounds.

Chemical ecology – studies the use by organisms of naturally occurring chemical compounds for various purposes (e.g., in defense against predators).

Chemical energy – potential energy stored in chemical bonds of molecules that a chemical reaction can release.

Chemoorganotroph (or *heterotroph*) – 1 an organism requiring organic substrates to obtain carbon for growth and development. 2. an organism incapable of synthesizing its food and must feed upon organic compounds produced by other organisms.

Chernobyl – a city in Ukraine where a nuclear power plant suffered a meltdown due to poor decisions made by power plant workers; the resulting explosions killed some workers and leaked radioactive particles into the atmosphere.

Clathrate gun hypothesis – the proposal that melting methane clathrates could trigger runaway or severe global warming.

Clean Development Mechanism (CDM) – an arrangement under the *Kyoto Protocol* allowing industrialized countries with a greenhouse gas reduction commitment (called *Annex 1 countries*) to invest in projects that reduce emissions in developing countries as an alternative to more expensive emission reductions in their own countries.

Chlorinated hydrocarbon (or *organochloride, organochlorine compound* and *chlorocarbon*) – an organic compound in which chlorine atoms have replaced most of the hydrogen atoms.

Chlorine (Cl) – a halogen element isolated as a heavy greenish-yellow gas of pungent odor; used primarily as a bleach, oxidizing agent, and disinfectant in water purification.

Chlorofluorocarbons (CFC) – widely known families of *haloalkanes*; gases used for refrigeration, air conditioning, packaging, insulation, solvents, or aerosol propellants. Since they are not destroyed in the lower atmosphere, CFCs drift into the upper atmosphere where, given suitable conditions, they break down ozone. These gases are being replaced by other compounds: hydrochlorofluorocarbons, an interim replacement for CFCs covered under the *Montreal Protocol*, and hydrofluorocarbons, which are covered under the *Kyoto Protocol*. These substances are greenhouse gases.

Chlorophyll – any group of green pigments essential in photosynthesis.

Chloroplasts – chlorophyll-containing organelles in eukaryotic organisms; sites of photosynthesis.

Chronic – a continuous, low-level, long-term event. Contrast *acute*.

Chronic effects – long-lasting results of exposure to a toxin; can be a permanent change caused by a single, acute exposure or, over time, by continuous, low-level exposure.

Chronic food shortages – long-term undernutrition and malnutrition, usually caused by people's lack of money to buy food or lack of opportunity to grow it themselves.

Circular metabolism – a system in which wastes, especially water, and materials, are reused and recycled. Compare *linear metabolism*.

CITES Treaty (Convention on International Trade in Endangered Species) – agreement among 167 governments aiming to ensure that cross-border trade in wild animals and plants does not threaten their survival; in 1989, participating countries agreed to ban all ivory trade.

Citizen science – projects where trained volunteers work with scientific researchers to answer real-world questions.

City – a differentiated community with enough population and resource base to allow residents to specialize in arts, crafts, services, and professional occupations.

Civil law – a body of laws regulating relations between individuals or individuals and corporations concerning property rights, personal dignity and freedom, and personal injury.

Class A pan (*water management*) – an open pan used as a standard for measuring water evaporation.

Classical economics – modern Western economic theories of the effects of resource scarcity, monetary policy, and competition on the supply of and demand for goods and services in the marketplace; the basis for the capitalist market system.

Clay – a fine-grained, firm earthy material that is plastic when wet and hardens when heated, consisting primarily of hydrated silicates of aluminum; widely used in making bricks, tiles, and pottery, as well as liners in landfills because it is *Impervious*.

Clean Air Act – long-standing federal legislation that is the legal basis for the national clean air programs; last amended in 1990.

Cleaner production – the continual effort to prevent pollution, reduce the use of energy, water, and material resources, and minimize waste – all without reducing production capacity.

Clearcutting (or *clear-cut*) – a forestry or logging practice in which most or all trees in a forest sector are *felled. Cutting every tree in an area, regardless of species or size; an appropriate harvest method for some species; can be destructive if not carefully controlled.*

Climate – the average weather variations in a region over an extended period. Variations of weather in a region over a long period (i.e., the "average weather"). 1. in a narrow sense, the average weather. 2. more rigorously, the statistical description of the mean and variability of relevant quantities over a period ranging from months to thousands of years. The classical period is 3 decades, as defined by the World Meteorological Organization (WMO). These quantities are often surface variables such as *temperature, precipitation,* and *wind.* In a broader sense, climate is the state of the climate system, including a statistical description. See *weather.*

Climate change – refers to any significant change in the measures of climate lasting for an extended period. In other words, climate change includes major changes in temperature, precipitation, or wind patterns, among others, that occur over several decades or longer. A change in weather over time or region, usually relating to changes in temperature, wind patterns, and rainfall. change in the details of a particular climate, such as cloud cover, wind, speed, temperature, rainfall, or humidity in a specific region. Includes global warming and its effects, such as changes in precipitation, rising sea levels, and impacts that differ by region. However, it may be natural or anthropogenic; common discourse asserts that climate change is anthropogenic (i.e., human-made).

Climate change feedback – a natural phenomenon of increasing or decreasing warming resulting from a change in radiative forcing.

Climate change refugia – areas relatively buffered from contemporary climate change are likely to increase species or ecosystem persistence.

Climate commitment – how much future warming is *"pre-determined,"* even if greenhouse gas levels do not rise, due to thermal inertia, mainly of the oceans.

Climate cycle – any recurring cyclical oscillation within global or regional climates. *They are quasiperiodic (not perfectly periodic), so a Fourier analysis of the data does not have sharp peaks in the spectrum. Many oscillations on different time scales have been found or hypothesized.* See *climate oscillation.*

Climate ethics – an area of research focusing on the ethical dimensions of climate change.

Climate feedback – a process that amplifies or reduces direct warming or cooling effects.

Climate forcing – an energy imbalance imposed on the climate system externally or by human activities.

Climate justice – viewing climate change as an ethical issue and considering how its causes and effects relate to social and political concepts of justice.

Climate lag – delay occurs in climate change because some factors change slowly. For example, the effects of releasing more carbon dioxide into the atmosphere occur gradually because the ocean takes a long time to warm in response to a change in radiation. See *climate* and *climate change.*

Climate legislation – laws regulating greenhouse gas emissions.

Climate model – a quantitative way of representing the interactions of the atmosphere, oceans, land surface, and ice. *Models can range from relatively simple to quite comprehensive.* See *general circulation model.*

Climate oscillation – any recurring cyclical oscillation within global or regional climates. *They are quasiperiodic (not perfectly periodic), so a Fourier analysis of the data does not have sharp peaks in the spectrum. Many oscillations on different time scales have been found or hypothesized.* See *climate cycle.*

Climate resilience – the capacity for a socio-ecological system to 1. absorb stresses and maintain function in the face of external stresses imposed upon it by climate change and 2. adapt, reorganize, and evolve into more desirable configurations that improve the sustainability of the system, leaving it better prepared for future climate change impacts, while still being able to benefit from it now.

Climate sensitivity – how responsive the temperature of the climate system is to a change in radiative forcing. The temperature change in °C is associated with a doubling of the concentration of CO_2 in the atmosphere (the most crucial factor of radiative forcing). Intergovernmental Panel on Climate Change (IPCC) reports equilibrium climate sensitivity refers to the equilibrium change in global mean surface temperature following a doubling of the atmospheric (equivalent) CO_2 concentration. More generally, equilibrium climate sensitivity refers to the equilibrium change in surface air temperature following a unit change in radiative forcing (degrees Celsius, per watts per square meter, (C/Wm-2). One equilibrium climate sensitivity evaluation requires long simulations with Coupled General Circulation Models (Climate model). Effective climate sensitivity is a related measure that circumvents this requirement. It is evaluated from model output for evolving non-equilibrium conditions. It measures the strengths of feedback at a particular time and may vary with forcing history and climate state. See *climate* and *radiative forcing.*

Climate science (or *climatology*) – the study of climate, defined as weather conditions averaged over time.

Climate system (or *Earth system*) – the five physical components (atmosphere, hydrosphere, cryosphere, lithosphere, and biosphere) are responsible for the climate and its variations.

Climate variability (or *natural variability*) – climate change with no presumption of cause. Natural climate changes within the observed range of extremes for a particular region, as measured by temperature, precipitation, and frequency of events. *Drivers of climate variability include the El Niño Southern Oscillation and other phenomena.*

Climatology (or *climate science*) – the study of climate, defined as weather conditions averaged over a long period.

Climax community – a relatively stable, long-lasting community arrived at through succession, usually determined by climate and soil type. *When the different species are best adapted to average conditions in each area.*

Closed canopy – a forest where tree crowns spread over 20 percent of the ground; has the potential for commercial timber harvests.

Cloud forests – high mountain forests where temperatures are uniformly cool, and fog or mist keeps vegetation always wet.

CO_2 (carbon dioxide) – the most abundant *greenhouse gas* emitted from fossil fuels. A naturally occurring gas and by-product of burning fossil fuels and biomass, land-use changes, and other industrial processes. *Carbon dioxide is the principal human-caused greenhouse gas affecting Earth's radiative balance. It is the reference gas against which other greenhouse gases are measured and has a Global Warming Potential of 1.* See *climate change* and *global warming.*

Coal gasification – the heating and partial combustion of coal to release volatile gases, such as methane and carbon monoxide; after the pollutants are washed out, these gases become efficient, clean-burning fuel.

Coal liquefaction – a chemical process by which solid coal is converted to a liquid; referred to as a "synfuel" or "synthetic fuel."

Coalbed methane – is contained in coal seams and is often referred to as virgin coalbed methane or coal seam gas.

Coal mine methane – the subset of coalbed methane released from the coal seams during coal mining.

Coal washing – coal technology that involves crushing coal and washing out soluble sulfur compounds with water or other solvents.

Coastal Zone Management Act (1972) – legislation appropriating federal money to 30 seacoasts and Great Lakes states for development and restoration projects.

Co-benefit – policies implemented for various reasons simultaneously, including climate change mitigation, acknowledge that most policies designed to address greenhouse gas mitigation also have other, often at least equally important, rationales (e.g., related to development objectives, sustainability, and equity).

Co-composting – microbial decomposition of organic materials in solid waste into useful soil additives and fertilizer; often, extra organic material in the form of sewer sludge, animal manure, leaves, and grass clippings are added to solid waste to speed the process and make the product more useful.

Coevolution – the process in which species exert selective pressure on each other and gradually evolve new features or behaviors due to those pressures.

Cogeneration – simultaneous electricity production and useful heat from combustion of the same fuel source. *A power generation process that increases efficiency by harnessing the heat that would otherwise be wasted in fuel combustion and using it to generate electricity, warm buildings, or other purposes.*

Cohousing – clusters of houses having shared dining halls and other spaces, encouraging stronger social ties while reducing the material and energy needs of the community.

Coir – the fiber of a coconut.

Cold front – a moving boundary of cooler air displacing warmer air.

Cold wave – a period of abnormally cold weather lasting days to weeks.

Coliform bacteria – bacteria that live in the intestines (including the colon) of humans and other animals; used to measure the presence of feces in water or soil.

Combustion – a chemical change, especially oxidation, accompanied by the production of heat and light.

Command and control – require polluters to meet specific emission-reduction targets and often requires the installation and use of specific types of equipment to reduce emissions.

Commensalism – a symbiotic relationship in which one member benefits and the other is neither harmed nor benefited.

Commercial and industrial waste (*waste management*) – solid waste generated by the business sector and created by State and Federal government, schools, and tertiary institutions. Does not include that from the construction and demolition industry.

Commercial breeding – propagating animals or plants for commercial purposes, such as breeding dogs.

Commercial harvesting – the harvesting of animals or cash crops for commercial reasons.

Commingled materials (*waste management*) – materials mixed, such as plastic bottles, glass, and metal containers. *Commingled recyclable materials require sorting after collection before they can be recycled.*

Common law – court decisions that constitute a working definition of individual rights and responsibilities where no statutes (i.e., legislation) define these issues.

Communal resource management systems – resources directed by a group of people for long-term sustainability.

Community – a group of various populations in each area. *An assemblage of various organisms living in the same environment.*

Community ecology (*or synecology*) – studies the interactions between the species comprising an ecological community.

Comparative risk assessment – a methodology that uses science, policy, economic analysis, and stakeholder participation to identify and address areas of greatest environmental risk; a method for assessing environmental management priorities. *The U.S. EPA offers free software which contains the history and methodology of comparative risk, as well as many case studies.*

Compensation point – where the amount of energy produced by photosynthesis equals the amount of energy released by respiration.

Competition – organisms from the same or different species competing for food, living space, reproductive success, or any other limited resource. *The most adapted individuals prosper and thus survive and reproduce.*

Competitive exclusion principle (or *Gause's law*) – states that two species cannot coexist in the same environment if competing for precisely the same resource, often summarized as "*complete competitors cannot coexist.*" The theory that no two populations of different species will be able to occupy the same niche and compete for the same resources in the same habitat for a very long time.

Complex system – composed of many components which may interact with each other.

Complexity (*ecological*) – the number of species at each trophic level and the number of trophic levels in a community.

Compost – the aerobically decomposed remnants of organic matter.

Composting – the biological decomposition of organic materials in the presence of oxygen that yields carbon dioxide (CO_2), heat, and stabilized organic residues that may be used as a soil additive.

Compound – a molecule of two or more kinds of atoms held together by chemical bonds.

Comprehensive Environmental Response, Compensation, and Liability Act of 1980 (CERCLA, Superfund) – established a fund to clean up abandoned hazardous waste sites; establishes strict liability, which means that any individual or corporation associated with the site can be held liable for the entire cost of the cleanup, regardless of their contribution to the pollution at the site; sets guidelines on how to clean up sites.

Concentration – the amount of a chemical in a particular volume or weight of air, water, soil, or another medium. See *parts per billion* and *parts per million*.

Condensation – 1. the change of state from a gas to a liquid (e.g., when water vapor in the air changes to liquid as it cools); 2. the aggregation of water molecules changing from vapor to liquid or solid when the saturation concentration is exceeded.

Condensation nuclei – tiny particles floating in air and facilitating condensation.

Conference of the Parties (COP) – the supreme body of the United Nations Framework Convention on Climate Change (UNFCCC). It comprises more than 180 nations that have ratified the Convention. Its first session was held in Berlin, Germany, in 1995, and it is expected to continue meeting yearly. COP's role is to promote and review the implementation of the Convention. It will periodically review existing commitments considering the Convention's objective, new scientific findings, and the effectiveness of national climate change programs. See *United Nations Framework Convention on Climate Change*.

Confined aquifer – with a water table above their upper boundary and typically found below unconfined aquifers.

Conifer – needle-bearing trees that produce seeds in cones.

Coniferous forest – one of the primary terrestrial biomes, culminating in the taiga.

Conservation biology – the study of Earth's biodiversity to protect and conserve natural habitats and plant and animal species.

Conservation development – consideration of landscape history, human culture, topography, and ecological values in subdivision design; using cluster housing, zoning, covenants, and other design features, at least half of a subdivision can be preserved as open space, farmland, or natural areas.

Conservation of matter – in any chemical reaction, matter changes form; it is neither created nor destroyed.

Conspicuous consumption – the lavish spending on goods and services acquired mainly to display income or wealth rather than satisfy basic needs. *A term coined by economist and social critic Thorstein Veblen.*

Construction and demolition waste (*waste management*) – includes waste from residential, civil, and commercial construction and demolition activities, such as fill material (e.g., soil), asphalt, bricks, and timber. C&D waste excludes construction waste which is included in the municipal waste stream. C&D waste does not generally include commercial and industrial waste stream waste.

Consumer – 1. an organism that obtains energy and nutrients by feeding on other organisms or their remains; see *heterotroph*; 2. an industry that maintains themselves by transforming a high–quality energy source into a lower one. Compare *primary producers* and *heterotroph*.

Consumer democracy – using the economic capacity to promote values.

Consumption – the fraction of withdrawn water lost in transmission or evaporated, absorbed, chemically transformed, or otherwise made unavailable for other purposes due to human use.

Consumption (*ecology*) – the use of resources by a living system, the inflow and degradation of energy used for system activity.

Consumption (*economics*) – part of disposable income (income after taxes paid and payments received) that is not saved, essentially the goods and services used by households; this includes purchased commodities at the household level (such as food, clothing, and utilities), the goods and services paid for by the government (such as defense, education, social services, and health care), and the resources consumed by businesses to increase their assets (such as business equipment and housing).

Consumptive – pertaining to consumption; having the quality of consuming or dissipating; consumptive uses of water include pumping water for irrigation or municipal uses and *evapotranspiration*.

Containment building – reinforced concrete building housing a nuclear reactor; designed to contain an explosion should one occur.

Contaminants – something that makes a place or substance no longer suitable for use.

Continental – characteristic of a continent (one of the large landmasses of the Earth).

Contour plowing (or *contour farming*) – the farming practice of plowing across a slope following its contours. The rows formed have the effect of slowing water runoff during rainstorms so that the soil is not washed away and allows the water to percolate into the soil.

Control rods – neutron-absorbing material inserted into spaces between fuel assemblies in nuclear reactors to regulate fission reactions.

Controlled burning – a technique in forest management, farming, prairie restoration, or greenhouse gas abatement.

Convection cell – the transfer of heat or other atmospheric properties by massive motion within the atmosphere, especially by such motion directed upward.

Convection currents – rising or sinking air currents that stir the atmosphere and transport heat from one area to another; they also occur in water. See *spring overturn.*

Convention on the International Trade in Endangered Species (CITES) – an international agreement among 167 governments aiming to ensure that cross–border trade in wild animals and plants does not threaten their survival. *The species covered by CITES are listed in three Appendices, according to the degree of protection they need.*

Conventional energy – energy from sources, such as fossil fuels, that are widely used.

Convert – to express a quantity in alternative units.

Cool deserts – characterized by cold winters and sagebrush (e.g., the American Great Basin).

Cooperation – the process by which organisms work together for mutual benefit.

Coral bleaching – the process in which a coral colony, under environmental stress, expels the microscopic algae (zooxanthellae) that live in symbiosis with their host organisms (polyps). The affected coral colony appears whitened.

Coral reefs – an underwater ecosystem characterized by reef-building corals. *Reefs are formed of colonies of coral polyps held together by calcium carbonate. Most coral reefs are built from stony corals, whose polyps cluster in groups.* Prominent oceanic features composed of hard, lime skeletons produced by coral animals; usually formed along the edges of shallow, submerged ocean banks or shelves in warm, shallow tropical seas.

Core – the dense, intensely hot mass of molten metal, mostly iron and nickel, that is thousands of kilometers in diameter at the Earth's center.

Core region – the primary industrial region of a country, usually located around the capital or largest port; has both the greatest population density and the greatest economic activity of the country.

Coriolis effect – the observed effect of the Coriolis force, especially the inertial force caused by the Earth's rotation in deflecting an object moving above the Earth, rightward in the northern hemisphere, leftward in the southern hemisphere.

Cornucopian fallacy – the belief that nature is limitless in its abundance and that perpetual growth is not only possible but essential.

Corporate Social Responsibility – integration of social and environmental policies into day-to-day corporate business.

Corridor – a strip of natural habitat that connects two adjacent nature preserves to allow migration of organisms from one place to another.

Corrosive – 1. causing damage to metal during chemical processes; 2. causing something to become weak; gradually destructive; steadily harmful.

Cost-benefit analysis – evaluates large-scale public projects by comparing the costs and benefits they will accrue.

Courtship display – ritual, social behavior between possible mates.

Covenants – formal agreements or contracts, often between government and industry sectors. *The national packaging covenant and sustainability covenants are voluntary covenants with a regulatory underpinning. Land covenants protect land for wildlife in the future.*

Cover crops – plants (e.g., rye, alfalfa, or clover) planted immediately after a harvest to hold and protect the soil.

Cracking – the breaking of the long carbon chains found in the hydrocarbons in crude oil by heating them at high temperatures to form smaller molecules that are more useful.

Criminal law – a body of court decisions based on federal and state statutes concerning wrongs against persons or society.

Criteria pollutants – the 1970 amendments to the Clean Air Act required EPA to set National Ambient Air Quality Standards for certain pollutants known to be hazardous to human health; the EPA has identified six criteria pollutants: sulfur dioxide, carbon monoxide, lead, nitrogen oxides, ozone, and particulate matter.

Critical factor – the single environmental factor closest to the tolerance limit for a given species at a given time. See *limiting factors*.

Critical thinking – an ability to systematically, purposefully, and efficiently evaluate information and opinions.

Crop coefficient (Kc) (*water management*) – a variable to calculate the *evapotranspiration* of a plant crop based on that of a reference crop.

Crop evapotranspiration (ETc) (*water management*) – crop water use as the daily water withdrawal.

Crop rotation (or *crop sequencing*) – the practice of growing a series of different crops in the same space in sequential seasons for various benefits, such as avoiding the buildup of pathogens and pests that often occurs when one species is continuously cropped.

Croplands – land that is suitable for growing crops.

Crude death rate (or *crude mortality rate*) – annual number of deaths per thousand persons.

Crude mortality rate (or *crude death rate*) – annual number of deaths per thousand persons.

Crude oil – a naturally occurring mixture (e.g., butane, octane) of hydrocarbons (i.e., molecules with carbon and hydrogen) under average temperature and pressure.

Crust – the cool, lightweight, outermost layer of the Earth's surface that floats on the soft, pliable underlying layers.

Cryosphere – the combined portions of Earth's surface where water is frozen solid as ice, including sea ice, lake ice, river ice, snow, glaciers, ice caps, ice sheets, and frozen ground such as permafrost. One interrelated component of Earth's system; the cryosphere is frozen water in the form of snow, permanently frozen ground (permafrost), floating ice, and glaciers. *Fluctuations in the volume of the cryosphere cause changes in ocean sea level, directly impacting the atmosphere and biosphere. There is a significant overlap with the hydrosphere.*

Curbside collection – a collection of household recyclable materials (separated or co-mingled) left at the curbside for collection by local government services.

Cullet – crushed glass that is suitable for recycling by glass manufacturers.

Cultural eutrophication – an increase in biological productivity and ecosystem succession caused by human activities. *The process that speeds up natural eutrophication because of human activity.*

Cultural services – the non-material benefits of ecosystems, including refreshment, spiritual enrichment, knowledge, and artistic satisfaction.

Culture jamming – altering existing mass media to criticize itself (e.g., defacing advertisements with an alternative message). *Public activism opposing commercialism is little more than propaganda for established interests and an attempt to find alternative expressions.*

Culvert – drain that passes under a road or pathway, maybe a pipe or other conduit.

Curbside collection – a collection of household recyclable materials (separated or co-mingled) left at the curbside for collection by local council services.

Cut and fill – mechanically removing earth from one place to another.

Cyanobacteria (*Cyanophyta* or *blue-green algae*) – a phylum of bacteria obtaining energy through photosynthesis.

Cyclones – intense low–pressure weather systems; mid-latitude cyclones are atmospheric circulations that rotate clockwise in the Southern Hemisphere and anti-clockwise in the Northern Hemisphere and are generally associated with stronger winds, unsettled conditions, cloudiness, and rainfall. Tropical *cyclones* (called *hurricanes* in the Northern Hemisphere) cause storm surges in coastal areas.

D

Daughter – a material formed from the parent material after a given process, such as nuclear decay or movement through the rock cycle.

DDT (dichlorodiphenyltrichloroethane) – a chlorinated hydrocarbon used as a pesticide, a persistent organic pollutant. A colorless, odorless water-insoluble crystalline insecticide $C_{14}H_9Cl_5$ that accumulates in ecosystems and has toxic effects on many vertebrates; became the most widely used pesticide from WWII to the 1950s; implicated in illnesses and environmental problems; now banned in the U.S.

Debt-for-nature swap – a financial transaction in which a portion of a developing nation's foreign debt is forgiven in exchange for local investments in conservation measures.

Deciduous – trees and shrubs that shed their leaves at the end of the growing season.

Deciduous broadleaf forest – any tree-canopied area in a temperate zone whose trees shed their leaves during the cold season.

Deciduous forest – tree-canopied area with trees that drop their leaves seasonally.

Decline spiral – a catastrophic deterioration of a species, community, or whole ecosystem; accelerates as functions are disrupted or lost in a downward cascade.

Decomposers – 1. any organism that breaks down decomposing bits of organic matter. 2. consumers, mostly microbial, that change dead organic matter into minerals and heat.

Decomposition – the process by which tissues of dead organisms break down into simpler forms of organic matter, thereby clearing the limited space in a biome.

Deductive reasoning – deriving testable predictions about specific cases from general principles.

Deep ecology – a philosophy that calls for a profound shift in our attitudes and behavior based on voluntary simplicity, rejection of anthropocentric attitudes, intimate contact with nature, decentralization of power, support for cultural and biological diversity, a belief in the sacredness of nature and direct personal action to protect nature, improve the environment and bring about fundamental societal change.

Deep-sea community – any group of organisms linked by a shared habitat in the deep sea.

Deforestation – the conversion of forested areas to non-forest land for agriculture, urban use, development, or wasteland. The removal of a forest or stand of trees from land converted to non-forest use. *Deforestation contributes to increasing carbon dioxide concentrations by 1) the burning or decomposition of wood releases CO_2, and 2) trees that remove carbon dioxide from the atmosphere in photosynthesis are no longer present. Deforestation can involve the conversion of forest land to farms, ranches, or urban use. The most concentrated deforestation occurs in tropical rainforests. About 31% of Earth's land surface is covered by forests.*

Degradation (*water resource*) – deterioration in water quality due to contamination or pollution; makes the water unsuitable for other desirable purposes.

Delaney Clause – an amendment to the Federal Food, Drug and Cosmetic Act added in 1958 prohibiting the addition of any known cancer-causing agent to processed foods, drugs, or cosmetics.

Delivered energy – energy delivered to and used by a household, usually gas and electricity.

Delta – fan-shaped sediment deposit found at the mouth of a river.

Demand – the amount of a product that consumers are willing and able to buy at various possible prices, assuming they are free to express their preferences.

Demanufacturing – disassembly of products so components can be reused or recycled.

Dematerialization – decreasing the consumption of materials and resources while maintaining the quality of life.

Demographic transition – 1. a change in the make-up of a human population or group from one set of characteristics to another; 2. a pattern of falling death rates and, often, birthrates in response to improved living conditions; could be reversed in deteriorating conditions.

Demographics – the characteristics of a human population or a part of it, especially its size, growth, density, distribution, and statistics regarding birth rate, marriage, the incidence of disease, and death rate.

Demography – 1. vital statistics about people: births, marriages, deaths, etc.; 2. the statistical study of human populations relating to growth rate, age structure, geographic distribution, etc., and their effects on social, economic, and environmental conditions.

Denitrification – the breakdown of nitrates (mostly in the soil) by anaerobic bacteria into their constituent chemical elements: nitrogen and oxygen.

Denitrifying bacteria – free-living soil bacteria that convert nitrates to gaseous nitrogen and nitrous oxide.

Density – the quantity of something per unit measure, especially per unit length, area, or volume; the mass per unit volume of a substance under specified pressure and temperature conditions.

Density dependence – the dependence of the growth rate of a population of a given species on its density.

Dependency ratio – the number of non-working members compared to working members for a given population.

Depository or repository – a place where something is kept for safekeeping or storage, such as a warehouse or store for furniture or valuables. Yucca Mountain in New Mexico is being studied as a potential depository for spent nuclear fuel.

Desalination – producing potable (i.e., drinking water) or recyclable water by removing salts from salty or brackish water. Three methods do this: 1. distillation or freezing, 2. reverse osmosis using membranes, electrodialysis, and 3. ion exchange. At present, these methods are *energy intensive*.

Desert – an area with average annual precipitation of less than 250 mm (9.8 in) or where more water is lost than falls as precipitation.

Desert ecology – the sum of the interactions between biotic and abiotic factors in a desert biome, including interactions between plant, animal, and bacterial populations in a desert community.

Desertification – 1. a process by which areas become desert-like wastelands with lower and different biodiversity. 2. land degradation in arid, semi-arid, and dry sub-humid areas resulting from climatic variations, primarily human activities. Denuding and degrading a once-fertile land, initiating a desert-producing cycle that feeds on itself and causes long-term changes in an area's soil, climate, and *biota*. land degradation in arid, semi-arid, and dry sub-humid areas results from various factors, including climatic variations and human activities. UNCCD (The United Nations Convention to Combat Desertification) defines land degradation as a reduction or loss, in arid, semi-arid, and dry sub-humid areas, of the biological or economic productivity and complexity of rain-fed cropland, irrigated cropland, or range, pasture, forest, and woodlands resulting from land uses or a process or combination of processes, including processes arising from human activities and habitation patterns, such as (i) soil erosion caused by wind or water; (ii) deterioration of the physical, chemical and biological or economic properties of soil; and (iii) long-term loss of natural vegetation. Conversion of forest to non-forest.

Design for assembly/disassembly (dfX) – re–use, and recycling.

Design for the environment (dfE) – considers cradle-to-grave costs and benefits of material acquisition, manufacture, use, and disposal.

Design for manufacturing (dfM) – designing products so that they are easy to manufacture.

Design for sustainability (dfS) – an integrated design approach aiming to achieve environmental quality and economic efficiency through redesigning industrial systems.

Detrital food web – a food web depicting the energy flow from photoautotrophs through detritivores and decomposers.

Detritivores (*detritus feeder*) – heterotrophs that consume decomposing bits of organic matter, such as plant litter. *Animals and plants that consume detritus (decomposing organic material) and, in doing so, contribute to the decomposition and the recycling of nutrients.*

Detritus – non-living particulate organic material (as opposed to dissolved organic material).

Detritus feeders – organisms that obtain their nutrients and energy by breaking down dead materials and organic compounds in an ecosystem.

Developing countries – development of a country is measured using a mix of economic factors (income per capita, GDP, degree of modern infrastructure, degree of industrialization, the proportion of economy devoted to agriculture and natural resource extraction) and social factors (life expectancy, the rate of literacy, poverty). UN–produced Human Development Index (HDI) is a compound indicator of the above statistics. A strong correlation exists between low-income and high population growth within and between countries. Developing countries have low per capita income, widespread poverty, and low capital formation.

Developed countries have continuous economic growth and a relatively high standard of living. The term is value-laden and prescriptive, implying a natural transition from "undeveloped" to "developed" when such transitions can be imposed instead. Although poverty and physical deprivation are undesirable, it does not follow that "undeveloped" economies should move towards affluent Western style "developed" free market economies.

Dewpoint – the temperature at which condensation occurs for a given water vapor concentration in the air.

Deoxyribonucleic acid (DNA) – the long, double-helix molecule in the nucleus of cells that contains the genetic code and directs the development and functioning of all cells.

Dichlorodiphenyltrichloroethane (DDT) – a chlorinated hydrocarbon used as a pesticide, a persistent organic pollutant. A colorless, odorless water-insoluble crystalline insecticide $C_{14}H_9C_{l5}$ that accumulates in ecosystems and has toxic effects on many vertebrates; became the most widely used pesticide from WWII to the 1950s; implicated in illnesses and environmental problems; now banned in the U.S.

Dieback (*arboriculture*) – 1. a condition in trees or woody plants in which peripheral parts are killed, either by parasites or due to conditions such as acid rain. 2. a sudden population decline. See *population crash.*

Diesel – 1. fuel made of hydrocarbons with 16 carbons; 2. a high-compression internal combustion engine.

Dietary energy supply – food available for human consumption, usually in kilocalories per person per day (kg/person/day).

Diminishing returns – a condition in which unrestrained population growth causes the standard of living to decrease to a subsistence level where poverty, misery, vice, and starvation make life permanently drab and miserable; this dreary prophecy has led economics to be called "the dismal science."

Dioxin – chemical compounds that are persistent organic pollutants and carcinogenic.

Direct action – civil disobedience, guerrilla street theater, picketing, protest marches, road blockades, demonstrations, and other techniques borrowed from the civil rights movement and applied to environmental protection.

Direct energy – used, mainly at home (delivered energy) and for fuels used for transport.

Disability-adjusted life years (DALY) – a measure of premature deaths and losses due to the onset of illnesses and disabilities in a population.

Discharge – the amount of water that passes a fixed point in a given time, usually expressed as liters or cubic feet of water per second.

Discharge rate – the amount of water that passes a fixed point in a given time, usually expressed as liters or cubic feet of water per second.

Disclimax community (or *equilibrium community*) – a community subject to periodic disruptions, usually by fire, that prevent it from reaching a climax stage.

Disease – a deleterious change in the body's condition in response to destabilizing factors, such as nutrition, chemicals, or biological agents.

Disinfection – to make free from infection by destroying harmful microorganisms.

Dispersal – the movement of individual organisms from their birth or breeding sites to another location.

Dissemination – to become widely scattered (seeds).

Dissolved Oxygen (DO) content – the amount of oxygen dissolved in a given volume of water at a given temperature and atmospheric pressure, usually expressed in parts per million.

Distillation – 1. the extraction of volatile components of a mixture by the condensation and collection of the vapors that are produced as the mixture is heated; 2. a process of desalinization in which water is evaporated and then re-condensed.

Distributed water (*water management*) – purchased water supplied to a user, usually through a reticulated mains system, pipes and open channels, and irrigation systems supplied to farms.

Diversion rate (*waste disposal*) – the proportion of a potentially recyclable diverted from the waste disposal stream and, therefore, not directed to a landfill.

Diversity (or *species diversity* or *biological diversity*) – the number of species present in a community (species richness) and the relative abundance of each species.

Divertible resource (or *water management*) – the proportion of water runoff and recharge accessed by humans.

DNA (deoxyribonucleic acid) – the long, double-helix molecule in the nucleus of cells that contains the genetic code and directs the development and functioning of all cells.

Dominance hierarchy – the organization of individual organisms into groups with a social structure.

Dominance species – characterizes and dominates an ecological community as measured by its primary productivity or biomass.

Dominant – 1. an organism that behaves in such a way as to be in a position over others of the same species; 2. the allele of a gene that requires only one copy to be present in an individual for that trait to be present.

Dominant plants – those plant species in a community that provide the food base for most of the community; usually take up the most space and have the largest biomass.

Dose threshold level – the maximum level of a substance before toxic levels are reached.

Downbursts – sudden, powerful downdrafts of cold air with an advancing storm front.

Downcycling (*waste management*) – recycling in which an item's quality is diminished with each recycling.

Downstream – the processes occurring after a particular activity (e.g., transporting a manufactured product from a factory to the wholesale or retail outlet). Compare *upstream*.

Drainage (*water management*) – irrigation or rainfall that runs off an area or is lost to deep percolation.

Drawdown (*water management*) – drop in water level, generally applied to wells or bores.

Dredging (*water management*) – the repositioning of soil from an aquatic environment using specialized equipment to initiate infrastructural or ecological improvements.

Drift net – a fishing net used in oceans, coastal seas, and freshwater lakes.

Drinking water (or *potable water*) – water fit for human consumption by the *World Health Organization* (WHO) guidelines.

Drip irrigation (*water management*) – a drip hose is placed near the plant roots to minimize deep percolation and evaporation. Using pipe or tubing perforated with tiny holes to deliver water one drop at a time directly to the soil around each plant; conserves water, prevents soil waterlogging, and reduces the salt content.

Driver (*ecology*) – any natural or human-induced factor that directly or indirectly causes a change in an ecosystem. *A direct driver unequivocally influences ecosystem processes and can be measured.*

Drop-off center (*waste management*) – where discarded materials can be left for recycling.

Drought – a period of abnormally dry weather marked by little or no rain that lasts long enough to cause water shortage for people and natural systems. *An acute water shortage relative to availability, supply, and demand in a region. An extended period of months or years when a region has a deficient water supply. Generally, this occurs when a region receives consistently below–average precipitation.*

Drought cycle – temporary, repetitive phases of dry conditions in an otherwise hospitable environment.

Dry alkali injection – spraying dry sodium bicarbonate into flue gas to absorb and neutralize acidic sulfur compounds. See *flue-gas scrubbing*.

Dryland farming – a technique that uses soil moisture conservation and seed selection to optimize production under dry conditions.

Dryland salinity (*water management*) – accumulation of salts in soils, soil water, and groundwater; may be natural or induced by land clearing.

Dry spell – a period with little or no rain. *Whether a dry spell becomes a drought depends on how long it lasts, expectations based on historical data and perceptions, and the water needs of people and natural systems.*

Dump (or *landfill*) – land waste disposal sites where waste is generally spread in thin layers, compacted, and regularly covered with fresh soil (e.g., each day). *A site for waste materials disposal by burial and is the oldest form of waste treatment. Solid waste disposal in which refuse is buried between soil layers. A method often used to reclaim low–lying ground. Landfill is sometimes used as a noun to refer to the waste itself.*

Dung – animal excrement (biomass); used as fuel for heating or cooking in many countries.

Dynamic state of equilibrium – a steady state in an ecosystem or a system where change is not observable because, even though there are changes in progress, they are being made at an equal rate with no net gain.

E

E-cycling – recycling electronic waste.

E–waste – electronic waste, especially mobile phones, televisions, and personal computers.

Earth's atmosphere – the layer of gases surrounding Earth and retained by Earth's gravity.

Earth Charter – a set of principles for sustainable development, environmental protection, and social justice developed by a council appointed by the United Nations.

Earth science – includes all fields of natural science related to Earth. This science focuses on the physical, chemical, and biological complex constitutions and synergistic linkages of Earth's four spheres: the biosphere, hydrosphere, atmosphere, and geosphere (or lithosphere). *Earth science is a branch of planetary science but with a much older history.*

Earthquakes – a sudden, violent movement of the Earth's crust.

Earthshine – sunlight reflected from Earth and illuminating the dark side of the Moon, which helps determine Earth's albedo.

Eccentricity – the extent to which Earth's orbit around the Sun departs from a perfect circle.

Eco- – prefix added indicating general environmental considerations (e.g., eco-housing, ecolabel, eco–material).

Eco-asset – a biological asset providing financial value to private landowners when maintained in or restored to their natural state.

Eco-efficiency – creating more goods and services while using fewer resources and creating less waste and pollution.

Ecocentric (or *ecologically centered*) – a philosophy that claims moral values and rights for organisms and ecological systems and processes.

Ecofeminism – a pluralistic, nonhierarchical, relationship-oriented philosophy that suggests how humans could reconceive themselves and their relationships to nature in non-dominating ways (devised as an alternative to patriarchal systems of domination).

Ecojustice – justice in the social order and integrity in the natural order.

Ecolabel – notion indicating a product has met specific environmental or social standards.

E. Coli (*Escherichia coli*) – a bacterium used to indicate fecal contamination and potential disease organisms in the water.

Ecological corridor – an area of habitat connecting wildlife populations separated by human activities or structures.

Ecological deficit – of a country or region; measures the amount by which its *Ecological Footprint* exceeds the ecological capacity of that region.

Ecological development – a gradual process of environmental modification by organisms.

Ecological economics – application of ecological insights to economic analysis in a holistic, contextual, value-sensitive, eco-centric manner.

Ecological equivalents – different species that occupy similar ecological niches in similar ecosystems in different parts of the world.

Ecological footprint (or *eco-footprint*, or *footprint*) – a measure of the area of biologically productive land and water needed to produce the resources and absorb the waste of a population using the prevailing technology and resource management schemes. *A measure of the consumption of renewable natural resources by a human population, be it that of a country, a region or the whole world given as the total area of productive land or sea required to produce all the crops, meat, seafood, wood, and fiber it consumes, to sustain its energy consumption and to give space for its infrastructure.*

Ecological literacy – the ability to understand the natural systems that make life on Earth possible.

Ecological niche – 1. the habitat of a species or population within its ecosystem; 2. the functional role and position of a species (population) within a community or ecosystem, including what resources it uses, how and when it uses the resources and how it interacts with other populations. The match of a species to a specific environmental condition. It describes how an organism or population responds to the distribution of resources and competitors. See *niche*.

Ecological pyramid (or *biomass pyramid*) – a graph illustrating the productivity within a trophic level.

Ecological recycling (or *nutrient cycle*) – the movement and exchange of organic and inorganic matter back into the production of living matter.

Ecological selection – ecological processes that operate on a species' inherited traits without reference to mating or secondary sex characteristics.

Ecological succession – 1. the process by which organisms occupy a site and gradually change environmental conditions so other species can replace the original inhabitants; 2. the predictable and orderly changes in the composition or structure of an ecological community over time. The change in the species structure of an ecological community over time.

Ecological sustainability – the capacity of ecosystems to maintain essential processes and functions and retain their biological diversity without impoverishment.

Ecologically sustainable development – using, conserving, and enhancing community resources so that ecological processes on which all life depends can be maintained and enriched into the future.

Ecology – 1. the scientific study of living organisms and their relationships to one another; concerned with the life histories, distribution, and behavior of individual species as well as the structure and function of natural systems at the level of populations, communities, and ecosystems; 2. the scientific study of the processes regulating the distribution and abundance of organisms. *The study of the design of ecosystem structure and function.*

Ecology of fear – a framework describing the psychological impact that predator-induced stress experienced by animals has on populations and ecosystems.

Economic development – a rise in real income per person, usually associated with new technology that increases productivity or resources.

Economic globalization – the emerging international economy characterized by free trade in goods and services, unrestricted capital flows, and more limited national powers to control domestic economies.

Economic growth – an increase in the total wealth of a nation; if the population grows faster than the economy, there may be macroeconomic growth, but the share per person may decline.

Economic thresholds – in pest management, the point at which the cost of pest damage exceeds the costs of pest control.

Ecophagy – the destruction of an ecosystem.

Ecophysiology – the study of the interaction of the physiological traits of an organism with its abiotic environment.

Ecopoiesis – the hypothetical shaping of a sustainable ecosystem by human action on a lifeless, sterile planet.

Ecoregion (*bioregion*) – 1. a region defined by its geography and ecology 2. the next smallest ecologically and geographically defined area beneath *biogeographic realm* or *ecozone*, which are divisions of Earth's surface defined by the distribution of organisms. See *bioregion*.

Ecosynthesis – the use of introduced species to fill niches in a disrupted environment to increase the speed of ecological restoration.

Ecosystem – a dynamic complex of plant, animal, and microorganism communities and their non-living environment, all interacting as a functional unit. *The total interacting organisms (biocoenosis) and non-living things (biotopes) in a specific environment. Any natural unit or entity, including living and non-living factors interacting to produce a stable system through the cyclic exchange of materials.*

Ecosystem boundary – the spatial delimitation usually based on discontinuities of organisms and physical environment.

Ecosystem ecology – studies how energy and matter flow interact with ecosystems' biotic elements. See *nutrient cycle efficiency*.

Ecosystem management –integration of ecological, economic, and social goals in a unified systems approach to resource management.

Ecosystem modeling – using mathematics, computer programs, and models to understand and predict ecosystem behavior.

Ecosystem restoration – to reinstate an entire community of organisms to as near its natural condition as possible.

Ecosystem services – 1. resources and processes provided in an ecosystem and beneficial organisms. 2. benefits humans get from many resources and processes supplied by natural ecosystems. 3. the benefits produced by ecosystems on which people depend. For example, fisheries, drinking water, fertile soils for growing crops, climate regulation, and aesthetic and cultural value. The role organisms play without charge in creating a healthy environment for humans, from oxygen production to soil formation, maintenance of water quality, and more. *These services are generally divided into four groups, supporting, provisioning, regulating, and cultural.*

Ecotage – direct action (e.g., guerrilla warfare) or sabotage to defend nature. See *monkeywrenching*.

Ecotax – a fiscal policy introducing taxes intended to promote ecologically sustainable activities via economic incentives.

Ecotone – a boundary between two types of ecological communities. *A transition area between two adjacent but different landscape patches.*

Ecotope – the smallest ecologically distinct landscape features in a landscape mapping and classification system.

Ecotourism – combines adventure travel, cultural exploration, and nature appreciation in native settings.

Ecotoxicology – the study of toxic chemicals' ecological role (often pollutants or natural compounds).

Ecozone (or *biographic realm*) – an area with characteristics natural origins such as climate, terrain, and vegetation; the largest division of the Earth's surface, filled with living organisms.

E-cycling – electronic recycling waste.

Edge effects – a change in species composition, physical conditions, or other ecological factors at the boundary between two ecosystems.

Effective rainfall – the volume of rainfall passing into the soil; that part of rainfall available for plants after runoff, leaching, evaporation, and foliage interception.

Effluent – a discharge or emission of liquid, gas, or other waste product.

Effluent sewerage – a low-cost alternative sewage treatment for cities in developing countries that combines some features of septic systems and centralized municipal treatment systems.

El Niño – a band of anomalously warm ocean water temperatures that occasionally develops off the coast of South America and can cause climatic changes across the Pacific Ocean. A warm water current periodically flows southwards along the coast of Ecuador and Peru in South America, replacing the usually cold northwards flowing current. *Occurs every five to seven years, usually during the Christmas season (the name refers to the Christ child).* The opposite phase is a *La Niña*.

El Niño Southern Oscillation (ENSO) – a set of specific interacting parts of a single global system of coupled ocean-atmosphere climate fluctuations resulting from oceanic and atmospheric circulations. The formation of an El Niño is linked with the cycling of a Pacific Ocean circulation pattern known as the southern oscillation; in a normal year, a surface low pressure develops in the region of northern Australia and Indonesia and a high-pressure system over the coast of Peru.

Pacific Ocean trade winds move strongly from east to west; the easterly flow of the trade winds carries warm surface waters westward, bringing convective storms to Indonesia and coastal Australia; along the coast of Peru, cold bottom water wells up to the surface to replace the warm water that is pulled to the west.

Electron – a negatively charged subatomic particle that orbits around the nucleus (protons and neutrons) of an atom.

Electrostatic – of or relating to electric charges at rest or produced or caused by such charges.

Electrostatic precipitators – the most common particulate controls in power plants; fly ash particles pick up an electrostatic surface charge as they pass between large electrodes in the effluent stream, causing particles to migrate to the oppositely charged plate.

Element – a molecule composed of one kind of atom; cannot be broken into simpler units by chemical reactions.

Embodied energy – 1. the energy expended over the lifecycle of a good or service; 2. the energy involved in the extraction of basic materials, processing/manufacture, transport, and disposal of a product; 3. the energy required to provide a good or service.

Embodied water – the hidden flow accompanying goods trade. See *virtual water*.

Emergent diseases – a new disease that has been absent for at least 20 years.

Emergent properties – not evident in the individual components of an object or system. characteristics of a complex system (or group) that arise from the interactions among the individual parts or changing membership of a larger system not possible when individual parts of the system act alone.

Emergy (short for *energy memory*) – all the available energy used in making a product directly and indirectly, expressed in units of one type of available energy (the work previously done to provide a product or service); the energy of one type required to make energy of another.

Emigration – 1. the movement of members from a population. 2. an organism leaving its native community for a new one.

Emission – substances, such as gases or particles, discharged into the atmosphere due to natural processes of human activities, including those from chimneys, elevated point sources, and tailpipes of motor vehicles.

Emissions – quantitative illustrations of how releasing different amounts of climate-altering gases and particles into the atmosphere from human and natural sources will produce different future climate conditions. Scenarios are developed using various assumptions about population growth, economic and technological development, and other factors.

Emissions factor – value for scaling emissions to activity data in terms of a standard emissions rate per unit of activity (e.g., grams of carbon dioxide emitted per barrel of fossil fuel consumed or per pound of product produced).

Emission intensity – the average emission rate of a given pollutant from a given source relative to the intensity of a specific activity. *For example, grams of carbon dioxide released per megajoule of energy produced or the ratio of greenhouse gas emissions produced to gross domestic product (GDP).*

Emission standard – a level of emissions that, under law, may not be exceeded.

Emission standards – requirements set specific limits to the number of pollutants released into the environment. *Regulations for restricting the amounts of air pollutants that can be released from specific point sources.*

Emissions intensity – emissions expressed as quantity per monetary unit.

Emissions trading (or *carbon trading*) – a system by which states and institutions receive permits to produce a specified amount of carbon dioxide (CO_2) and other greenhouse gases, which they may trade with others. A system that limits aggregate emissions from a group of emitters by setting a "cap" on maximum emissions. It is a market-based policy to reduce emissions of pollutants and encourage business investment in fossil fuel alternatives and energy efficiency. See *cap and trade*.

Endangered species – the imminent risk of becoming extinct; at risk of becoming extinct because they are either few or threatened by changing environmental or predation parameters.

Endemism – a state in which species are restricted to a region.

Energetics – the study of how energy flows within an ecosystem: the routes it takes, flow rates, where it is stored, and how it is used.

Energy – 1. the capacity to do work (i.e., to change the physical state or motion of an object); 2. a property of all systems which can be turned into heat and measured in heat units.

Atomic energy (or *nuclear energy*) – released by reactions within atomic nuclei, as in nuclear fission or fusion.

Available energy – with the potential to do work (exergy).

Delivered energy – delivered to and used by a household, usually gas and electricity.

Direct energy – currently used mainly at home (delivered energy) and for fuels used mainly for transport.

Embodied energy – expended over the entire life cycle of a good or service *or* energy involved in the extraction of basic materials, processing/manufacture, transport, and disposal of a product *or* energy required to provide a good or service.

Geothermal energy – heat emitted from within the Earth's crust as hot water or steam and used to generate electricity after transformation.

Hydro energy – *potential* (stored) and *kinetic* (motion) energy of water used to generate electricity.

Indirect energy – generated in and accounted for by the broader economy from actions or demands.

Kinetic energy – possessed by a body because of its motion.

Nuclear energy (or *atomic energy*) – released by reactions within atomic nuclei, as in nuclear fission or fusion.

Operational energy – used in carrying out a particular operation.

Potential energy – possessed by a body because of its position or condition (e.g., coiled springs and charged batteries have potential energy).

Primary energy – obtained directly from nature, the energy in raw fuels (electricity from the grid is not primary), used primarily on energy statistics when compiling energy balances.

> ***Solar energy*** – solar radiation used for hot water production and electricity generation (does not include passive solar energy to heat and cool buildings etc.).

> ***Secondary energy*** – primary energies are transformed in energy conversion processes to more convenient secondary forms such as electrical energy and cleaner fuels.

> ***Stationary energy*** – other than transport fuels and fugitive emissions, used mainly to produce electricity but also for manufacturing and processing and in agriculture, fisheries etc.

> ***Tidal/ocean/wave energy*** – mechanical energy from water movement used to generate electricity.

> ***Useful energy*** – available to increase system production and efficiency.

> ***Wind energy*** – kinetic energy of wind used for electricity generation using turbines.

Energy accounting – measuring value by the energy input required for a good or service. *A form of accounting builds in measuring human impact on nature (rather than being restricted to human–based items).*

Energy audit – a systematic gathering and analysis of energy use information that can be used to determine energy efficiency improvements. Energy Audits define three levels for consistency: *basic, detailed,* and *precision energy audits.*

Energy crisis – a significant rise in price due to scarcity of energy supplies within an economy.

Energy cycle – how energy is cycled through the biosphere (e.g., when the sun's energy is taken up by plants, from plants to animals, and from animals to other animals through ingestion).

Energy efficiency – using less energy to provide the same level of energy service. *A measure of energy produced compared to the energy consumed.*

Energy footprint – the area required to provide or absorb the waste from coal, oil, gas, fuelwood, nuclear energy, and hydropower. *Fossil Fuel Footprint* is required to sequester the emitted CO_2, considering CO_2 absorption by the sea, etc.

Energy-for-land ratio – the amount of energy produced per hectare of ecologically productive land. The units used are gigajoules per hectare and year (GJ/ha/yr). For fossil fuel (calculated as CO_2 assimilation), the ratio is 100 GJ/ha/yr.

Energy management – a program of well-planned actions to reduce energy use, recurrent energy costs, and harmful greenhouse gas emissions.

Energy pyramid – a representation of the loss of useful energy at each step in a food chain. A graphical representation designed to show the biomass or biomass productivity at each trophic level in each ecosystem.

Energy recovery – 1. incineration of solid waste to produce useful energy; 2. the productive extraction of energy, usually electricity or heat, from waste or materials that would otherwise have gone to landfill.

ENERGY STAR – U.S. Environmental Protection Agency voluntary program that helps businesses and individuals save money and protect our climate through superior energy efficiency.

Energy systems – the infrastructure and systems of electricity production, transport, storage, and consumption.

Enhanced greenhouse effect – the increase in the natural greenhouse effect resulting from increases in atmospheric concentrations of greenhouse gases due to emissions from human activities. *Natural greenhouse effect has been enhanced by increased atmospheric concentrations of greenhouse gases (e.g., CO_2 and methane) emitted by human activities. These added greenhouse gases cause the Earth to warm up.*

Enriched uranium – uranium (U) ore occurs naturally in a state that cannot be used in most reactors or to make nuclear weapons. Enrichment it makes it easier to use in reactors; the enrichment process increases the amount of the fissionable ^{235}U isotope; uranium enriched to contain less than 20% ^{235}U is low-enriched uranium; uranium enriched to contain 20% or greater ^{235}U is highly-enriched uranium that can be directly used to make nuclear weapons.

ENSO (El Niño–Southern Oscillation) – events occurring during El Niño; at one extreme of the cycle, when the central Pacific Ocean is warm, and the atmospheric pressure over Australia is relatively high, the ENSO causes drought conditions over eastern Australia. Compare *El Niño* and *Southern Oscillation*.

Enteric fermentation – anaerobic metabolism in the digestive systems of ruminant animals. *Enteric fermentation is a cause of methane (CH_4) emissions. Livestock, especially cattle, produce methane during digestion, representing one-third of emissions from agriculture.*

Entropy – for a closed thermodynamic system, a quantitative measure of the amount of thermal energy not available to do work; the symbol is S.

Evapotranspiration – evaporation of water from soil and plant leaves.

Environment – 1. the external conditions, resources, stimuli etc., with which an organism interacts. 2. the conditions surrounding an organism (or group of organisms) and the complex social or cultural conditions affecting an individual or community. *The biotic and abiotic surroundings of an organism or population and the chemical interactions between these factors influence their survival, development, and evolution. An environment can vary in scale from microscopic to global.*

Environmental backlash (or *greenlash*) – dramatic changes in ecosystems' structure and dynamic behavior.

Environmental crime – a crime against environmental legislation subject to prosecution.

Environmental ethics – 1. decisions humans make concerning the environment. 2. a search for moral values and ethical principles in human relations with the natural world.

Environmental flows – river or creek water flow allocated to maintain the waterway ecosystems.

Environmental hormones – chemical pollutants that, over time, come to substitute for or interfere with naturally occurring hormones in our bodies; these chemicals may trigger reproductive failure, developmental abnormalities, or tumor promotion.

Environmental impact statement (EIS) – an analysis, required by the *National Environmental Policy Act* of 1970, of the effects of any major program a federal agency plans to undertake.

Environmental indicator – 1. physical, chemical, biological, or socio–economic measures used to assess natural resources and environmental quality. 2. organisms with these characteristics are "bioindicators."

Environmental justice – a recognition that access to a clean, healthy environment is a fundamental right of all humans. *The fair treatment and meaningful involvement of all people regardless of race, color, national origin, or income with respect to the development, implementation, and enforcement of environmental laws, regulations, and policies.*

Environmental law – the special body of official rules, decisions, and actions concerning environmental quality, natural resources, and ecological sustainability.

Environmental literacy – fluency in the principles of ecology that gives us a working knowledge of the basic grammar and underlying syntax of environmental wisdom.

Environmental migrant – a displaced person caused by climate change-induced environmental disasters.

Environmental movement (or *environmentalism*) – conservation and green movements; a diverse scientific, social, and political movement. *The movement is centered around ecology, health, and human rights in recognizing humanity as an ecosystem participant. Environmentalists generally advocate the sustainable management of resources and stewardship of the natural environment through changes in public policy and individual behavior.*

Environmental noise (or *noise pollution*) – displeasing human or machine–created sound that disrupts the activity or happiness of human or animal life.

Environmental policy – the environmental rules or regulations adopted, implemented, and enforced by some governmental agency.

Environmental racism – decisions that restrict certain groups of people to polluted or degraded environments by race.

Environmental resistance – all the limiting factors that tend to reduce population growth rates and set the maximum allowable population size or ecosystem carrying capacity. Compare *biotic potential*.

Environmental resources – anything an organism needs that the environment can provide.

Environmental restoration – undoing the damage caused to an area by human activity or natural disasters.

Environmental science – the study of interactions among the environment's physical, chemical, and biological components and human's role in it.

Environmentalism – 1. active participation in attempts to solve environmental pollution and resource problems. 2. conservation and green movements; a diverse scientific, social, and political movement. *The movement is centered around ecology, health, and human rights in recognizing humanity as an ecosystem participant. Environmentalists generally advocate the sustainable management of resources and stewardship of the natural environment through changes in public policy and individual behavior.*

Enzymes – molecules, usually proteins or nucleic acids, acting as catalysts (i.e., increase reaction rates) in biochemical reactions.

Ephemerality – the concept of things being transitory, existing only briefly.

Epidemiology – the study of factors affecting the health and illness of populations and serves as the foundation and logic of interventions made in public health and preventive medicine.

Epiphyte – a plant that grows on a substrate other than soil, such as the surface of another organism.

Equilibrium community (or *disclimax community*) – a community subject to periodic disruptions, usually by fire, that prevent it from reaching a climax stage.

Erosion – displacement of solids, such as sediment, soil, rock, and other particles, usually by the agents of currents such as wind, water, or ice by downward or down-slope movement in response to gravity or by living organisms. *Removal of vegetation and trees can increase erosion of topsoil.*

***Escherichia coli* (*E. Coli*)** – a bacterium used to indicate fecal contamination and potential disease organisms in the water.

Estimated reserves – reserves of resources whose quantities have only been estimated and are not known for certain.

Estuary – 1. the broad lower course of a river where the tide flows in, causing fresh and saltwater to mix; 2. a semi-enclosed coastal body of water with one or more rivers or streams flowing into it and with a free connection to the open sea.

Ethical consumerism – buying things that are made ethically (i.e., without harm to or exploitation of humans, animals, or the natural environment); *generally, it entails favoring products and businesses that take account of the greater good in their operations.*

Ethical living – adopting lifestyles, consumption, and shopping habits that minimize our negative impact and maximize our positive impact on people, the environment, and the economy. See *consumer democracy.*

Ethology – the study of animal behavior. See *animal behavior.*

Eukaryotic cell – a cell containing a membrane-bounded nucleus and membrane-bounded organelles.

Eutectic fluid – eutectic salts (salts that melt at low temperatures) are phase-changing chemicals used in active solar heating to store solar energy; heating melts these materials and cools them to the original phase.

Eutrophic [*eu* = well and *trophic* = nutritious] – rivers and lakes rich in organisms and organic material, often due to runoff from land.

Eutrophication – the enrichment of water bodies with nutrients, primarily nitrogen and phosphorus, stimulates aquatic organisms' growth. An increase in natural or chemical nutrients in an ecosystem. This nutrient increase typically stimulates the growth of some aggressive plant species and hampers that of others, thereby harming biodiversity. *In aquatic ecosystems, it may result in hypoxia.*

Euxinic – with insufficient oxygen. See *anoxic.*

Evaporation – 1. water converted to water vapor. 2. the process of changing liquid into vapor (the gas phase) due to increased temperature or pressure. 3. the slow vaporization of water from soil or surface water.

Evapotranspiration (ET) – 1. the water evaporating from the soil and transpired by plants. 2. the sum of water evaporation and plant transpiration. *The combined process of evaporation from the Earth's surface and transpiration from vegetation. Actual evapotranspiration can never be greater than precipitation and will usually be less because some water will run off in rivers and flow to the oceans.*

Evergreen – coniferous trees and broad-leaved plants that retain their leaves year-round.

Evolution – 1. change in heritable characteristics over successive generations. 2. a theory that explains how random changes in genetic material and competition for scarce resources cause species to change gradually.

Evolutionary ecology – changes occurring to an organism within its population or the wider community.

E-waste – electronic waste, especially mobile phones, televisions, and personal computers.

Exhaustible resources – generally considered the Earth's geologic endowment: minerals, non-mineral resources, fossil fuels, and other materials present in finite amounts in the environment.

Existence value – an economic value in which the benefit of knowing that a particular species, organism, or resource exists is appraised.

Exotic organisms – alien species introduced by the human agency into biological communities where they would not naturally occur.

Exotic species – an introduced species not native or endemic to a habitat.

Exponential curve – describes growth at a constant rate of increase per unit of time; it can be expressed as a constant fraction or exponent.

Exponential growth – growth at a constant rate of increase per unit of time; it can be expressed as a constant fraction or exponent. See *geometric growth*.

Extended producer responsibility (EPR) (or *product take-back*) – a requirement (often in law) that producers take back and accept responsibility for the responsible disposal of their products; this encourages the design of products easily repaired, recycled, reused, or upgraded.

External costs – monetary or otherwise expenses borne by someone other than the individuals or groups using a resource.

External water footprint – the embodied water of imported goods. Compare *internal water footprint*.

Externality (*environmental economics*) – a cost or benefit not borne by the producer or supplier of a good or service. In many situations, environmental deterioration may be caused by a few while the community bears the cost. *For example, overfishing, pollution (e.g., production of greenhouse emissions that are not compensated for by taxes etc.), and the environmental cost of land–clearing etc.*

By-products of activities that affect the well-being of people or damage the environment, where those impacts are not reflected in market prices; the costs or benefits associated with externalities do not enter standard cost accounting schemes; in many environmental situations environmental deterioration may be caused by a few while the cost is borne by the community (e.g., overfishing, the production of greenhouse emissions not compensated for by taxes); the environment is often cited as a negatively affected externality of the economy.

Extinction – 1. the cessation of a species or group of taxa, reducing biodiversity. 2. the irrevocable elimination of species; it can be a normal process of the natural world as species out-compete or kill off others or as environmental conditions change, causing a reduction in biodiversity. 3. the termination of an organism or a taxon, usually a species, occurs when the last individual organism dies. Compare *functional extinction.*

Extinction event (or *mass extinction, extinction-level event* or ELE) – a sharp decrease in the number of species in a relatively short period.

Extirpate – to eradicate a species; extinction caused by direct human action, such as hunting, trapping, etc.

Extreme events (or *extreme weather*) – a weather event that is rare at a particular place and time of year, including, for example, heat waves, cold waves, heavy rains, periods of drought and flooding, and severe storms. *Extreme is a statistical concept that varies depending on location, season, and length of the historical record.*

Extreme environment – an environment in which few living organisms can survive.

Extreme points of Earth – the geographical locations that differ relative to other land masses, continents, or countries.

Extreme precipitation (*events*) – an abnormally high rain or snow episode. *Extreme is a statistical concept that varies depending on location, season, and length of the historical record.*

Extremophile – an organism that thrives in physically or geochemically extreme conditions.

Eye – the center of a hurricane, where no storm activity occurs.

Eye wall – the area between the eye and the storm.

F

Fair trade – a guarantee that a fair price is paid to producers of goods or services; includes a range of other social and environmental standards, including safety standards and the right to form unions.

Fall overturn – the mixing (or *turning over*) of lake water occurs in autumn, facilitating its re-oxygenation.

Family planning – controlling reproduction; planning the timing and the number of births to have babies.

Famines – acute food shortages characterized by large-scale loss of life, social disruption, and economic chaos.

Fauna – all the animals in a region.

Feces – food waste discharged from the bowels after it has been digested.

Fecundity – the physical ability to reproduce.

Feedback – flow from outputs back to interact with the action. An amplification (i.e., *positive feedback*) or a reduction (i.e., *negative feedback*) of the rate of global warming caused by its effects.

Feedback mechanisms – factors that increase or amplify (*positive feedback*) or decrease (*negative feedback*) the rate of a process. *An example of positive climatic feedback is ice-albedo feedback. The process through which a system is controlled, changed, or modulated in response to its output. Positive feedback results in the amplification of the system output; negative feedback reduces the output of a system.*

Feedlot (or *feed yard*) – a type of *Confined Animal Feeding Operation* (CAFO, or *factory farming*) used for finishing livestock, notably beef cattle, before slaughter.

Fen – an area of waterlogged soil that tends to be peaty; fed mainly by upwelling water; low productivity.

Feral – 1. in a natural, wild state; 2. a once domestic animal that has taken up a wild existence.

Fermentation – any of a group of chemical reactions induced by living or nonliving ferments that split complex organic compounds into relatively simple substances, especially the anaerobic conversion of sugar to carbon dioxide and alcohol by yeast.

Fertigate – applying fertilizer through an irrigation system.

Fertility – a measurement of the number of offspring produced through sexual reproduction; usually described regarding the number of offspring of females since paternity can be difficult to determine.

Fertility rate – number of live births per 1,000 women aged 15 to 44. Compare *mortality rates*.

Fertilization – the union of two gametes whereby the somatic chromosome number is restored, and the development of a new individual is initiated; the addition of materials to the soil to increase the available nutrient content.

Fertilizers – compounds given to plants to promote growth; they are usually applied either through the soil, for uptake by plant roots, or by foliar feeding, for uptake through leaves.

Fetal alcohol syndrome – a tragic set of permanent physical, mental and behavioral congenital disabilities that can result when the mother drinks alcohol during pregnancy.

Fibrosis – the general name for accumulating scar tissue in the lung.

Fidelity – a principle that forbids misleading or deceiving any creature capable of being misled or deceived.

Filters – a porous mesh of cotton cloth, spun glass fibers, or asbestos-cellulose that allows air or liquid to pass through but holds back solid particles.

Fire-climax community – an equilibrium community maintained by periodic fires (e.g., grasslands, chaparral shrubland, and some pine forests).

Fire ecology – a branch of ecology that studies the ecological role of naturally occurring wildfires.

First law of thermodynamics – energy is conserved; energy is neither created nor destroyed; it is only changed to a different state (e.g., from chemical energy such as gasoline, into mechanical energy to power an engine and finally into heat from friction).

Fitness – an individual organism's reproductive success.

Fixed action pattern (*ethology*) – an instinctive behavioral pattern.

Flagship species – representative of an environmental cause, such as an ecosystem in need of conservation.

Flood control devices – measures to protect areas that are easily flooded by either reducing flood flows or confining the flow; devices include building dams or levees or modifying the river or stream channel.

Flood Disaster Protection Act of 1973 – this law signaled a shift in federal policy from reducing floods through structural controls to reducing damages by limiting the development in flood-prone areas by making federally-subsidized flood insurance available to property owners in flood-prone areas only in those communities which adopted *Floodplain* zoning.

Floodplains – lowlands along riverbanks, lakes, and coastlines subjected to periodic inundation.

Flora – all of the plants in a given region.

Fluorinated gases – powerful synthetic greenhouse gases such as hydrofluorocarbons, perfluorocarbons, and sulfur hexafluoride are emitted from various industrial processes. Fluorinated gases sometimes substitute stratospheric ozone-depleting substances (e.g., chlorofluorocarbons, hydrochlorofluorocarbons, and halons). *They are used in coolants, foaming agents, fire extinguishers, solvents, pesticides, and aerosol propellants. These gases are emitted in small quantities compared to carbon dioxide (CO_2), methane (CH_4), or nitrous oxide (N_2O). However, because they are potent greenhouse gases, they are High Global Warming Potential gases (High GWP gases).*

Fluorocarbons – carbon-fluorine compounds often contain other elements such as hydrogen, chlorine, or bromine. Common fluorocarbons include chlorofluorocarbons (CFCs), hydrochlorofluorocarbons (HCFCs), hydrofluorocarbons (HFCs), and perfluorocarbons (PFCs). See *chlorofluorocarbons, hydrochlorofluorocarbons, hydrofluorocarbons,* and *ozone-depleting substances.*

Fluctuations – rising and falling, such as population numbers; a variant.

Flue-gas scrubbing – treating combustion exhaust gases with chemical agents to remove pollutants; spraying crushed limestone and water into the exhaust gas stream to remove sulfur is a common scrubbing technique.

Fluidized bed combustion – high-pressure air is forced through a mixture of crushed coal and limestone particles, lifting the burning fuel and causing it to move like a boiling fluid.

Flyway – the flight paths used in bird migration. *Flyways generally span over continents and often oceans.*

Food aid – financial assistance intended to boost less-developed countries' living standards.

Food chain (*food webs, food networks,* or *trophic networks*) – the feeding relationships between species within an ecosystem. *The sequence of organisms through which energy and materials are transferred, in the form of food, from one trophic level to another. A group of organisms interrelated because each member feeds upon the one below it.*

Food density – the amount of food available within a given *ecotope.* (i.e., distinct landscape).

Food miles – the emissions produced, and resources needed to transport food and drink around the globe.

Food network (*food chain, food webs,* or *trophic networks*) – the feeding relationships between species within an ecosystem. *The sequence of organisms through which energy and materials are transferred, in the form of food, from one trophic level to another.*

Food security – enough to meet the complete requirements of all people (i.e., total global food supply equals total global demand). Food security always has components of production, access, and utilization. *For households, the ability to purchase or produce the food needed for a healthy and active life (disposable income is crucial). For national food security, the focus is on sufficient food for all people in a nation, and it entails a combination of national production, imports, and exports.*

Food surpluses – excess food supplies.

Food webs (*food chain, food networks,* or *trophic networks*) – feeding relationships between species within an ecosystem. A set of interconnected food chains by which energy and nutrients circulate within an ecosystem. *A complex, interlocking series of individual food chains in an ecosystem.*

Footprint (or *ecological footprint*) – in a general environmental sense, *footprint* measures environmental impact. However, this is usually expressed as an area of productive land (*footprint*) needed to counteract the impact. *A measure of the consumption of renewable natural resources by a human population, be it that of a country, a region or the whole world given as the total area of productive land or sea required to produce all the crops, meat, seafood, wood, and fiber it consumes, to sustain its energy consumption and to give space for its infrastructure.*

Forage – the plant material (mainly plant leaves) eaten by grazing animals.

Forcing – factors that affect the Earth's climate. *For example, natural factors such as volcanoes and human factors such as the emission of heat-trapping gases and particles through fossil fuel combustion.*

Forcing mechanism – a process altering the energy balance of the climate system (i.e., changes the relative balance between incoming solar radiation and outgoing infrared radiation from Earth). *Such mechanisms include changes in solar irradiance, volcanic eruptions, and enhancement of the natural greenhouse effect by emissions of greenhouse gases.* See *radiation*, *infrared radiation*, and *radiative forcing*.

Forest – land with a canopy cover greater than 30%.

Forest ecology – a branch of ecology that studies the interrelated patterns, processes, flora, fauna, and ecosystems within forests.

Forest management – scientific planning and administration of forest resources for sustainable harvest, multiple uses, regeneration, and maintenance of a healthy biological community.

Formula for photosynthesis – CO_2 (from the air) + H_2O + sun's energy (light) * $C_6H_{12}O_6$ (glucose) + O_2

Fossil fuel – a general term for organic materials formed from decayed plants and animals that have been converted to crude oil, coal, natural gas, or heavy oils by exposure to heat and pressure in the Earth's crust over hundreds of millions of years. *Hydrocarbons within the top layer of the Earth's crust. Any hydrocarbon deposit burned for heat or power, such as coal, oil, and natural gas (produces carbon dioxide when burnt); fuels formed from once–living organisms that have become fossilized over geological time. (e.g., petroleum, natural gas, coal).*

Fossil water – groundwater that has remained in an aquifer for thousands or millions of years; when geologic changes seal the aquifer preventing further replenishment, the water becomes trapped inside and is *fossil water. Fossil water is a limited resource and can only be used once.*

Foundation species – a dominant primary producer in its ecosystem in terms of abundance and influence on other organisms and the environment.

Founder effect – the accumulation of random genetic changes in an isolated population.

Fourth World – a political/economic category describing very developing nations with neither market economies nor central planning and either not developing or developing very slowly; also used to describe poor indigenous communities within wealthier nations.

Freegan – a person using alternative strategies for living based on limited participation in the conventional economy and minimal consumption of resources. Freegans embrace community, generosity, social concern, freedom, cooperation, and sharing – contrary to materialism, moral apathy, competition, conformity, and greed. The most notorious freegan strategy is "urban foraging" or "dumpster diving." This technique involves rummaging through the garbage of retailers, residences, offices, and other facilities for useful goods. Freegan is compounded from "free" and "vegan." Compare *affluenza, Froogle*.

Freezing condensation – a process that occurs in clouds when ice crystals trap water vapor; as the ice crystals become larger and heavier, they begin to fall as rain or snow.

Freon – DuPont's trade name for odorless, colorless, nonflammable, and noncorrosive chlorofluorocarbon and hydrochlorofluorocarbon refrigerants, used in air conditioning and refrigeration systems.

Freshwater – 1. water containing no significant amounts of salt. 2. water other than seawater covers only about 2% of the Earth's surface, including streams, rivers, lakes, ponds, and water associated with several kinds of wetlands. Compare *potable water*.

Freshwater ecosystems – where fresh (non-salty) water of streams, rivers, ponds, or lakes play a defining role.

Friction – the rubbing of two objects against each other when one or both is moving; a significant percentage of the energy produced by an automobile engine is dissipated in friction, reducing the system's overall efficiency.

Front (*weather*) – the boundary between warm (*high-pressure*) and cold (*low-pressure*) air masses.

Frontline communities – those communities that experience climate change first and often feel the worst effects. They are communities that have higher exposures, are more sensitive, and are less able to adapt to climate change impacts for various reasons.

Froogle – a play on the word frugal; people who lead low–consumption lifestyles: a person who is part of a new movement towards self–sufficiency and waste–reduction achieved by bartering goods and services mainly through the internet, making their products, soap, clothes, and breeding chickens and goats, growing their food, baking bread, harvesting water and energy, and helping to develop a sense of community. Sometimes referring to people who have resolved to only buy essentials for a particular period. Compare *freegan, affluenza*.

Frost-free season – the time between the last occurrence of an air temperature of 32 °F in spring and the first occurrence of 32 °F in the subsequent fall.

Fuel assembly – hollow metal rods containing uranium oxide pellets used to fuel a nuclear reactor.

Fuel cell – an electrochemical device with no moving parts that converts the chemical energy of a fuel, such as hydrogen, and an oxidant, such as oxygen, directly into electricity; clean, quiet, and highly efficient sources of electricity.

Fuel-switching – generally, this is substituting one fuel type for another. In the climate-change discussion, it is implicit that the substituted fuel produces lower carbon emissions per unit of energy produced than the original fuel (e.g., natural gas for coal).

Fuelwood – branches, twigs, logs, wood chips, and other wood products harvested for use as fuel.

Fugitive emissions – 1. in the context of the National Greenhouse Gas Inventory, these are greenhouse gases emitted from fuel production itself, including processing, transmission, storage, and distribution processes, and including emissions from oil and natural gas exploration, venting and flaring, as well as the mining of black coal; 2. substances that enter the air without going through a smokestack, such as dust from soil erosion, strip mining, rock crushing, construction, and building demolition.

Fujita Scale – measures the intensity of a tornado based on its wind speed, diameter, and the amount of damage caused.

Full-cost pricing – the cost of commercial goods, such as electric power, that includes the private costs of inputs and the costs of the externalities required by their production and use. See *externality*.

Functional ecology – a branch of ecology that studies the roles or functions that species (or groups of species) play in an ecosystem.

Functional extinction – the effective extinction of a species or other taxon such that reports of its existence cease, the reduced population no longer plays a significant role in ecosystem function, or the population is no longer viable because it is unable to sustain healthy reproduction, even if the last individual organism of the species has not yet died.

Functional response – the intake rate of a consumer as a function of food density.

Fungi or Fungus – one of the five-kingdom classifications; consist of non-photosynthetic, eukaryotic organisms with cell walls, filamentous bodies, and absorptive nutrition. *Bacteria and fungi are the major decomposers in terrestrial (and some aquatic) ecosystems and play a crucial role in nutrient cycles.*

Fungicide – a chemical that kills *fungi*.

G

G8 (Group of Eight) – an international forum for the world's major industrialized democracies that emerged following the 1973 oil crisis and subsequent global recession. It includes Canada, France, Germany, Italy, Japan, Russia, the UK, and the US, representing about 65% of the world economy.

Gaia's hypothesis – proposes that living and nonliving parts of Earth are a complex interacting system thought of as a single organism., named after the Greek Earth mother goddess Gaia.

Gamma rays – very short wavelength forms of the electromagnetic spectrum.

Gap analysis – a biogeographical technique of mapping biological diversity and endemic species to find gaps between protected areas that leave endangered habitats vulnerable to disruption.

Garden city – a new town designed with special emphasis on landscaping and rural ambiance.

Garden organics – organics derived from garden sources (e.g., prunings, grass clippings).

Gasohol – a mixture of gasoline and ethyl alcohol; used in the internal combustion engine.

Gasoline – a volatile flammable liquid made from petroleum and used as fuel in internal combustion engines; made up of hydrocarbons made of 8 carbon chains.

Gause's law (or *competitive exclusion principle*) – states that two species cannot coexist in the same environment if competing for precisely the same resource, often memorably summarized as "complete competitors cannot coexist."

Gene – 1. a unit of heredity; a segment of DNA nucleus of the cell that contains information for the synthesis of a specific protein, such as an enzyme. 2. a locatable region of a genomic sequence corresponding to a unit of inheritance, associated with regulatory regions, transcribed regions, or other functional sequence regions.

Gene banks – storage for seed varieties for future breeding experiments.

Gene pool – 1. the collective genetic information contained within a population of sexually reproducing organisms. 2. the complete set of unique alleles in a species or population.

General circulation mode (**GCM**; or *global climate model*) – a computer model of the world's climate system, including the atmosphere and oceans. a global, three-dimensional computer model of the climate system that can be used to simulate human-induced climate change. *GCMs are highly complex and represent the effects of such factors as reflective and absorptive properties of atmospheric water vapor, greenhouse gas concentrations, clouds, annual and daily solar heating, ocean temperatures, and ice boundaries. The most recent GCMs include global representations of the atmosphere, oceans, and land surface. See climate modeling.*

General fertility rate – the crude birthrate multiplied by the percentage of women of reproductive age.

Generalist species – organisms able to thrive in a wide variety of environmental conditions and use various resources.

Genetic assimilation – the disappearance of a species as its genes are diluted through crossbreeding with a closely related species.

Genetic bottleneck – an evolutionary event in which a significant percentage of a population or species is killed or prevented from reproducing.

Genetic diversity – one of the three levels of biodiversity that refers to the total number of genetic characteristics.

Genetic engineering – 1. the use of various experimental techniques to produce molecules of DNA containing new genes or novel combinations of genes, usually for insertion into a host cell for cloning; 2. the technology of preparing recombinant DNA in vitro by cutting up DNA molecules and splicing together fragments from more than one organism; 3. the laboratory modification of genetic material that would otherwise be subject to the forces of nature only; 4. laboratory manipulation of genetic material using molecular biology techniques to create desired characteristics in organisms.

Genetic rescue – a conservation tool used to increase the fitness of a small, imperiled population by adding genetic variation through a small number of immigrants.

Genetically modified organisms (GMO) – any organism whose genetic material has been altered using genetic engineering techniques.

Genome – the total genetic composition of an organism.

Geoengineering – intentional modifications of the Earth system, usually technological, to reduce future climate change.

Geometric growth – growth that follows a geometric pattern of increase, such as 2, 4, 8, 16, etc. See *exponential growth*.

Geosphere – the solid part of planet Earth, the main divisions being the crust, the mantle, and the liquid core. *Lithosphere* is the geosphere's part consisting of the crust and the upper mantle.

Geothermal energy – derived from Earth's natural heat through geysers, fumaroles, hot springs, or other natural geothermal features or through deep wells that pump heated groundwater. *It is used to generate electricity after transformation.*

Germplasm – genetic material that may be preserved for future agricultural, commercial, and ecological values (plant seeds or parts or animal eggs, sperm, and embryos).

Glacial earthquake – a large-scale temblor occurs in glaciated areas where glaciers move faster than one kilometer yearly.

Glacier – a multi-year surplus accumulation of snowfall above snowmelt on land resulted in a mass of ice at least 0.1 km^2 in an area showing some evidence of movement in response to gravity. *A glacier may terminate on land or in water. Glacier ice is the largest reservoir of fresh water on Earth, second only to the oceans as the largest reservoir of total water. Glaciers are on every continent except Australia.*

Global acres – acres/hectares adjusted according to world average biomass productivity to be compared meaningfully across regions; 1 global acre is 1 acre of biologically productive space with average world productivity. See *global hectares*.

Global average temperature – an estimate of Earth's mean surface air temperature averaged over the entire planet.

Global change – differences in the global environment may alter the capacity of the Earth to sustain life. Global change encompasses climate change, but it also includes other critical drivers of environmental change that may interact with climate change, such as land use change, the alteration of the water cycle, changes in biogeochemical cycles, and biodiversity loss. See *climate change*.

Global climate model (GCM) (or *general circulation model*) – a computer model of the world's climate system, including the atmosphere and oceans.

Global cooling – a concern during the 1970s of imminent cooling of the Earth's surface and atmosphere and a posited glaciation commencement.

Global dimming – the observed decrease in surface insolation that may have recently reversed. *A reduction in the amount of direct solar radiation reaching the earth's surface due to light diffusion because of air pollution and increasing levels of cloud. A phenomenon of the last 30–50 years.*

Global ecology (or *macroecology*) – studies the relationships between organisms and their environment at large spatial scales to characterize and explain statistical patterns of abundance, distribution, and diversity.

Global ecophagy – the destruction of Earth's ecosystems.

Global environmentalism – a concern for and action to help solve global environmental problems.

Global hectares – acres/hectares adjusted according to world average biomass productivity so they can be compared meaningfully across regions; 1 global hectare is 1 hectare of biologically productive space with average world productivity. See *global acres*.

Global temperature record (or historical temperature record) – the temperature fluctuations of the atmosphere and oceans through various periods.

Global warming (GW) – the increase in the average temperature of Earth's near-surface atmosphere and oceans. The increase in global temperatures mainly caused by human-induced enhanced greenhouse effect trapping the sun's heat in Earth's atmosphere; Earth's average temperature has risen and fallen over millions of years, such as during the Ice Ages. *Also, any period in which the temperature of Earth's atmosphere increases; the theory of such changes. The current concern is that the increase in greenhouse gases generated by humans, particularly carbon dioxide emissions from fossil fuels, will contribute to global warming; the preferred term is "global climate change" because changes in average temperatures have effects on other aspects of weather and climate, including the amount of rainfall.*

Global warming controversy – socio-political issues surrounding the theory of global warming.

Global warming period – any period in which the temperature of the Earth's atmosphere increases.

Global warming potential – a system of multipliers devised to enable the warming effects of different gases to be compared. *Measures how much a given mass of greenhouse gas is estimated to contribute to global warming. A measure of the total energy that a gas absorbs over a particular period (usually 100 years), compared to carbon dioxide.*

Globalization – 1. the expansion of interactions to a global or worldwide scale; 2. the increasing interdependence, integration, and interaction among people and organizations worldwide; 3. a mix of economic, social, technological, cultural, and political interrelationships.

Glyphosate – a nonselective herbicide particularly effective against perennial weeds. the active ingredient in the herbicide *Roundup*™.

Governance – the decision-making procedure; who makes decisions, how they are made, and with what information; the structures and processes for collective decision-making involving governmental and non-governmental actors.

Grasslands – an area where grasses dominate the vegetation. *A biome dominated by grasses and associated herbaceous plants.*

Green (*sustainability*) – indicates consideration for the environment (e.g., green plumbers, green purchasing, etc.). *Sometimes used as a noun* (e.g., the Greens, green plumbers, green purchasing etc.).

Green architecture – building design that moves towards self-sufficient sustainability by adopting *circular metabolism.*

Green design – 1. environmentally sustainable design. 2. designing objects, services, and buildings to achieve environmental sustainability.

Green manure – a cover crop grown primarily to add nutrients and organic matter to the soil.

Great Pacific garbage patch – a gyre of marine debris particles discovered in the central North Pacific Ocean between 1985 and 1988. *The patch is characterized by exceptionally high relative pelagic concentrations of plastic, chemical sludge, and other debris that the currents of the North Pacific Gyre have trapped.*

Green plans – integrated national environmental plans for reducing pollution and resource consumption while achieving sustainable development and environmental restoration.

Green political parties – political organizations promoting environmental protection, participatory democracy, grassroots organization, and sustainable development.

Green power – electricity generated from clean, renewable energy sources (such as solar, wind, biomass, or hydropower) and supplied through the grid.

Green products and services – have a reduced effect on health and the environment compared with competing products or services. *Green products or services contain recycled content, reduce waste, conserve energy or water, use less packaging, and reduce the number of toxins disposed of or consumed.*

Green purchasing – purchasing goods and services that minimize environmental impacts and are socially just.

Green Revolution – the ongoing transformation of agriculture that led in some places to significant increases in agricultural production between the 1940s and 1960s. *It usually requires high inputs of water, plant nutrients, and pesticides.*

Green Star – a voluntary rating system for buildings for green design, covering nine impact categories. *The highest rating is six stars, which equals a world leader in sustainability.*

Green waste – plant material discarded as non–putrescible waste – includes tree and shrub cuttings and pruning, grass clippings, leaves, natural (untreated) timber waste, and weeds (noxious or otherwise).

Greenhouse debt – the measure to which a person, incorporated association, business enterprise, government instrumentality, or geographic community exceeds its permitted greenhouse footprint and emits greenhouse gases contributing to global warming and climate change.

Greenhouse effect – 1. the insulating effect of atmospheric greenhouse gases (e.g., water vapor, carbon dioxide, methane) that keeps Earth's temperature about 60 °F (16 °C) warmer than otherwise. 2. the process in which the emission of infrared radiation by the atmosphere warms a planet's surface. T the warming of Earth's climate from solar irradiance trapped in the atmosphere.

The phenomenon is caused by atmospheric gases, which allow the Sun's energy to reach the Earth's surface but subsequently absorb heat that is radiated back from the warmed surface. trapping and build-up of heat in the atmosphere (troposphere) near the Earth's surface. Some heat flowing back toward space from Earth's surface is absorbed by water vapor, carbon dioxide, ozone, and other atmospheric gases and reradiated toward the Earth's surface. *If these greenhouse gases' atmospheric concentrations rise, the lower atmosphere's average temperature will gradually increase.* See *greenhouse gas, anthropogenic, climate,* and *global warming.* Compare *enhanced greenhouse effect.*

Greenhouse gas (GHG) – 1. any gas that absorbs infrared radiation (i.e., greenhouse effect) and traps heat in the atmosphere. 2. contributes to the greenhouse effect; gaseous atmospheric constituents, both natural and from human activity, absorb and re–emit infrared radiation. Greenhouse gases include carbon dioxide, methane, nitrous oxide, ozone, chlorofluorocarbons, hydrochlorofluorocarbons, hydrofluorocarbons, perfluorocarbons, and sulfur hexafluoride.

Greenhouse gases are a natural part of the atmosphere, including carbon dioxide (CO_2), methane (CH_4, persisting 9–15 years with a greenhouse warming potential (GWP) 22 times CO_2), nitrous oxide (N_2O persists 120 years with a GWP of 310), ozone (O_3), hydrofluorocarbons, perfluorocarbons, and sulfur hexafluoride. *Water vapor (H_2O) is the most abundant greenhouse gas.*

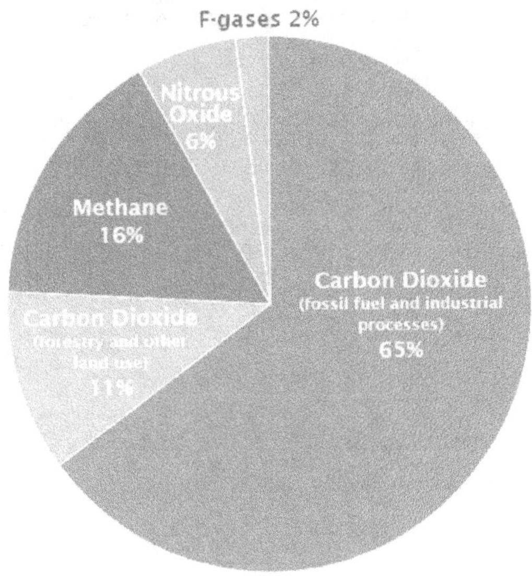

Global greenhouse gases by gas emitted, EPA, 2014

Carbon dioxide (CO_2) – a gas entering the atmosphere through burning fossil fuels (coal, natural gas, and oil), solid waste, trees, and wood products, and because of specific chemical reactions (e.g., manufacture of cement). Carbon dioxide is removed from the atmosphere (or *sequestered*) when plants absorb it as part of the biological carbon cycle during photosynthesis.

Methane (CH_4) – a gas emitted while producing and transporting coal, natural gas, and oil. Methane emissions also result from livestock and other agricultural practices and the decay of organic waste in municipal solid waste landfills.

Nitrous oxide (N$_2$O) – a gas emitted during agricultural and industrial activities and during the combustion of fossil fuels and solid waste.

Fluorinated gases – hydrofluorocarbons, perfluorocarbons, sulfur hexafluoride, and nitrogen trifluoride are synthetic, potent greenhouse gases emitted from various industrial processes. Fluorinated gases sometimes substitute stratospheric ozone-depleting substances (e.g., chlorofluorocarbons, hydrochlorofluorocarbons, and halons). These gases are typically emitted in smaller quantities, but because they are potent greenhouse gases, they are High Global Warming Potential gases (*High GWP gases*).

Greenhouse gas inventory – a type of emission inventory that includes greenhouse gas emissions from source categories and removal by carbon sinks.

Greenlash (or *environmental backlash*) – dramatic changes in ecosystems' structure and behavior.

Greenwashing – companies that portray themselves as environmentally friendly when their business practices do not back this up. *Generally, applies to excessive use of green marketing and packaging when this does not consider the total ecological footprint.*

Greenwater – water replenishing soil moisture, evaporating from soil, plant, and other surfaces, and transpired by plants. In nature, the global average amount of rainfall becoming green water is about 60%. Of the green water, about 55% falls on forests, 25% on grasslands, and 20% on crops. *Green water productivity increases through rainwater harvesting, infiltration, and runoff collection. Green water cannot be piped or drunk (cannot be sold) and is generally ignored by water management authorities. However, it is crucial to plants and agriculture and needs careful management as an essential part of the global water cycle.*

Greywater – household wastewater that has not encountered toilet waste; includes water from baths, showers, bathrooms, washing machines, laundry, and kitchen sinks. *It can be reused without purification for some purposes.*

Gross domestic product (GDP) – the total economic activity within national boundaries.

Gross national product (GNP) – the total of all goods and services produced in a national economy; *Gross domestic product* (GDP) distinguishes economic activity within a country from that of off-shore corporations.

Gross primary productivity – total carbon assimilation.

Ground cover – any plant that grows over an area of ground, protecting the topsoil from erosion and drought.

Groundwater – 1. water found below the surface – usually in porous rocks, soil, or underground aquifers. 2. water located beneath the ground surface in soil pore spaces and the fractures of lithologic formation. *It does not include water or crystallization held by chemical bonds in rocks or moisture in upper soil layers.*

Group of Eight (G8) – an international forum for the world's major industrialized democracies that emerged following the 1973 oil crisis and subsequent global recession. It includes Canada, France, Germany, Italy, Japan, Russia, the UK, and the US, representing about 65% of the world economy.

Growth – increase in size, weight, power, etc.

Guest – a generic term for parasitic, mutualistic, and commensalist symbionts.

Gulf Stream – a powerful, warm, and swift Atlantic Ocean current that originates in the Gulf of Mexico, exits through the Strait of Florida, and follows the eastern coastlines of the United States and Newfoundland before crossing the Atlantic Ocean.

Gully erosion – removal of soil layers, creating channels or ravines too large to be removed by normal tillage operations.

H

Habitat – an ecological or environmental area that is inhabited by a species. A specific ecological area inhabited by specific plant and animal species.

Habitat conservation plans – agreements under which property owners are allowed to harvest resources or develop the land if habitats are conserved or replaced to benefit resident endangered or threatened species; *some incidental "taking" or loss of endangered species is generally allowed in such plans.*

Habitat fragmentation – the discontinuation of a species' habitat caused by environmental change. A process during which larger habitat areas are broken into several smaller patches of smaller total area, isolated by a matrix of habitats, unlike the original habitat.

Hadley cells – circulation patterns of atmospheric convection currents as they sink and rise in several intermediate bands.

Halocarbons – compounds containing chlorine, bromine, fluorine, and carbon. Such compounds can act as potent greenhouse gases in the atmosphere. *Chlorine and bromine-containing halocarbons are involved in the depletion of the ozone layer.*

Halophyte – a *salt-loving* plant.

Halophile – a *salt-loving* organism.

Hard waste (or *municipal sold waste*) – household trash (or rubbish) not generally accepted into garbage bins (e.g., old stoves, mattresses). Generally, garbage means food waste while rubbish or trash refers to other solid, nonhazardous waste.

Hard water – water with high mineral content.

Hazardous chemicals – dangerous chemicals, including flammables, explosives, irritants, sensitizers, acids, and caustics; many are hazardous in high concentrations but harmless when diluted.

Hazardous waste – any discarded material containing substances known to be toxic, mutagenic, carcinogenic, or teratogenic to humans or other life forms; ignitable, corrosive, explosive, or highly reactive alone or with other materials.

Health – a state of physical and emotional wellbeing; the absence of disease or ailment.

Heap-leach extraction – a technique for separating gold from highly low-grade ores; crushed ore is piled in huge heaps and sprayed with a dilute alkaline-cyanide solution, which percolates through the pile to extract the gold, which is separated from the effluent in a processing plant; this process has a high potential for water pollution.

Heat – energy derived from the motion of molecules; *a form of energy into which all other forms of energy may be degraded.*

Heat capacity – the amount of heat energy that must be added or subtracted to change the temperature of a body; water has a high heat capacity.

Heat island (or *urban heat island*) – an urban area with temperatures higher than the surrounding non-urban area. *As urban areas develop, buildings, roads, and other infrastructure replace open land and vegetation. These surfaces absorb more solar energy, creating higher temperatures in urban areas.*

Heat of vaporization – the heat energy required to convert water from a liquid to a gas.

Heat stress – the negative health impacts, such as heat stroke or heat exhaustion, caused by exposure to extreme heat or long periods in hot environments.

Heat tax – a tax imposed on the use of energy supplies.

Heat waves – prolonged excessive heat, often combined with excessive humidity. *A period of abnormally hot weather lasting days to weeks.*

Heath – low-growing woody vegetation found on free-draining acidic soils.

Heavy metals – mercury, lead, cadmium, and nickel; highly toxic in very small quantities; can be fatal and accumulate in the environment with long-term cumulative effects in humans.

Heavy precipitation events – an episode of abnormally high rain or snow. *Extreme is a statistical concept that varies depending on location, season, and length of the historical record.*

Heiligendamm process – an initiative to institutionalize high-level dialogue between the G8 countries and the five crucial emerging economies, known as Outreach 5 (O 5), consisting of China, Mexico, India, Brazil, and South Africa.

Hemoglobin – the iron-containing respiratory pigment in red blood cells of vertebrates, consisting of about 6 percent heme and 94 percent globin.

Herbicide – a chemical that kills or inhibits plant growth.

Herbivore – an organism that eats only plants.

Herbivory – predation in which an organism known as an *herbivore* primarily consumes autotrophs such as plants, algae, and photosynthesizing bacteria.

Heterarchy – a way of organizing that does not include rank (i.e., each element possesses the same level of importance or authority). Compare *hierarchy*.

Heterotroph (or *chemoorganotroph*) – 1. an organism requiring organic substrates to obtain carbon for growth and development. 2. an organism incapable of synthesizing its food and must feed upon organic compounds produced by other organisms.

Hexafluoroethane (C_2F_6) – the perfluorocarbon counterpart to the hydrocarbon ethane; a non-flammable gas negligibly soluble in water and slightly soluble in alcohol. It is an extremely potent and long-lived greenhouse gas. *Due to the high energy of C-F bonds, hexafluoroethane is inert and thus is an extremely stable greenhouse gas, with an atmospheric lifetime of 10,000 years. It has a global warming potential (GWP) of 9200 and an ozone depletion potential (ODP) of 0. Hexafluoroethane is included in the IPCC list of greenhouse gases.*

Hidden energy – energy within a system that one is not aware of.

Hierarchy – an organization of parts in which control from the top (generally with few parts) proceeds through a series of levels (ranks) to the bottom (generally consisting of many parts). Compare *heterarchy*.

High-density polyethylene (HDPE) – a polyethylene plastic used to make products such as milk bottles, pipes, and shopping bags. HDPE may be colored or opaque.

High-level wastes – highly radioactive wastes.

High-level waste repository – a place where intensely radioactive wastes can be buried and will be kept unexposed to groundwater and earthquakes for tens of thousands of years.

High-quality energy – intense, concentrated, and high-temperature energy considered high-quality because of its usefulness in performing work.

Histogram – a statistical graph of a frequency distribution in which vertical rectangles of different heights are proportionate to corresponding frequencies; used to graph distributions of populations, such as the population percentage in distinct age groups.

Historical temperature record (or *global temperature record*) – the fluctuations of the temperature of the atmosphere and the oceans through various periods.

Hockey stick graph – reconstructions of the Northern Hemisphere or *global mean temperature* changes during the past 600 to 11,300 years, a name coined by Mann, Bradley, and Hughes in 1999.

Holistic science – the study of entire integrated systems rather than isolated parts; often takes a descriptive or interpretive approach.

Holocene – a geological period that began approximately 11,550 calendar years BP (before present; about 9600 BC) and continued to the Anthropocene.

Holocene Climatic Optimum – a warm period during 9,000 to 5,000 years AD.

Home energy audits – auditing or analyzing the energy expenditure in a home, including the loss of energy.

Homeostasis – a system that regulates its internal environment and maintains a constant and stable condition (e.g., endothermic animals maintain a constant body temperature). *The property of an open or closed system, especially a living organism. Regulating internal environment to maintain a stable, constant condition.*

Homestead Act – a U.S. legislation passed in 1862 allowing any citizen or applicant for citizenship over 21 years old and the head of a family to acquire 160 acres of public land by living on it and cultivating it for five years.

Homoclime – a region with the same patterns of weather (i.e., climate) as the one under investigation.

Horsepower (hp) – a unit of power in physics equal to 550 foot-pounds/sec or 745.7 watts.

Horton overland flow – the tendency of water to flow horizontally across land surfaces when rainfall has exceeded infiltration capacity and depression storage capacity..

Host – an organism that harbors a parasitic, mutualistic, or commensal symbiont.

Host organism – an organism that provides lodging for a parasite.

Hot desert – deserts of the American Southwest and Mexico; characterized by extreme summer heat and cacti.

House energy rating – an assessment of the energy efficiency of a residential house or unit design using a 5-star scale.

Household metabolism – the passage of food, energy, water, goods, and waste through the household unit, like the metabolic activity of an organism. Compare *industrial metabolism.*

Human ecology – the study of the interactions of humans with the environment. *A branch of ecology that studies the relationships between humans and their natural, social, and built environments.*

Human equivalent (He) – the approximate human daily energy requirement of 12,500 kJ or its approximate energy generating capacity at a basal metabolic rate, which is equivalent to about 80 watts or 3.47222 kWh per day; a 100-watt light bulb, therefore, runs at 1.25 He.

Human resources – human wisdom, experience, skill, labor, and enterprise.

Humus – 1. organic material in soil lending it a bark brown or black coloration. 2. semi–persistent organic matter in the soil that can no longer be recognized as tissue. 3. sticky, brown, insoluble residue from the bodies of dead plants and animals. *Humus gives soil its structure, coating mineral particles and holding them together; serves as a major source of plant nutrients.*

Hurricanes – large cyclonic oceanic storms with heavy rain and winds exceeding 119 km/hr (74 mph). Intense low–pressure weather systems; mid-latitude cyclones are atmospheric circulations that rotate clockwise in the Southern Hemisphere and anti-clockwise in the Northern Hemisphere and are generally associated with stronger winds, unsettled conditions, cloudiness, and rainfall. Tropical *cyclones* (called *hurricanes* in the Northern Hemisphere) cause storm surges in coastal areas.

Hurricane Nor'easter – a hurricane that generates from the northeast and moves southwest.

Hybrid gas-electric motor – automobiles that run on electric power and small gasoline or diesel engine.

Hydro energy – potential and kinetic energy of water used to generate electricity.

Hydrocarbons – molecules made from carbon and hydrogen found in raw materials such as petroleum, coal, and natural gas and derived products such as plastics. An organic chemical compound containing only hydrogen and carbon atoms, arranged in rows or rings or both, and connected by single, double, or triple bonds; constitute a very large group, including alkanes, alkenes, and alkynes (e.g., petroleum, coal, methane).

Hydrochlorofluorocarbons (HCFCs) – compounds containing hydrogen, fluorine, chlorine, and carbon atoms. However, ozone-depleting substances are less potent at destroying stratospheric ozone than chlorofluorocarbons (CFCs). They have been introduced as temporary replacements for CFCs and are also greenhouse gases. See *ozone-depleting substances.*

Hydroelectric power – the electrical power generated using the power of falling water.

Hydrofluorocarbons (HFCs) – compounds containing only hydrogen, fluorine, and carbon atoms. They were introduced as alternatives to ozone-depleting substances for industrial, commercial, and personal needs. HFCs are emitted as by-products of industrial processes and used in manufacturing. They do not significantly deplete the stratospheric ozone layer but are powerful greenhouse gases with global warming potential ranging from 140 (HFC-152a) to 11,700 (HFC-23).

Hydrologic cycle (or *water cycle*) – the cyclic process of evaporation and condensation of water and its distribution across Earth as driven by solar energy. *The natural cycle of water from evaporation, transpiration in the atmosphere, condensation (rain and snow), and flows back to the ocean (e.g., rivers). The evaporation process, vertical and horizontal transport of vapor, condensation, precipitation, and water flow from continents to oceans. It is a major factor in determining climate through its influence on surface vegetation, clouds, snow and ice, and soil moisture. Hydrologic cycle is responsible for 25 to 30 percent of the mid-latitudes heat transport from the equatorial to polar regions.*

Hydrophyte (or *aquatic plants*) – plants adapted to living in aquatic environments. They are *hydrophytes* or *macrophytes* to distinguish them from algae and other microphytes. *Macrophytes are plants that grow in or near water and is emergent, submergent, or floating.*

Hydrosphere – the combined mass of water found on, under, and above the surface of the Earth. All Earth's water, including water in the sea, streams, lakes, waterbodies, soil, groundwater, and air.

Hydrothermal vent – an underwater steaming fissure that has a unique ecosystem.

Hydroxyl radical ($\cdot$OH) – the monovalent group $\cdot$OH in such compounds as bases and some acids and alcohols; this radical is characteristic of hydroxides, oxygen acids, alcohols, glycols, phenols, and hemiacetals.

Hyperalimentation (or *overnutrition*) – when the amount of nutrients ingested exceeds what is needed for normal growth, metabolism, and development.

Hypothesis – a tentative explanation that accounts for facts and can be tested for further investigation.

Hypoxia – reduced oxygen content of air or a body of water detrimental to aerobic organisms.

I

Ice age – a long-term reduction in the temperature of Earth's climate, resulting in expansions of continental ice sheets, polar ice sheets, and alpine glaciers. *A cylindrical section of ice removed from a glacier or ice sheet to study past climate patterns. By performing chemical analyses on air trapped in ice, scientists estimate the percentage of carbon dioxide and trace gases in the atmosphere at a given time. Analysis of the ice itself can give some indication of historic temperatures.*

Ice core – a sample from snow and ice accumulation over many years that have re-crystallized and trapped air bubbles from previous periods.

Igneous rocks – crystalline minerals solidified from molten magma from deep in the Earth's interior (e.g., basalt, rhyolite, andesite, lava, and granite).

Illegitimate receiver – an organism that intercepts a signal intended for another organism to the fitness detriment of either the signaler or the legitimate signal receiver.

Impervious – incapable of being penetrated.

Inaccessible – not available.

Inbreeding depression – in a small population, an accumulation of harmful genetic traits (through random mutations and natural selection) that lowers the viability and reproductive success of enough individuals to affect the whole population.

Incineration – combustion (i.e., *chemical oxidation*) of waste material to treat or dispose of that waste material.

Incinerator – an apparatus, such as a furnace, for burning waste.

Indicators – 1. quantitative markers for monitoring progress towards desired goals. 2. an observation or calculation that allows scientists, analysts, decision-makers, and others to track environmental trends, understand key factors that influence the environment, and identify effects on ecosystems and society.

Indicator species – any biological species that defines a trait or characteristic of the environment. *Any species that defines a characteristic of its environment. The presence or abundance of organisms of these species indicates the health of a given ecosystem.*

Indigenous knowledge – in brief, refers to Indigenous peoples' systems of observing, monitoring, researching, recording, communicating, and learning that is required, as for any group, to support survival and flourishing in an ecosystem and the social adaptive capacity to adjust to or prepare for changes.

Indirect emissions – release of greenhouse gases that result from the generation of electricity used in a building, home, or business. These emissions are "indirect" because the actual emissions occur at the power plant which generates the electricity, not at the building using the electricity.

Indirect energy – the energy generated in and accounted for by the wider economy as a consequence of an agent's actions or demands.

Inductive reasoning – inferring general principles from specific examples.

Industrial agriculture – a form of modern farming involving industrialized production of livestock, poultry, fish, or crops.

Industrial ecology (the term originated by Harry Zvi Evan, 1973) – 1. a period in the late 18th and early 19th centuries when significant changes in agriculture, manufacturing, and transportation profoundly affected socioeconomic and cultural conditions. 2. the observation that nature produces no waste, providing an example of sustainable waste management. Natural Capitalism espouses industrial ecology as one of its four pillars: energy conservation, material conservation, redefinition of commodity markets, and product stewardship in a service economy.

Industrial metabolism – the processes to which materials and components are subjected in industrial ecosystems. It is analogous to the metabolic processes that occur with food and nutrients in biological systems. Like biological metabolism, industrial metabolism may be addressed at several levels. Compare *household metabolism*.

Industrial Revolution – a period in the late 18th and early 19th centuries when major changes in agriculture, manufacturing, and transportation profoundly affected socioeconomic and cultural conditions. *A period of rapid industrial growth with far-reaching social and economic consequences, beginning in England during the second half of the 18th century and spreading to Europe and later to other countries, including the United States. The industrial revolution marked the beginning of a strong increase in the combustion of fossil fuels and related emissions of carbon dioxide.*

Industrial timber (or *roundwood*) – trees used for lumber, plywood, veneer, particleboard, chipboard, and paper.

Inertial confinement – a nuclear fusion process in which a small pellet of nuclear fuel is bombarded with extremely high-intensity laser light.

Infrared radiation – light whose wavelength is longer than the red color in the visible spectrum but shorter than microwave radiation. Infrared radiation can be perceived as heat. The Earth's surface, atmosphere, and clouds emit infrared radiation, terrestrial or long-wave radiation. In contrast, solar radiation is mainly short-wave radiation because of the temperature of the Sun.
See *radiation, greenhouse effect, enhanced greenhouse effect,* and *global warming.*

Infiltration – 1. water movement below topsoil to the plant roots and below. 2. the process by which water on the ground surface enters the soil. 3. the act or process of infiltrating water into a porous substance or fluid into the cells of an organ or part of the body.

Informal economy – small-scale individual or family businesses in temporary locations outside the control of normal regulatory agencies.

Inherent value – ethical values or rights that exist as an intrinsic or essential characteristic of a particular thing or class of things simply by their existence.

Inholdings – private lands within public parks, forests, or wildlife refuges.

Insecticide – a pesticide used to control insects in all developmental forms.

Insolation – incoming solar radiation. The amount of solar radiation reaching the surface of the Earth. The amount of solar energy reaching the Earth is 70 percent. The surface of the Earth absorbs 51 percent of the insolation. Water vapor and dust account for 16 percent of the energy absorbed.

Instinctive behavior – the inherent inclination of an organism towards a particular complex behavior.

In-stream – the use of freshwater where it occurs, usually a river or stream. *Includes hydroelectricity, recreation, tourism, scientific and cultural uses, ecosystem maintenance, and dilution of waste.*

Instrumental temperature record – the fluctuations of the temperature of the atmosphere and the oceans as measured by temperature sensors. *The longest-running quasi-global record started in 1850.*

Instrumental value – value or worth of objects that satisfy the needs and wants of moral agents; objects that can be used as a means to some desirable end.

Insular biogeography – the study of the distributions of biological communities on islands.

Intangible resources – factors that cannot be contained or measured, such as open space, beauty, serenity, wisdom, diversity, and satisfaction.

Intergovernmental Panel on Climate Change (IPCC) – jointly by the United Nations Environment Program and the World Meteorological Organization in 1988. The purpose of the IPCC is to assess information in the scientific and technical literature related to all significant components of the issue of climate change. *IPCC draws upon hundreds of the world's expert scientists as authors and thousands as expert reviewers. Leading experts on climate change and environmental, social, and economic sciences from some 60 nations have helped the IPCC to prepare periodic assessments of the scientific underpinnings for understanding global climate change and its consequences. With its capacity for reporting on climate change, its consequences, and the viability of adaptation and mitigation measures, the IPCC is considered the official advisory body to the world's governments on the state of the science of the climate change issue. For example, the IPCC developed internationally accepted methods for conducting national greenhouse gas emission inventories.*

Integrated pest management (IPM) – a pest control strategy using several complementary methods. For example, natural predators and parasites, pest–resistant varieties, cultural practices, biological controls, various physical techniques, and the strategic use of pesticides. *An ecologically-based pest-control strategy that relies on natural mortality factors, such as natural enemies, weather, cultural control methods, and carefully applied doses of pesticides. Minimizes chemical use by combining pest control options. IPM does not eliminate pests but reduces pest populations to acceptable levels, an ecologically based pest control strategy relying on natural mortality and control tactics that minimally disrupt these factors.*

Integrated product life-cycle management – managing all phases of goods and services to be environmentally friendly and sustainable.

Intercropping – the agricultural practice of cultivating two or more crops simultaneously in the same space.

Interdecadal Pacific Oscillation (IPO) – a cycle of 15 to 30- years cycles between warm or cool waters in the north and the south Pacific Ocean.

Intergenerational equity – the intention to leave the world in the best possible condition for future generations.

Intergovernmental Panel on Climate Change (IPCC, 1988**)** – established by the World Meteorological Organization and the UN Environment Program to provide the scientific and technical foundation for the United Nations Framework Convention on Climate Change (UNFCCC), primarily through periodic assessment reports.

Intermediate disturbance hypothesis – predicting how species diversity will change with varying levels of disturbance.

Intermittent – any phenomenon that stops and starts at intervals.

Internal costs – the monetary or otherwise expenses borne by those who use a resource.

Internal water footprint – the water embodied in goods produced within a country (although these may be subsequently exported). Compare *external water footprints*.

Internalizing costs – those who reap the benefits of resource use will bear all the external costs.

Interplanting – the system of planting two or more crops, either mixed or in alternating rows, in the same field; protects the soil and makes more efficient land use.

Interpretive science – an explanation based on observation and description of entire objects or systems rather than isolated parts.

Interspecific competition – competition for resources between members of different species in a community. *A form of competition between individuals of different species (e.g., when different species try to use the same resources in an environment).* Contrast *intraspecific competition.*

Intertidal zone – a coastal area periodically submerged underwater by tides.

Intraspecific competition – a form of competition between individuals of the same species, e.g., when members of the same species compete for territories or access to mates. Compare *interspecific competition.*

Intrinsic value – the value of something independent of its utility.

Introduced species (*alien species* or *exotic species*) – organisms living outside its native distributional range, but which has arrived there by human activity, directly or indirectly, and either deliberately or accidentally. *A non-native species that has been brought to an area either by accident or intentionally. An introduced species may prey upon or compete more successfully with one or more species that are native to the community and thereby alter the entire nature of the community.*

Inundation – the submergence of land by water, particularly in a coastal setting.

Invasive species – any non-native, introduced species that adversely affect the habitats and bioregions it invades economically, environmentally, or ecologically. *A non-native species whose introduction to an area causes economic, environmental or harm to human health.*

Ion exchange – a reversible chemical reaction where ions with the same charge are switched. *This principle is used in the purification of wastewater.*

Ionizing radiation – high-energy electromagnetic radiation or energetic subatomic particles released by nuclear decay.

Ionosphere – the lower part of the thermosphere.

Ions – electrically charged atoms that have gained or lost electrons.

Iris hypothesis (Richard Lindzen et al., 2001) – increased sea surface temperature in the tropics would result in reduced cirrus clouds and, thus, more infrared radiation leakage from Earth's atmosphere.

Irradiance – the amount of electromagnetic radiation reaching a surface measured in watts per square meter.

Irrigation – 1. watering of plants, no matter what system is used. 2. an essential component of agriculture developed across cultures.

Irrigation index (Ii) – an efficiency indicator showing the degree of match between water supplied and water used. Ideal rating = 1 with an Ii of 1.5 for a 50% oversupply of water.

Irrigation scheduling – watering plants according to their needs.

Irruptive growth – an expansion in population followed by a dramatic decrease in population. See *Malthusian growth.*

Island biogeography – the study of colonization rates and species extinction rates on islands or other isolated areas based on size, shape, and distance from other inhabited regions.

ISO 14001 (1996) – an international standard for companies seeking to certify their environmental management system. The International Organization for Standardization (ISO) specifies the requirements for environmental management systems in companies and institutions to minimize harmful environmental effects and the goal of continually improving environmental performance.

Isobars (or *isopiestic*) – lines on a weather map connecting points of equal atmospheric pressure.

Isolated – a population separated from other populations of the species (as on an island).

Isotopes – forms of a single element that differ in atomic mass due to a different number of neutrons in the nucleus.

J

J curve (or *J-shaped curve*) – a growth curve that depicts exponential growth; called a J curve because of its shape; it looks like a "J."

Jet stream – a high-speed, meandering wind current, generally moving from a westerly direction at altitudes of 10 to 15 miles and speeds often exceeding 250 miles per hour; like oceanic currents in extent and effect on climate.

Joule (J) – the basic unit of energy; the equivalent of 1 watt of power radiated or dissipated for 1 second; natural gas consumption is usually measured in megajoules (MJ), where 1 MJ = 1, 000,000 J. On large accounts, it may be measured in gigajoules (GJ), where 1 GJ = 1,000,000,000 J.

Jungle – a dense, wet, humid forest, often tropical, which supports many wild plant and animal species.

K

k-selected species – a species that forms a group of strong competitors in a crowded environment and has fewer but stronger offspring. Contrast *r-selected species*.

Karst – an area of irregular limestone in which erosion has produced fissures, sinkholes, underground streams, and caverns.

Keeling Curve – a graph showing the variation in atmospheric carbon dioxide concentration since 1958.

Kerosene – a colorless, flammable oil distilled from petroleum and used as a fuel for jet engines, heating, cooking, and lighting.

Keystone species – an organism with a disproportionate environmental effect relative to its abundance, affecting many other organisms in an ecosystem and determining the types and numbers of other species in a *community*.

Kinetic energy – energy contained in a body because of its motion; equal to one-half the mass of the body times the square of its speed (e.g., a rock rolling down a hill, the wind blowing through the trees, water flowing over a dam).

Known resources – those that have been located and are not completely mapped but are likely to become economical in the foreseeable future.

Kwashiorkor – a widespread human protein deficiency disease resulting from a starchy diet low in protein and essential amino acids.

Kyoto Protocol (1997) – an international agreement adopted in Kyoto, Japan, sets binding emission targets for developed countries to reduce emissions by 5.2 percent below 1990 levels. A United Nations Framework Convention on Climate Change modification. *See post–Kyoto Protocol negotiations on greenhouse gas emissions.*

Kyoto unit (or *Removal unit*) – a tradable carbon credit represents an allowance to emit one metric ton of greenhouse gases absorbed by a removal or carbon sink activity in an Annex I country.

L

Lake – an inland body of water localized in a basin and often fed by a river.

Lake effect snow – lake-generated snow squalls form when cold air passing for long distances over the relatively warm waters of a large lake picks up moisture and heat from the lake and then deposits the moisture in the form of snow upon reaching the downwind shore.

Land cover – the physical characteristics of the land surface, such as crops, trees, or concrete.

Land reform – democratic redistribution of land ownership to recognize the rights of those who work the land to a fair share of the products of their labor.

Land use – activities taking place on land, such as growing food, cutting trees, or building cities.

Land use, land-use change, and forestry (LULUCF) – land uses and land–use changes can act as sinks or emission sources. *Kyoto Protocol* allows parties to receive emissions credit for certain LULUCF activities to reduce net emissions. *An estimated one–fifth of global emissions result from LULUCF activities.*

Land use planning – a branch of public policy encompassing various disciplines that seek to order and regulate land use efficiently and ethically.

Landfill (or *dump*) – land waste disposal sites where waste is generally spread in thin layers, compacted, and regularly covered with fresh soil (e.g., each day). *A site for waste materials disposal by burial and is the oldest form of waste treatment. Solid waste disposal in which refuse is buried between soil layers. A method often used to reclaim low–lying ground. Landfill is sometimes used as a noun to refer to the waste itself.*

Landfill gas – emissions from biodegrading waste in landfills, including CO_2, CH_4, and small amounts of nitrogen and oxygen with traces of toluene, benzene, and vinyl chloride. The gas emissions from biodegrading waste in a landfill, including carbon dioxide (CO_2), methane (CH_4), and small amounts of nitrogen (N) and oxygen (O) with traces of toluene, benzene, and vinyl chloride.

Landfill levy – 1. taxes applied (at differential rates) to municipal, commercial, and industrial wastes and prescribed wastes disposed to licensed landfills; 2. taxes to foster the environmentally sustainable use of resources and best practices in waste management.

Landfill prohibition – banning a particular material or product type from disposal to landfills. Occurs occasionally, for example, where a preferable waste management option is available.

Landscape ecology – the study of the reciprocal effects of spatial patterns on ecological processes (i.e., how landscape history shapes the features of the land and the organisms that inhabit it, as well as our reaction to and interpretation of the land). *An interdisciplinary branch of ecology combining aspects of ecology, botany, biogeography, physical geography, and environmental planning.*

Landslide – the sudden fall of earth from a hill or cliff, often triggered by an earthquake or heavy rain.

La Niña – is a coupled ocean-atmosphere phenomenon that is the colder counterpart of El Niño, as part of the broader El Niño–Southern Oscillation climate pattern. La Niña means "the little girl," analogous to El Niño, meaning *"the little boy."* During La Niña, the sea surface temperature across the equatorial Eastern Central Pacific Ocean is below normal by 5.4 to 9 °F (3 to 5 °C). La Niña persists for at least five months and has effects on the weather across the globe.

Large marine ecosystems – 64 global extensive coastal sea areas by the National Oceanic and Atmospheric Administration, where primary production and biomass are higher than in the open ocean.

Latitude – 1. the angular distance north or south of the Earth's equator, measured in degrees along a meridian, as on a map or globe; 2. a region of the Earth considered with its distance from the equator (e.g., the temperate latitudes). 3. north or south of the equator, designated at zero (0) degrees. Lines of latitude are parallel to the equator and circle the globe. The North and South poles are at 90 degrees North and South latitude.

Lava (or *magma*) – magma spewing from an erupting volcano. Magma is molten rock that sometimes forms beneath the surface of the Earth (or terrestrial planet) that often collects in a magma chamber and is ejected by volcanoes; called *lava* when it.

Law of the minimum – the concept that the growth or survival of a population is directly related to the life requirement in the least supply and not to a combination of factors.

Leachate (*waste*) – the mixture of water and dissolved solids (possibly toxic) that accumulates as water passes through waste and collects at the bottom of a landfill site.

Leaching – the movement of a chemical from the upper layers of soil into the lower layers or groundwater by being dissolved in water.

Lead – a soft, malleable, ductile, bluish-white, dense metallic element, extracted chiefly from galena and used in containers and pipes for corrosives, solder and type metal, bullets, radiation shielding, paints, and antiknock compounds (atomic number 82; atomic weight 207.19; melting point 327.5 °C; boiling point 1,744 °C; specific gravity 11.35; valence 2, 4).

Leaf area index (LAI) – the ratio of photosynthetic leaf area to the ground area covered (optimal for photosynthesis = 3–5). *Shifts in leaf angle, a form of solar tracking, often optimize LAI.*

Least developed country – low indicators of socioeconomic development and human resources, as well as economic vulnerability, as determined by the United Nations.

Lee – the side or part sheltered or turned away from the wind, such as with a mountain.

Legionnaires Disease – an acute bacterial respiratory illness caused by the gram-negative bacterium *Legionella pneumophila*, a member of the family *Legionellaceae*; the bacteria have been found in water systems and can survive in the air conditioning systems of large buildings; risk factors for infection include smoking, Chronic Obstructive Pulmonary Disease (COPD), renal failure, cancer, diabetes, and alcoholism.

Lek mating – an animal mating system in which an aggregation of male animals gathers to engage in competitive displays to entice females during the breeding season.

Less-developed countries (LDC) – non-industrialized nations characterized by low per capita income, high birthrates and death rates, high population growth rates, and low levels of technological development.

Lethal dose (LD50) – a chemical dose lethal to 50 percent of a test population. *The amount of a material, given all at once, which causes the death of 50% (one half) of test animals.*

Leukemia – malignant neoplasm of blood-forming tissues; characterized by abnormal proliferation of leukocytes; one of the four major types of cancer.

Level (scale, context, or framework) – a context, frame of reference, or degree of organization within an integrated system; may or may not be spatially delimited.

Lichen – a composite organism that results from a symbiosis between algae or cyanobacteria and the hyphae of a fungus. The combined lichen has properties different from those of its component organisms.

Lifecycle (*of a product*) – all stages of a product's development, from its raw materials and manufacturing process to its consumption and ultimate disposal.

Life-Cycle Assessment (LCA) – an objective process to evaluate the environmental impacts associated with a product, process, or activity. Measures the material and energy inputs and outputs at each stage of manufacture, use, and disposal of a product; a means of identifying resource use and waste released to the environment and to assess management options.

Life expectancy – the average age that a newborn infant can expect to attain in a particular time and place.

Life form – an entity or being that is living.

Life history – the sequence of events experienced by an organism, from birth to reproduction to death.

Lifespan – the longest period of life reached by a type of organism.

Life support systems (World Conservation Union (IUCN)) – the biophysical processes "*that sustain the productivity, adaptability, and capacity for renewal of lands, waters, or the biosphere as a whole.*"

Lilac water – recycled water unsuitable for drinking.

Limiting factor – any essential resource in short supply in each environment and therefore limits the possibilities for change in other aspects of the same environment. Chemical or physical factors that limit an organism's existence, growth, abundance, or distribution. See *tolerance limits*.

Limnology – the study of inland waters, regarded as forming part of ecology or environmental science.

Linear low-density polyethylene – a polyolefin plastic; a strong and flexible plastic usually used in film for packaging, bags, and industrial products such as pressure pipes.

Linear metabolism – direct conversion of resources into wastes often sent directly to landfill.

Lipid – a non-polar organic compound that is insoluble in water but soluble in solvents, such as alcohol and ether; includes fats, oils, steroids, phospholipids, and carotenoids.

Liquid metal fast breeder – a nuclear power plant that converts ^{238}U (uranium 238) to ^{239}Pu (plutonium 239). *Breeder creates more nuclear fuel than it consumes; because of the extreme heat and density of its core, the breeder uses liquid sodium as a coolant.*

Lithosphere – the solid outermost shell of a rocky planet.; considered ideal for gardening and agricultural uses.

Little Ice Age – a historical period of cooling that followed a warmer period known as the Medieval climate optimum.

Loam – a soil composed of sand, silt, and clay in relatively even concentration (about 40–40–20% concentration respectively),

Locally existing capacity – the total ecological production within a country's territories. It is usually expressed in hectares based on average world productivity.

Lobbying – using personal contacts, public pressure, or political action to persuade legislators to vote in a particular manner.

Locally Unwanted Land Uses (LULU) – an acronym for toxic waste dumps, incinerators, smelters, airports, freeways, and other environmental, economic, or social degradation sources.

Logistic curve – an S-shaped curve representing population growth of a given species.

Logistic growth – growth rates regulated by internal and external factors that establish an equilibrium with environmental resources. See *S curve.*

Longevity – the length or duration of life.

Long-wave radiation – emitted in the spectral wavelength greater than 4 micrometers, corresponds to the radiation emitted from the Earth and atmosphere, sometimes called *terrestrial radiation* or *infrared radiation*, although somewhat imprecise. See *infrared radiation.*

Lotka–Volterra equation – a mathematical equation describing predator-prey interactions between two species.

Love Canal – an area in Niagara Falls, New York, where seepage from buried toxic wastes contaminated local soil and water. *In 1968, President Carter relocated almost all the residents of Love Canal, the impetus for the 1980 Superfund legislation.*

Lovelock Retreats (or *polar city*) – a proposed human refuge located in northern regions of Earth and in Tasmania, New Zealand, and Antarctica, where people might live to survive global warming events.

Low-density polyethylene – a flexible polyolefin plastic usually used as a film for packaging or as bags.

Low entropy energy – carriers with the lowest entropy (i.e., highest quality) transformed into mechanical energy at efficiency rates well above 90%. *In contrast, fossil fuel chemical energy can be converted into mechanical energy at a typical efficiency rate of 25% (for cars) to 50 percent (for modern power plants). The chemical energy of biomass is lower.*

Low-head hydropower – small-scale hydro technology that can extract energy from small headwater dams; causes much less ecological damage.

Low-level wastes – wastes that are not highly radioactive.

Low-quality energy – diffuse, dispersed energy at a low temperature that is difficult to gather and use for productive purposes.

LULU (Locally Unwanted Land Uses) – an acronym for toxic waste dumps, incinerators, smelters, airports, freeways, and other environmental, economic, or social degradation sources.

M

Macroecology (or *global ecology*) – studies the relationships between organisms and their environment at large spatial scales to characterize and explain statistical patterns of abundance, distribution, and diversity. A branch of ecology examining ecological phenomena at the largest scale. Compare *microecology*.

Macrophyte (or *aquatic plants*) – a plant that grows in or near water and is either emergent, submergent, or floating. Plants that have adapted to living in aquatic environments. They are hydrophytes or macrophytes to distinguish them from algae and other microphytes.

Magma (or *lava*) – molten rock that sometimes forms beneath the surface of the Earth (or terrestrial planet) that often collects in a magma chamber and is ejected by volcanoes; called *lava* when it spews from an erupting volcano.

Magnetosphere – the region around an astronomical object in which phenomena are dominated or organized by its magnetic field.

Magnetic confinement – a technique for enclosing a nuclear fusion reaction in a powerful magnetic field inside a vacuum chamber.

Malignant tumor – a mass of cancerous cells that have left their site of origin, migrated through the body, invaded normal tissues, and grown out of control.

Malnourishment – a nutritional imbalance caused by a lack of specific dietary components or an inability to absorb or utilize essential nutrients.

Malthusian growth – a population explosion followed by a population crash. See *irruptive growth.*

Man and Biosphere (MAB) program – a design for nature preserves that divides protected areas into zones with different purposes. *A highly protected core is surrounded by a buffer zone and peripheral regions in which multiple-use resource harvesting is permitted.*

Mangrove wetland – shrubs or small trees that grow in coastal saline or brackish water in the tropics and provide a habitat to many marine organisms.

Mantle – a hot, pliable rock layer surrounding Earth's core and underlying the cool outer crust.

Manure – organic matter used as fertilizer in agriculture.

Marasmus – a widespread human protein deficiency disease caused by a diet low in calories and protein or imbalanced in essential amino acids.

Marginal costs – the cost to produce one additional unit of a good or service.

Marine – living in or pertaining to the sea.

Marine climate – as its name suggests, west coast marine climates (Cfb) are generally found on the western sides of continents in the belt of the westerly winds between roughly 40 to 60 degrees latitude; this location produces a humid climate, often quite rainy, with mild temperatures considering the fairly high latitudes. *This is the effect of having large bodies of water to windward; water is a great modifier of temperatures because it heats and cools slowly. The proximity of water to windward leads to much milder winter temperatures and somewhat cooler summer temperatures that are experienced at continental locations at the same latitudes (some consider Cfb climates to be gloomy climates because they are the world's cloudiest climates; distinctive kind of biological community adapted to those conditions).*

Marine ecosystem – an aquatic ecosystem dominated and defined by saline water.

Marine snow – tiny particles, including dead organic matter from the ocean's upper layers, sinking deep into the ocean.

Mark and recapture – an observational methodology used to estimate variables of a population under study, including population density, survival rates, movement, and growth.

Market benefits – benefits of climate policy can be measured in terms of avoided market impacts such as changes in resource productivity (e.g., lower agricultural yields, scarcer water resources) and damages to the human–built environment (e.g., coastal flooding due to sea–level rise).

Market equilibrium – the dynamic balance between supply and demand under a given set of conditions in a "free" market (where there are no monopolies or government interventions).

Marsh – a wetland dominated by herbaceous rather than woody plant species and often found at the edges of lakes and streams, where it forms a transition between the aquatic and terrestrial ecosystems. *Wetland without trees; in North America, this type of land is characterized by cattails and rushes.*

Mass burn – incineration of unsorted solid waste.

Mass extinction (or *extinction event, extinction–level event, ELE*) – a sharp decrease in species in a relatively short period.

Material flow – the cycling of materials driven by the flow of energy.

Material identification – words, numbers, or symbols used to designate the composition of a product or packaging components. Note: a material identification symbol does not indicate whether an item can be recycled.

Materials recovery facility (MRF) – a center for receiving and transferring materials recovered from the waste stream. MRF sort materials by type and treatment (e.g., cleaned, compressed).

Matter – anything that takes up space and has mass.

Mauna Loa – home to the longest instrumental CO_2 record.

Mauna Loa record (1958) – the measurements of atmospheric CO_2 concentrations taken at Mauna Loa Observatory, Mauna Loa, Hawaii. The record shows the continuing increase in average annual atmospheric CO_2 concentrations.

Maunder Minimum – a historical period from 1645 to 1715 when sunspots became exceedingly rare, as noted by solar observers of the time.

Maximum soil water deficit – the amount of water stored in the soil readily available to plants.

Meander – a turning or winding of a stream.

Mediation – an informal dispute resolution process in which parties discuss issues but in which all decisions are reached by consensus, and any participant can withdraw at any time.

Mediterranean climate areas – specialized landscapes with warm, dry summers, cool, wet winters, many unique plants and animal adaptations, and many levels of endemism.

Medieval Warm Period – a warm historical period from about the 10th century to the 14th century.

Megacity (or *megacity* and *super city*) – a large city, typically with a population above ten million.

Megadiverse countries – 17 countries home to the largest fraction of wild species (e.g., Australia).

Megalopolis (or *megacity* and *super city*) – an urban area with more than 10 million inhabitants.

Megawatt (MW) – a unit of electrical power equal to 1,000 kilowatts or 1 million watts.

Mesosphere – the atmospheric layer above the stratosphere and below the thermosphere; the middle layer; temperatures are usually very low.

Mesopredators – a predator which occupies a mid-ranking trophic level in a food web. *There is no standard definition of a mesopredator, but they are usually referred to as being medium-sized, compared to the apex predator and the prey in the food web. Mesopredators typically prey on smaller animals.*

Mesopredator release hypothesis – as top predators dwindle in an ecosystem, different populations of mesopredators occur.

Metabolic theory of ecology – explains the relationship between an organism's body mass and metabolic rate.

Metabolism – all the energy and matter exchanges that occur within a living cell or organism; collectively, the life processes.

Metalimnion – a layer within a lake where the temperature changes rapidly with depth.

Metamorphic rock – igneous and sedimentary rocks modified by heat, pressure, and chemical reactions.

Meteorology – the interdisciplinary scientific study of the atmosphere and weather processes, focusing on weather forecasting.

Methane (CH_4) – a greenhouse gas released by enteric fermentation in livestock, rice production, and fossil fuel extraction. A hydrocarbon greenhouse gas with global warming potential recently estimated at 25 times that of carbon dioxide (CO_2). Methane is produced through anaerobic (i.e., without oxygen) decomposition of waste in landfills, animal digestion, decomposition of animal wastes, production and distribution of natural gas and petroleum, coal production, and incomplete fossil fuel combustion. GWP is from the IPCC's Fourth Assessment Report (AR4).

Methane hydrate – tiny bubbles or individual molecules of methane (CH_4: natural gas) trapped in a crystalline matrix of frozen water.

Metric ton – common international measurement for the quantity of greenhouse gas emissions. A metric ton is equal to 2205 lbs. or 1.1 short tons. See *short ton*.

Microbial ecology – studies microorganisms.

Micro-climate – a local set of atmospheric conditions that differ from surrounding areas.

Microecology – studies ecological phenomena at tiny scales, a large field that includes many topics such as evolution, biodiversity, exobiology, ecology, bioremediation, recycling, and food microbiology. In humans, gut microecology is the study of the microbial ecology of the human gut which includes gut microbiota composition, its metabolic activity, and the interactions between the microbiota, the host, and the environment. Contrast *macroecology*.

Micro-hydro generators – small power generators that can be used in low-level rivers to provide economical power for four to six homes, freeing them from dependence on large utilities and foreign energy supplies.

Microorganism – an organism visible only through a microscope.

Microwave – a high-frequency electromagnetic wave, one millimeter to one meter in wavelength, intermediate between the infrared and short-wave radio wavelengths.

Middle East – a region in western Asia and northeast Africa including 15 countries, including Bahrain, Islamic Rep. Iran, Iraq, Israel, Jordan, Kuwait, Lebanon, Oman, Qatar, Saudi Arabia, Syria, United Arab Emirates, and Yemen.

15 countries: Bahrain, Islamic Republic of Iran, Iraq, Israel, Jordan, Kuwait, Lebanon, Oman, Qatar, Saudi Arabia, Syria, the United Arab Emirates, and Yemen.

Migration – the moving of one species or a group of species from one area to another.

Milankovitch cycles – periodic variations in the tilt, eccentricity, and wobble of the Earth's orbit; Milutin Milankovitch suggested they are responsible for cyclic weather changes.

Milpa agriculture – an ancient farming system in which small patches of tropical forests are cleared and perennial polyculture (growing many crops in the same space) agriculture is practiced, followed by many years of fallow to restore the soil. See *Swidden agriculture*.

Mineral – a naturally occurring, inorganic, crystalline solid with definite chemical composition and characteristic physical properties.

Mimicry – an adaption of one species to another that protects one or both species from predators.

Mitigation – repairing or rehabilitating a damaged ecosystem or compensating for damage by providing a substitute area. *Measures to reduce the amount and speed of climate change by reducing emissions of heat-trapping gases or removing carbon dioxide from the atmosphere. Human intervention to reduce the human impact on the climate system includes strategies to reduce greenhouse gas sources and emissions and enhance greenhouse gas sinks.*

Mitigation of global warming – any procedure involving reducing greenhouse gas emissions and enhancing sinks to reduce the degree of global warming.

Mixed perennial polyculture – growing a mixture of different perennial crop species (where the same plant persists for more than one year) together in the same plot.

Mobile garbage bin – a wheeled curbside container for collecting garbage or other materials.

Mode of variability – a pattern of climate change, usually oscillatory, with specific regional effects.

Moderators – a substance, for example, graphite or beryllium, that slows neutrons in a nuclear reactor so that they can bring about the fission of uranium.

Molecule – a combination of two or more atoms.

Molecular ecology – applies molecular population genetics, molecular phylogenetics, and genomics to traditional ecological questions. It is essentially the same as ecological genetics.

Monitored, retrievable storage – holding wastes in underground mines or secure surface facilities such as dry casks where they can be watched and repackaged, if necessary.

Monkeywrenching – environmental sabotage, such as driving large spikes in trees to protect them from loggers, vandalizing construction equipment, pulling up survey stakes for unwanted developments, and destroying billboards. See *ecotage*.

Mono Lake – an oasis in the dry Great Basin in California and a vital habitat for millions of migrating and nesting birds.

Monoculture – producing or growing one crop over a wide area.

Monoculture agroforestry – intensive planting of a single species; an efficient wood production approach, but one that encourages pests and disease infestations and conflicts with wildlife habitat or recreation uses.

Monsoon – 1. a wind system that influences large climatic regions and reverses direction seasonally; 2. a wind from the southwest or south that brings heavy rainfall to southern Asia in the summer or the rain accompanying this wind. *The predictable occurrence of dramatic seasonal changes in atmospheric circulation and precipitation patterns.*

Montane coniferous forests – coniferous forests of mountains consisting of belts of different forest communities along an altitudinal gradient.

Montreal Protocol (1987) – an international treaty to protect the ozone layer by phasing out the production of numerous substances responsible for ozone depletion, especially CFCs. *The treaty governs stratospheric ozone protection and research and the production and use of ozone-depleting substances. Provides for ending the production of ozone-depleting substances such as CFCs; under the Montreal Protocol, various research groups continue to assess the ozone layer. The Multilateral Fund provides resources to developing nations to promote their transition to ozone-safe technologies.*

Moral agents – beings capable of distinguishing between right and wrong and acting accordingly (i.e., those held responsible for their actions).

Moral extensionism – expansion of our understanding of the inherent value or rights to persons, organisms, or things that might not be considered worthy of value or rights under some ethical philosophies.

Moral subjects – beings that are incapable of distinguishing between right or wrong or cannot act on moral principles and yet are capable of being wronged by others.

Morals – a set of ethical principles that guide our actions and relationships.

Morbidity – describes how often a disease afflicts a certain area (e.g., "how many people have lung cancer in New York City").

More-developed countries (MDC) – industrialized nations characterized by high per capita incomes, low birth, and death rates, low population growth rates, and high levels of industrialization and urbanization.

Mortality – 1. the death rate in a population; 2. the probability of dying.

Mortality rate – the total number of deaths per 1,000 people of a given age group.

Mount Pinatubo – a volcano in the Philippine Islands that erupted in 1991. The eruption of Mount Pinatubo ejected enough particulate and sulfate aerosol matter into the atmosphere to block some of the incoming solar radiation from reaching Earth's atmosphere. *This effectively cooled the planet from 1992 to 1994, masking the warming occurring for most of the 1980s and 1990s.*

Mullerian mimicry – the evolution of two noxious species who share common predators to resemble each other; the theory is that predators, who associate the unique characteristics of one noxious species with danger, will also choose to ignore the mimicking species.

Mulch – any composted or non–composted organic material, excluding plastic, suitable for placing on soil surfaces to restrict moisture loss from the soil and provide a source of nutrients to the soil.

Multiple uses – many coincidences. Used in forest management; limited to mutually compatible uses.

Municipal sewage – the wastewater from households, offices, and other buildings in a city; can be sanitary sewage only or sanitary sewage and stormwater. *Collected at treatment plants where solids are removed by "primary sewage treatment" and then treated by various other methods including using aerobic bacteria to remove organic wastes in "secondary treatment" and advanced or "tertiary treatment" with various chemical and physical processes.*

Municipal solid waste (MSW) – residential solid waste (i.e., garbage and hard waste) and some non-hazardous commercial, institutional, and industrial wastes such as street sweeping litter, tree lopping, waste dropped at transfer stations, and construction waste from owner/occupier renovations. *This material is generally sent to municipal landfills for disposal.* See *landfill.*

Mutagens – agents, such as chemicals or radiation, that damage or alter genetic material (DNA) in cells.

Mutation – a change, either spontaneous or by external factors, in the genetic material of a cell; future generations of organisms can inherit mutations in the gametes (egg or sperm cells).

Mutualism – a symbiotic relationship between individuals of two different species in which both species benefit from the association. *Both individual organisms derive a fitness benefit.*

N

NF$_3$ – Nitrogen trifluoride

N$_2$O – Nitrous oxide

NAAQS – *"National Ambient Air Quality Standard;"* federal standards specifying the maximum allowable levels (averaged over specific periods) for regulated pollutants in *Ambient air.*

Natality – the production of new individuals by birth, hatching, germination, or cloning.

National ambient air quality standards – health-based pollutant concentration limits established by the EPA that apply to the outside air.

National Packaging Covenant – a self–regulatory agreement between packaging industries and the government.

National Priority List (NPL) – established by the EPA as part of the *Superfund* program; locates and sets priorities for cleaning up hazardous waste sites.

Native species – species that are initially in a specific area.

Natural – the existing air, water, land, and energy resources from which all resources derive. Primary functions include resource production (such as fish, timber, or cereals), waste assimilation (such as CO_2 absorption and sewage decomposition), and life support services (UV protection, biodiversity, water cleansing, and climate stability). *Environmental services must be maintained so that human development can be sustainable.*

Natural capital – natural resources and ecological processes equivalent to financial capital.

Natural gas – underground deposits of gases consist of 50 to 90 percent methane (CH_4) and small amounts of heavier gaseous hydrocarbon compounds such as propane (C_3H_8) and butane (C_4H_{10}).

Natural history – the study of where and how organisms carry out their lifecycles.

Natural increase – the crude death rate subtracted from the crude birth rate.

Natural resources – naturally occurring substances valuable in their relatively unmodified (i.e., natural) form. *Natural biotic and abiotic resources combined.*

Natural selection – the process by which favorable heritable traits become more common in successive generations of reproducing organisms, and unfavorable heritable traits become less common.

Natural variability (or *climate variability*) – variations in the mean state and other statistics (such as standard deviations or statistics of extremes) of the climate on all time and space scales beyond that of individual weather events. *Natural variations in climate over time are caused by internal processes of the climate system, such as El Niño as well as changes in external influences, such as volcanic activity and variations in the Sun's output.*

Negative feedback loop – a process in which the effects of a change in a system act to reduce or counteract the change. Negative feedback loops promote stability and settle to equilibrium, reducing the effects of perturbations in the system. Contrast *positive feedback loop.*

Neighborhood environment improvement plan – developed by a local community, including residents, special interest groups, local government, local industry, and government agencies.

Nematocide – a chemical that kills nematodes (e.g., roundworms and threadworms).

Neutralism – the belief that changes in evolution are caused by random mutation rather than by natural selection.

Neo-classical economics – a branch of economics that attempts to apply the principles of modern science to economic analysis in a mathematically rigorous, non-contextual, abstract, predictive manner.

Neo-Luddites – people who reject technology, believing it is the cause of environmental degradation and social disruption; named after the followers of Ned Ludd, who tried to turn back the Industrial Revolution in England by wrecking factories.

Neo-Malthusian – a belief that the world is characterized by scarcity and competition in which too many people fight over too few resources, named for Thomas Malthus, predicted a dismal cycle of misery, vice, and starvation due to human overpopulation.

Net energy yield – total useful energy produced during the lifetime of an entire energy system minus the energy used, lost, or wasted in making useful energy available.

Net primary production – the energy or biomass content of plant material accumulated in an ecosystem over some time through photosynthesis. It is the amount of energy left after subtracting the respiration of primary producers (primarily plants) from the total amount of solar energy fixed biologically; gross primary productivity minus respiratory losses (carbon gain).

Neurotoxins – toxic substances, such as lead or mercury, that poison nerve cells.

Neutron – a subatomic particle found in the atom's nucleus with no electromagnetic charge.

New towns – experimental urban environments that combine the best features of the rural village and the modern city.

Niche – a position or function of an organism in a community of related organisms. *A specific category that an organism fits into in an environment and its role in carrying out the processes in that ecosystem.*

Niche construction – the process by which an organism alters its or another organism's ecological niche.

Niche differentiation – in a biological community, various populations share environmental resources through specialization, thereby reducing direct competition. See *resource partitioning*.

Nickel-cadmium batteries – typically used in appliances such as power tools and mobile phones. Cadmium is a heavy metal that risks human and ecosystem health.

Nihilists [Latin, nihil for nothing] – those who reject moral or religious beliefs, often concluding that the world and everything in it amounts to nothingness or is meaningless.

NIMBY – an acronym for "Not In My BackYard;" the rallying cry opposing *LULUs*.

Nitrates – 1. salt or ester of nitric acid; 2. sodium nitrate or potassium nitrate used as a fertilizer.

Nitrate-forming bacteria – bacteria that combine ammonia with oxygen to form nitrites that green plants can use to build proteins.

Nitrification – the oxidation of ammonia with oxygen into nitrite.

Nitrogen cycle – the continuous cycle by which atmospheric nitrogen and compounded nitrogen are exchanged through the soil into substances taken up and used by green plants; the remainder returns to the atmosphere due to denitrification. The circulation and utilization of nitrogen in nature, consisting of a cycle of chemical reactions in which atmospheric nitrogen is compounded, dissolved in the rain, and deposited in the soil, where it is assimilated and metabolized by bacteria and plants, eventually returning to the atmosphere by bacterial decomposition of organic matter. *Specific principles include: N_2 is the most abundant gas in the atmosphere (78%), nitrogen-fixing bacteria convert it to NH_3, and nitrate-forming bacteria combine NH_3 with oxygen to form NO_2 and then NO_3, plants absorb and make NH_4, consumers eat plants, nitrogen re-enters the environment when these organisms die, shed, urinate, produce excrement, which de-nitrifying bacteria break down into N_2, and the process repeats.*

Nitrogen fixation – the conversion of nitrogen into nitrogen compounds (e.g., nitrate, nitrite) carried out naturally by certain bacteria and algae.

Nitrogen-fixing bacteria – bacteria that convert nitrogen from the atmosphere or soil solution into ammonia that can then be converted to plant nutrients by nitrite- and nitrate-forming bacteria.

Nitrogen oxides (NOx) – highly reactive gases formed when nitrogen in fuel or combustion air is heated to over 650 °C (1,200 °F) in the presence of oxygen or when bacteria in soil or water oxidize nitrogen-containing compounds; often mentioned in discussions of nitrogen-based air pollution as a reference to both nitric oxide (NO) and nitrogen dioxide (NO_2). *In addition to particulates and sulfur dioxide, NOx is one of the major pollutants related to energy use; can transform to nitrates in the atmosphere.*

Nitrous oxide (N_2O) – a potent greenhouse gas with a global warming potential 298 times that of carbon dioxide (CO_2). *Major sources include soil cultivation practices, especially commercial and organic fertilizers, fossil fuel combustion, nitric acid production, and biomass burning. The global warming potential (GWP) is from the IPCC's Fourth Assessment Report (AR4). Natural emissions of N_2O are mainly from bacteria breaking down nitrogen in soils and the oceans. Nitrous oxide is mainly removed from the atmosphere through destruction in the stratosphere by ultraviolet radiation and associated chemical reactions. However, certain types of bacteria can also consume it in soils.*

Noise pollution (or *environmental noise*) – displeasing human or machine–created sound that disrupts the activity or happiness of human or animal life.

Non-criteria pollutants – not explicitly mentioned in NAAQS or the *Hazardous Air Pollutants* (HAPs) in the Clean Air Act (e.g., benzene, dioxins, pesticides). See *unconventional air pollutants*.

Nongovernmental organizations (NGO) – a not–for–profit or community–based organization. *Refer collectively to advocacy and research groups, advisory agencies, political parties, professional societies, and other groups concerned about environmental quality, resource use, and other issues.*

Non-ferrous metals – contain little or no iron (e.g., copper, brass, and bronze).

Non-Methane Volatile Organic Compounds (NMVOCs) – organic compounds, other than methane, participate in atmospheric photochemical reactions.

Nonpoint source pollution – affecting a water body from diffuse sources rather than a point source discharging to a water body at a single location.

Nonpoint sources – scattered, diffuse sources of pollutants, such as runoff from farm fields, golf courses, construction sites, etc.

Nonradiative forcing – a type of climate forcing that creates an energy imbalance that does not immediately involve radiation.

Nonrenewable resources – minerals, fossil fuels, and other materials present in essentially finite amounts (within human time scales) in our environment.

Nor'easter – a storm blowing from the northeast.

North/South division – describes that most of the world's wealthier countries tend to be in North America, Europe, and Japan, while the poorer countries tend to be closer to the equator.

North Atlantic Deep Water – one of the water masses of the ocean.

North Atlantic oscillation – an atmospheric climate model. See *arctic oscillation.*

No-till farming (or *zero tillage*) – a conservation tillage system. An agricultural technique for growing crops or pasture without disturbing the soil through tillage. *No-till farming decreases soil erosion tillage caused in certain soils, especially in sandy and dry soils on sloping terrain. Benefits include an increase in the amount of water infiltrating into the soil, soil retention of organic matter, and nutrient cycling.*

Nuclear energy – energy released by reactions within atomic nuclei, as in nuclear fission or fusion; also called "atomic energy."

Nuclear fission – the radioactive decay in which isotopes split apart to create two smaller atoms.

Nuclear fusion – when two smaller atomic nuclei fuse into one larger nucleus and release energy; the power source is a hydrogen bomb.

Nucleic acids – large organic molecules made of nucleotides that transmit hereditary traits, protein synthesis, and control of cellular activities.

Nucleus – 1. the center of the atom, occupied by protons and neutrons; 2. in cells, the organelle that contains the chromosomes (DNA).

Nuées ardentes – deadly, denser-than-air mixtures of hot gases and ash ejected from volcanoes.

Numbers pyramid – a diagram showing the relative population sizes at each trophic level in an ecosystem; usually corresponds to the biomass pyramid.

Numerical response – a change in predator density as a function of change in prey density.

Nutrients – chemicals required for the growth of organisms; chemicals (e.g., nitrogen and phosphorus) that plants and animals need to live and grow. At high concentrations, particularly in water, nutrients can become pollutants. *Phosphorus, nitrogen, and potassium are major plant nutrients. However, many trace elements are needed in small quantities for growing and developing animal and plant life.*

Nutrient cycle (or *ecological recycling*) – the movement and exchange of organic and inorganic matter back into the production of living matter.

Nutrient cycle efficiency – studies how energy and matter flow interact with ecosystems' biotic elements. See *ecosystem ecology*.

O

O₃ – (Tropospheric) Ozone

Ocean – a vast body of saltwater. Oceans cover almost 75% of the Earth's surface.

Ocean acidification – reduction in pH from increased carbon dioxide concentrations in seawater cause a measurable increase in acidity (i.e., a reduction in ocean pH). The process by which ocean waters have become more acidic due to the absorption of human-produced carbon dioxide, which interacts with ocean water to form carbonic acid and lower the ocean's pH. *Acidity reduces the capacity of crucial plankton species and shelled animals to form and maintain shells. This may lead to reduced calcification rates of calcifying organisms such as corals, mollusks, algae, and crustaceans. Caused by their uptake of anthropogenic carbon dioxide from the atmosphere.*

Ocean heat content (OHC) – the energy absorbed and stored by oceans. To calculate the ocean heat content, measurements of ocean temperature at many different locations and depths are required. *Integrating the areal density of ocean heat over an ocean basin, or entire ocean, gives the total ocean heat content.*

Ocean planet – the opposite concept of *Snowball Earth*.

Ocean shorelines – rocky coasts and sandy beaches along the oceans; support prosperous, stratified communities.

Ocean thermal electric conversion (OTEC) – energy derived from the temperature differential between warm ocean surface waters and cold, deep waters. *This temperature differential can be used to drive turbines attached to electric generators.*

Oceania – the southern, western, and central Pacific Ocean islands, including Melanesia, Micronesia, and Polynesia; in some definitions, Oceania encompasses Australia, New Zealand, and Maritime Southeast Asia.

Oceanic islands – islands in the ocean; formed by breaking away from a continental landmass, volcanic action, coral formation, or a combination of sources; support distinctive communities.

Offset – something that balances, counteracts, or compensates.

Offset allowances – a controversial component of air quality regulations that allows a polluter to avoid installation of control equipment on one source by an "offsetting" pollution reduction at another source.

Ogallala aquifer – the largest aquifer in North America, located under the Great Plains in U.S.A.

Oil glut – when oil supply on the market dramatically exceeds demand, resulting in lower oil prices.

Oil shale – a fine-grained sedimentary rock rich in solid organic material called "kerogen;" when heated, the kerogen liquefies to produce a fluid petroleum fuel.

Old-growth forests (or *ancient forest*) – an area with great age exhibits unique biological features. Forests without disturbances for long enough (generally 150 to 200 years) to have mature trees, ideal physical conditions, species diversity, and other characteristics of equilibrium ecosystems. Dominated by mature trees with little or no evidence of disturbance such as logging, ground clearing, and building.

Oligotrophic [*oligo* = little; *trophic* = nutrition] – the condition of rivers and lakes with clear water and low biological productivity. *Oligotrophic waters are usually clear, cold, infertile headwater lakes and streams.*

Omnivore – a species of animal eating both plants and animals as its primary food source.

OPEC (Organization of Petroleum Exporting Countries) – founded in 1960 to unify and coordinate the members' petroleum policies.

Open access system – a commonly held resource for which there are no management rules.

Open burning – uncontrolled fires in an open dump.

Open canopy – a forest where tree crowns cover less than 20 percent of the ground. See *woodland*.

Open-pit mining (or *opencast mining* and *open–cut mining*) – a method of extracting rock or minerals from the earth by removing them from an open pit or borrow.

Open range – unfenced, natural grazing lands; includes woodland and grassland.

Open system – a system that exchanges energy and matter with its environment.

Operational energy – the energy used in carrying out a particular operation.

Optimum – the most favorable condition regarding an environmental factor.

Orbital – the space or path in which an electron orbits the nucleus of an atom.

Organic – derived from a living organism, containing *carbon*.

Organic agriculture – a holistic production management system that avoids synthetic fertilizers, pesticides, and genetically modified organisms (GMO), minimizes air, soil, and water pollution, and optimizes the health and productivity of interdependent communities of plants, animals, and people.

Organic compounds – complex molecules organized around skeletons of carbon atoms arranged in rings or chains; includes biomolecules, molecules synthesized by living organisms.

Organic gardening – gardening that follows, in general principle, the philosophy of organic agriculture.

Organic matter – compounds that contain carbon and hydrogen covalently bonded together in molecules; molecules from living matter; organic wastes in sewage and runoff from lawns and farms in freshwaters can cause oxygen depletion and degradation of water quality.

Organics – plant or animal matter originating from domestic or industrial sources (e.g., grass clippings, tree pruning, food waste).

Orographic effect (Chinook winds) – a moist wind blowing from the sea on the Northwestern U.S. coast.

Overburden – overlying layers of noncommercial sediments that must be removed to reach a mineral or coal deposit.

Overdrawn – taking too much out or depleting resources (e.g., pumping water from an aquifer faster than it can be replenished or recharged by rainfall).

Overnutrition (or *hyperalimentation*) – when the amount of nutrients ingested exceeds what is needed for normal growth, metabolism, and development.

Overshoot – growth beyond an area's carrying capacity; ecological deficit occurs when human consumption and waste production exceed the capacity of the Earth to create new resources and absorb waste. *Natural capital is being liquidated during overshot to support current use, so the Earth's ability to support future life declines.*

Oxidation – the act or process of oxidizing (i.e., to change a compound by increasing the proportion of the electronegative part or charge (an element or ion) from a lower to a higher positive valence); removing one or more electrons from an atom, ion, or molecule to combine with oxygen.

Oxidize – to chemically transform a substance by combining it with oxygen.

Oxygen cycle – the circulation and utilization of oxygen in the biosphere.

Oxygen sag – oxygen decline downstream from a pollution source that introduces materials with high biological oxygen demands.

Ozone (O$_3$) – the triatomic form of oxygen, is a gaseous atmospheric constituent as an inorganic pale blue gas with a distinctively pungent smell. It is an allotrope of oxygen much less stable than the diatomic allotrope O$_2$, breaking down to O$_2$ (dioxygen) in the lower atmosphere. Ozone is formed from dioxygen by ultraviolet (UV) light and electrical discharges within the Earth's atmosphere. *A colorless, highly reactive molecule containing three oxygen atoms; a dangerous pollutant in ambient air that is soluble in alkalis and cold water; in the stratosphere, ozone forms an ultraviolet absorbing shield that protects us from mutagenic radiation; a strong oxidizing agent and can be produced by electric discharge in oxygen or by the action of ultraviolet radiation on oxygen in the stratosphere.*

In the troposphere, it is created by photochemical reactions involving gases resulting from natural sources and human activities (photochemical smog). In high concentrations, tropospheric ozone can harm many living organisms. Tropospheric ozone acts as a greenhouse gas. In the stratosphere, ozone is created by the interaction between solar ultraviolet radiation and molecular oxygen (O$_2$). Stratospheric ozone plays a decisive role in the stratospheric radiative balance. Depleting stratospheric ozone due to chemical reactions that may be enhanced by climate change results in an increased ground-level flux of ultraviolet (UV-) B radiation. See *atmosphere* and u*ltraviolet radiation.*

Ozone-depleting substance (ODS) – **family** of manufactured compounds that includes, but are not limited to, chlorofluorocarbons (CFCs), bromofluorocarbons (halons), methyl chloroform, carbon tetrachloride, methyl bromide, and hydrochlorofluorocarbons (HCFCs). These compounds have been shown to deplete stratospheric ozone and are typically called ODSs. See *ozone.*

Ozone depletion – two related events observed since the late 1970s: a steady lowering of about four percent in the total amount of ozone in Earth's atmosphere and a much more significant springtime decrease in stratospheric ozone (i.e., the ozone layer) around Earth's polar regions. The latter phenomenon is referred to as the *ozone hole.*

Ozone layer – begins approximately 15 km above Earth and thins to an almost negligible amount at about 50 km shielding the Earth from harmful ultraviolet radiation from the Sun. The highest natural ozone concentration (approximately 10 parts per million by volume) occurs in the stratosphere approximately 25 km above Earth. Stratospheric ozone concentrations change during the year as stratospheric circulation changes with seasons. Natural events such as volcanoes and solar flares can produce changes in ozone concentration, but manufactured changes are of the most significant concern.

A region of Earth's stratosphere that absorbs most of the Sun's ultraviolet radiation. It contains a high concentration of ozone (O$_3$) in other parts of the atmosphere, although still small in relation to other gases in the stratosphere. The ozone layer contains less than 10 parts per million, while the average ozone concentration in Earth's atmosphere is about 0.3 parts per million. The ozone layer is mainly found in the lower portion of the stratosphere, from approximately 15 to 35 kilometers (9 to 22 mi) above Earth, although its thickness varies seasonally and geographically. See *stratosphere* and *ultraviolet radiation.*

Ozone precursors – chemical compounds, such as carbon monoxide, methane, non-methane hydrocarbons, and nitrogen oxides, in the presence of solar radiation, react with other chemical compounds to form ozone, mainly in the troposphere. See *troposphere*.

P

Pacific Decadal Oscillation (PDO) – a 23–30-year pattern of warm or cool water in the north Pacific Ocean. A large pool of warm water moves north and south in the Pacific Ocean and dramatically affects North America's climate.

Paleocene–Eocene Thermal Maximum (PETM) – a historical warming event that suddenly and fundamentally altered the geological and biological aspects of the planet.

Paleoclimate – the climate that existed during the period before modern record-keeping. Paleoclimate can be measured with "natural thermometers" such as ice cores or tree rings.

Paleoclimatology – the study of climate change taken on the scale of Earth's history.

Paleoecology – a branch of ecology that uses data from fossils to reconstruct past ecosystems.

Parabolic mirrors – curved mirrors that focus light from a large area onto a single central point, concentrating solar energy and producing high temperatures.

Paradigm – a model that provides a framework for interpreting observations.

Parasite – an organism that lives in or on another organism, deriving nourishment at the expense of its host, usually without killing it. An organism that depends on a symbiotic relationship with a host which it does not usually kill directly but does negatively affect.

Parasitoid – an organism that is a parasite for most of its life and usually kills its host.

Parent – an original radioactive atom or any material.

Parsimony – the reluctance to use resources or spend money.

Particulate material (PM) – tiny pieces of solid or liquid matter such as particles of soot, dust, fumes, mist, or aerosols. *The physical characteristics of particles and how they combine with other particles are part of the feedback mechanisms of the atmosphere. Atmospheric aerosols, such as dust, ash, soot, lint, smoke, pollen, spores, algal cells, and other suspended materials; originally applied only to solid particles but now extended to liquid droplets.* See *aerosol* and *sulfate aerosols*.

Parts per billion (ppb) – number of chemical parts in 1 billion parts of a gas, liquid, or solid mixture.

Parts per million (ppm) – number of chemical parts in 1 million parts of a gas, liquid, or solid mixture.

Parts per trillion (ppt) – number of chemical parts in 1 trillion parts of a gas, liquid, or solid mixture.

Passive heat absorption – using natural materials or absorptive structures without moving parts to gather and hold heat; the simplest and oldest use of solar energy.

Patchiness – within a larger ecosystem, the presence of smaller areas that differ in some physical conditions and support somewhat different communities; a diversity-promoting phenomenon.

Pathogen – an organism that produces disease in a host organism, the disease being an alteration of one or more metabolic functions in response to the organism's presence.

Pathogenic – describes any microorganism capable of causing disease.

Patterns in nature – visible regularities of form found in the natural world.

Pay-by-weight systems – financial approaches to managing waste by charging according to the quantity of waste collected rather than a price per pick–up or fixed annual charge, as typical for households with curbside services. *Pay–by–weight systems may provide an incentive to reduce waste generation.*

Peat – deposits of moist, acidic, semi-decayed organic matter.

Pedosphere – the outermost layer of the Earth composed of soil and subject to soil formation processes. It exists at the interface of the lithosphere, atmosphere, hydrosphere and biosphere.

Pellagra – a disease characterized by lassitude, torpor, dermatitis, diarrhea, and sometimes dementia and death, brought about by a diet deficient in tryptophan and niacin.

Peptides – two or more amino acids linked by a peptide bond.

Per capita consumption – the average amount of commodity used per person.

Percolation – water slowly moving through soil and gravel into an aquifer.

Perennial species – plants that grow for more than two years.

Perfluorocarbons (PFCs) – a group of chemicals composed of carbon and fluorine only. These chemicals (predominantly CF_4 and C_2F_6) were introduced as alternatives, along with hydrofluorocarbons, to the ozone-depleting substances. In addition, PFCs are emitted as by-products of industrial processes and used in manufacturing. PFCs do not harm the stratospheric ozone layer but are powerful greenhouse gases. CF_4 has a global warming potential (GWP) of 7,390, and C_2F_6 has a GWP of 12,200. These chemicals are predominantly human made, though there is a small natural source of CF_4. See *ozone-depleting substances.*

Permafrost – a permanently frozen layer of soil that underlies the arctic tundra; perennially (continually) frozen ground occurs where temperatures remain below 0 °C for years.

Permanent retrievable storage – placing waste storage containers in a secure building, salt mine, or bedrock cavern where they can be inspected periodically and retrieved, if necessary.

Persistent organic pollutants (POPs) – organic compounds resistant to environmental degradation through chemical, biological, and photolytic processes.

Pervious surface – penetrated by air and water.

Pest – any organism that reduces a useful resource's availability, quality, or value.

Pest resurgence – the rebound of pest populations due to acquired resistance to chemicals and nonspecific destruction of their natural predators and competitors by broad-scale pesticides.

Pesticide – any substance or mixture of substances intended for preventing, destroying, or controlling any pest. *Includes substances intended for use as a plant growth regulator, defoliant, desiccant, or agent for thinning fruit or preventing the premature fall of fruit and substances applied to crops either before or after harvest to protect the commodity from deterioration during storage and transport.*

Pesticide treadmill – a need for constantly increasing pesticide doses or new, more potent pesticides to prevent pest resurgence.

Petrochemicals – chemicals synthesized from oil.

pH – a value that indicates the acidity or alkalinity of a solution on a scale of 0 to 14, based on the proportion of H+ ions present.

pH scale – p(potential of) H(hydrogen); the logarithm of the reciprocal of hydrogen-ion concentration in gram atoms per liter. pH measures the acidity (pH < 7) or alkalinity (pH > 7) of a solution on a scale of 0 to 14 (where 7 is neutral).

Phenology – 1. the pattern of seasonal life cycle events in plants and animals, such as the timing of blooming, hibernation, and migration. 2. the study of periodic events in biological life cycles and how these are influenced by seasonal and interannual variations in climate, as well as habitat factors (e.g., such as elevation). *The timing of natural events, such as flower blooms and animal migration, is influenced by changes in climate. Phenology is the study of such important seasonal events. Climate factors influence phenological events, including light, temperature, rainfall, and humidity.*

Phenotypic plasticity – the ability of an organism to change its behavior, physiology, or physical characteristics in response to its environment. This change occurs within an organism's lifetime and therefore does not require genetic change.

Pheromone – a chemical excreted into the environment as a signal, causes a natural behavioral response in members of the same population.

Phosphates – 1. a salt or ester of phosphoric acid. 2. the trivalent anion PO_{43}, derived from phosphoric acid H_3PO_4, an organic compound of phosphoric acid in which the acid group is bound to nitrogen or a carboxyl group in a way that permits valuable energy to be released (as in metabolism). 3. a phosphatic material used for fertilizers.

Phosphorous (phosphorus) cycle – the biogeochemical cycle that describes the movement of phosphorus through the environment. *The movement of phosphorus atoms from rocks and soil through the biosphere and hydrosphere and back to the soil.*

Photochemical oxidants – products of secondary atmospheric reactions. See *smog*.

Photodegradable plastics – materials that break down when exposed to sunlight or a specific wavelength of light.

Photosynthesis – the transformation of radiant energy to chemical energy by plants; the manufacture by plants of carbohydrates from carbon dioxide and water. The capture of the Sun's energy (*primary production*) to power all life on Earth (*consumption*). *The reaction is driven by energy from sunlight, catalyzed by chlorophyll, and releases oxygen as a byproduct. The process by which plants take CO_2 from air (or bicarbonate in water) to build carbohydrates, releasing O_2. There are several pathways of photosynthesis with responses to atmospheric CO_2 concentrations.* See *carbon sequestration* and *carbon dioxide fertilization*.

Photosynthetic efficiency – the percentage of available sunlight captured by plants and used to make useful products.

Photovoltaic – the direct conversion of light into electricity.

Photovoltaic cell – an energy-conversion device that captures solar energy and directly converts it to electrical current.

Physical or abiotic factors – nonliving factors, such as temperature, light, water, minerals, and climate that influence an organism.

Phytophysiognomy – the overall physiognomy (i.e., appearance) and physical characteristics of a plant community.

Phytoplankton (or *plant plankton*) – microscopic, free-floating, autotrophic organisms that function as producers in aquatic ecosystems. The autotrophic (i.e., self-feeding) components of the plankton community and a crucial part of ocean and freshwater ecosystems. *Phytoplankton obtain their energy through photosynthesis, like plants and trees on land. Phytoplankton must have sunlight, so they live in well-lit surface layers (euphotic zone) of oceans and lakes.* See *autotroph* and *plankton*.

Pioneer species – in primary succession on a terrestrial site, the plants, lichens, and microbes that first colonize the site. A species that is the first to inhabit a previously unoccupied environment or niche.

Plague – a disease that spreads rapidly, infecting many people and killing many of them, an outbreak of such a disease.

Plankton – mostly microscopic animal and plant life suspended in water and a valuable food source for fish and marine animals. See *phytoplankton*.

Plant litter – the layer of dead plant material on the ground providing habitat to plants, microorganisms, and animals. It plays a vital role in the nutrient cycle.

Plant quality – a standard of plant appearance or yield.

Plasma – a hot, electrically neutral gas of ions and free electrons.

Plastic – high–polymeric substances, including natural and synthetic products, excluding rubbers. *At some stage in its manufacture, every plastic can flow, under heat and pressure, if necessary, into the desired final shape.*

PM-10 – particulates less than 10 microns in diameter; present in the smoke created by burning wood.

Poachers – those who hunt wildlife illegally.

Point sources – specific locations of highly concentrated pollution discharge, such as factories, power plants, sewage treatment plants, underground coal mines, and oil wells.

Polar amplification – greater temperature increases in the *Arctic* than on Earth due to the collective effect of positive feedback loops and other processes. *Despite its name, polar amplification only applies to the Arctic, not the Antarctic, because the Southern Ocean acts as a heat sink.*

Polar City (or *Lovelock Retreats*) – a proposed human refuge located in northern regions of Earth and in Tasmania, New Zealand, and Antarctica, where people might live to survive global warming events.

Policy – a societal plan or statement of intentions intended to accomplish some social good.

Policy cycle – the process of identifying and acting on problems in the public arena.

Political ecology – a branch of ecology that studies how political and economic power affects ecosystems and how environmental factors influence social activity.

Political economy – the branch of economics concerned with modes of production, distribution of benefits, social institutions, and class relationships.

Pollination – a type of fertilization when pollen grains are transported through air from a seed plant to the ovule-bearing organs of another. *Either wind, water, or animal assistance helps this transport.*

Polluter Pays Principle (PPP) – pollution producers compensate others for their pollution.

Pollution – to make foul, unclean, or dirty; any physical, chemical, or biological change that adversely affects the health, survival, or normal activities of living organisms or alters the environment in undesirable ways.

Pollution charges – fees assessed per unit of pollution based on the *polluter pays principle.*

Polycentric complex – cities with several urban cores surrounding a once-dominant central core.

Polyethylene terephthalate (PET) – a clear, tough, light, and shatterproof plastic used to make products such as soft drink bottles, film packaging, and fabrics.

Polypropylene (PP) – a polyolefin plastic. PP is light, rigid, and glossy and is used to make products such as washing machine agitators, clear film packaging, carpet fibers, and housewares.

Polystyrene (PS) – a styrene plastic. PS is easy to mold and is used to make refrigerator and washing machine components. It can be foamed to make single–use packaging, such as cups, meat, and produce trays.

Polyvinyl chloride (PVC) – a vinyl plastic. PVC can be clear, flexible, or rigid, making products like fruit juice bottles, credit cards, pipes, and hoses.

Population – a group of individuals of the same species occupying a given area.

Population crash – a sudden decline caused by predation, waste accumulation, or resource depletion. See *population dieback.*

Population density – the number of individuals of a species living in a defined area.

Population dieback – when the growth of a population slows due to some factor.

Population distribution (or *range*) – the prevalence of a species in the geographical area within which that species can be found.

Population ecology (or *autecology*) – a branch of ecology focused on the dynamics of populations within species and interactions of these populations with environmental factors.

Population explosion – the population growth at exponential rates to a size that exceeds environmental carrying capacity, usually followed by a *population crash.*

Population momentum – a potential for increased population growth as young members reach reproductive age.

Population size – the number of individuals of a species in a particular population.

Pore spaces – the amount of space available for groundwater due to the topography of the area.

Porosity – the ratio of the volume of all the pores in a material to the whole volume.

Positive feedback loop – a process in which the effects of a slight change in a system include an increase in the magnitude of the change; "A produces more of B, which in turn produces more of A." Contrast *negative feedback loop*.

Postconsumer material or waste – refuse that served its intended purpose and has been discarded for disposal or recovery. *This includes returns of material from the distribution chain, waste collected and sorted after use, and curbside waste.* Compare *pre–consumer waste*.

Post-materialist values – a philosophy emphasizing quality of life over acquiring material goods.

Post-modernism – a philosophy that rejects and often mocks modern positivism's optimism and universal claims.

Potable water (or *drinking water*) – water that is safe to drink. Water fit for human consumption by *World Health Organization* (WHO) guidelines.

Potential energy – the energy of a particle or system of particles derived from its position or condition rather than motion (e.g., a raised weight, coiled spring, or charged battery).

Power – the rate at which work is done; electrically, power = current × voltage (P = I V)

Precautionary principle – where there are threats of severe irreversible environmental damage, lack of scientific certainty should not be used as a reason for introducing measures to prevent degradation (*Rio Declaration*).

Precedent – a decision used as an example in addressing subsequent similar situations.

Precession – the wobble over thousands of years of Earth's axis tilt with respect to the plane of the solar system.

Precipitation (*weather*) – any liquid or solid water particles falling from the atmosphere to Earth's surface. Includes drizzle, rain, snow, snow, ice crystals, and ice pellets.

Precipitator – pollution control device that collects particles from an air stream.

Pre-consumer waste – material diverted to the waste stream during a manufacturing process, *waste from manufacture and production.*

Precycling – making environmentally sound decisions at the store and reducing waste.

Predation – the act of feeding by a *Predator.*

Predator – an organism that feeds directly on other organisms to survive; live-feeders, such as herbivores and carnivores.

Pre-industrial – referring to the time before industrialization (i.e., before the Industrial Revolution c. 1750-1850).

Preparedness – actions taken to build, apply, and sustain the capabilities necessary to prevent, protect against, and ameliorate negative effects.

Prescribed waste and industrial waste (1998) – Environment Protection (*Prescribed Waste*) Regulation lists requirements under the industrial waste management policy. *Prescribed wastes carry special handling, storage, transport, and often licensing requirements and attract substantially higher disposal levies than non–prescribed solid wastes.*

Prevention of significant deterioration – a clause of the Clean Air Act that prevents degradation of existing clean air; opposed by the industry as an unnecessary barrier to development.

Prey – an organism upon which a predator feeds.

Price elasticity – a situation in which the supply of and the demand for a commodity will fluctuate with price changes.

Primary energy – forms of energy obtained directly from nature; the energy in raw fuels (electricity from the grid is not primary) is used primarily on energy statistics when compiling energy balances.

Primary pollutants – chemicals released directly into the air in a harmful form.

Primary producers (or *producer*) – producers responsible for a substantial amount of the food for the rest of the food chain in an ecosystem. *An organism that produces food from inorganic material in the environment through photosynthesis or chemosynthesis in the deep sea. A plant that can produce its food from inorganic substances; (energetics) an organism or process generating concentrated energy from sunlight beyond its own needs.*

Primary production – synthesis of organic compounds from carbon dioxide (CO_2) in Earth's atmosphere. *All life on Earth, directly or indirectly, depends on it.*

Primary productivity – 1. the fixation rate at which plants fix energy. 2. synthesizing organic materials (*biomass*) by green plants using the light energy captured in photosynthesis.

Primary (sewage) treatment – a process that removes solids from sewage before it is discharged or treated further.

Primary standards – regulations of the 1970 Clean Air Act; intended to protect human health.

Primary succession – an ecological succession that begins in an area where no biotic community previously existed.

Principle of competitive exclusion – a result of natural selection whereby two similar species in a community occupy different ecological niches, thereby reducing competition for food.

Producer (or *primary producer*) – an organism that produces food from inorganic material in the environment through photosynthesis or chemosynthesis in the deep sea. *A plant that can produce its food from inorganic substances; (energetics) an organism or process generating concentrated energy from sunlight beyond its own needs.*

Producer responsibility – the legal responsibilities of producers/manufacturers for their products' lives.

Product – 1. a thing produced by labor; 2. material items bought in shops; 3. in ecology, the results of photosynthesis.

Product stewardship – shared responsibility by all sectors involved in manufacturing, distributing, using, and disposing of products for the consequences of these activities. *Manufacturing responsibility extends to the product's entire life.*

Production frontier – the maximum output of two competing commodities at different production levels.

Productivity (*ecology*) – the rate at which producers use radiant energy to form organic substances as food for consumers.

Prokaryotic – cells that do not have a membrane-bounded nucleus or membrane-bounded organelles.

Promethean environmentalism (or *technological optimists*) – those believing technology and human enterprise will find solutions for all problems.

Promoters – agents that are not carcinogenic but that assist in the progression and spread of tumors; sometimes called "co-carcinogens."

Pronatalist pressures – influences that encourage people to have children.

Proteins – chains of amino acids linked by peptide bonds.

Protocooperation – a type of mutualism without necessity.

Proton – a positively charged subatomic particle in the nucleus of an atom.

Proven resources – those that have been thoroughly mapped and are economical to recover at current prices with available technology.

Provisioning services – one of the major ecosystem services: the products obtained from ecosystems (e.g., genetic resources, food, fiber, and freshwater).

Proximity – the state, quality, sense, or fact of being near or next to; closeness.

Proxy – a variable related to one of interest (e.g., tree rings can be proxies for temperature variations).

Public trust – a doctrine obligating the government to maintain public lands in a natural state as guardians of the public interest.

Pull factors – in urbanization, conditions attracting people from the country to cities.

Push factors – in urbanization, conditions forcing people from the country into cities.

Pyrolysis – advanced thermal technology involving the thermal decomposition of organic compounds in the complete absence of oxygen under pressure and at elevated temperatures.

Q

Quadrat (or *quad*) – a rectangular plot of land extensively studied for its ecology.

Qualitative – of or concerning a trait, characteristic, or property.

Quantitative – relating to or expressed as a specified or indefinite number or amount.

R

Radiation – energy transfer in the form of electromagnetic waves or particles that release energy when absorbed by an object. See *ultraviolet radiation, infrared radiation, solar radiation*, and *long-wave radiation*.

Radiative forcing – the change in energy flux in the atmosphere caused by natural or anthropogenic climate change factors as measured by watts / meter^2. A change in Earth's energy balance–atmosphere system in response to a change in factors such as greenhouse gases, land–use change, or solar radiation. *It is a scientific concept to quantify and compare the external drivers of change to Earth's energy balance. Positive radiative forcing increases the temperature of the lower atmosphere, which increases temperatures at Earth's surface. Negative radiation cools the lower atmosphere. Radiative forcing is most measured in watts per square meter (W/m^2) units.*

Radiatively active gases – a gas that occurs naturally or is produced anthropogenically that affects atmospheric radiation by absorption or emission.

Radioactive – an unstable isotope that decays spontaneously and releases subatomic particles or units of energy.

Radioactive decay – a change in the nuclei of radioactive isotopes that spontaneously emit high-energy electromagnetic radiation or subatomic particles while gradually changing into another isotope or a different element.

Radionuclides – isotopes that exhibit radioactive decay.

Radon – a radioactive gaseous element formed by the disintegration of radium; the heaviest of the inert gases; occurs naturally (especially in areas over granite) and is considered a health hazard.

Rain garden – an engineered area for the collection, infiltration, and evapotranspiration of rainwater runoff, mostly from impervious surfaces. *It reduces rain runoff by allowing stormwater to soak into the ground (as opposed to flowing into storm drains and surface waters, which can cause erosion, water pollution, flooding, and diminished groundwater). Rain gardens absorb water contaminants that would enter water bodies. Terminology arose in Maryland, USA, in the 1990s as a more marketable expression for bioremediation.*

Rainshadow – an area with a consistently arid or semi-arid climate due to its position on the lee (i.e., sheltered side) of a mountain range. *A dry area on the downwind side of a mountain.*

Rainforest – a forest with high humidity, constant temperature, and abundant rainfall (generally over 150 inches per year); it can be tropical or temperate.

Rainwater harvesting (or *water harvesting*) – collecting rainwater either in storage or the soil mainly close to where it falls; the attempt to increase rainwater productivity by storing it in ponds, wetlands etc., and helping to avoid the need for infrastructure to bring water from elsewhere. *Practiced on a large scale upstream, this reduces available water downstream.*

Range (or *population distribution*) – the prevalence of a species in the geographical area within which that species can be found.

Rangeland – grasslands and open woodlands suitable for livestock grazing.

Range shift – change in the total areal extent of a species or the geographic limits within which a species can be found.

Rational choice – public decision-making based on reason, logic, and science-based management.

Raw materials – materials extracted from the ground and processed (e.g., bauxite is processed into aluminum).

Reasonably Available Control Technology (RACT) – the lowest emissions limit that a source can meet by applying control technology that is reasonably available considering technological and economic feasibility.

Recharge zones – an area where water filters into aquifers.

Reclaimed water – water taken from a waste (effluent) stream and purified to a level suitable for further use.

Reclamation – chemical, biological or physical cleanup and reconstruction of severely contaminated or degraded sites to return them like their original topography and vegetation.

Recoverable resources – those accessible with current technology but deemed not economical under current conditions.

Recovered material (*waste*) – material that would have otherwise been disposed of as waste or used for energy recovery but has instead been collected and recovered (reclaimed) as material input, thus avoiding using new primary materials.

Recovery rate (*waste*) – the percentage of materials consumed and recovered for recycling.

Re-creation – construction of an entirely new biological community to replace one destroyed on that or another site.

Recreational fishing – by the 1890s, most states in the U.S. had restrictions on fishing; today, a fishing license is needed to fish for recreation in lakes and inland bodies of water.

Recyclables – strictly, all materials may be recycled, but this may include the recyclable containers and paper or cardboard component of curbside waste (excluding garden organics).

Recycled content – mass proportion of recycled material in a product or packaging. *Only pre-consumer and post-consumer materials are considered recycled content.*

Recycled material – waste converted into usable forms, not necessarily in its original use. See *recovered material.*

Recycled water – treated stormwater, greywater, or blackwater suitable for toilet flushing, irrigation, industry etc. *Non–drinking water and is indicated using a lilac non–drinking label.*

Recycling – 1. includes collection, sorting, reprocessing, and manufacturing products into new goods. 2. reprocessing discarded materials into new, useful products; not the same as reusing materials for their original purpose, but the terms are often used interchangeably. Collecting and reprocessing a resource so it can be used again. *An example is collecting aluminum cans, melting them, and using them to make new cans or other aluminum products.*

Red tide – a population explosion or bloom of minute, single-celled marine organisms called *dinoflagellates. Billions of these cells can accumulate in protected bays where the toxins they contain can poison other marine life.*

Reduced tillage systems – such as minimum-till, conserve-till, and no-till preserve soil, save energy and water, and increase crop yields.

Reducing Emissions from Deforestation and Forest Degradation (REDD) – mechanisms using market and financial incentives to reduce the emission of greenhouse gases from deforestation and forest degradation.

Reflected – to return light rays from a surface so that the angle at which a given ray is returned equals the angle at which it strikes the surface.

Reflectivity – the ability of surface material to reflect sunlight, including the visible, infrared, and ultraviolet wavelengths.

Reforestation – 1. replanting of forests on lands that have recently been harvested; 2. the direct human conversion of non-forested land to forested land through planting, seeding, or promotion of natural seed sources on land that was once forested but now no longer. According to *Kyoto Protocol*, for the first commitment period (2008–2012), reforestation activities are limited to reforestation occurring on lands without forest at the beginning of 1990.

Reformer – a device that strips hydrogen from fuels such as natural gas, methanol, ammonia, gasoline, or vegetable oil so they can be used in a fuel cell.

Refracted – to alter the course of a wave of energy that passes into something from another medium, as water does to light entering it from the air, caused by differences in wave speed.

Refuse-derived fuel – the processing of solid waste to remove metal, glass, and other unburnable materials; the organic residue is shredded, formed into pellets, and dried to make fuel for power plants.

Regenerative farming – farming techniques and land stewardship that restore the health and productivity of the soil by rotating crops, planting ground cover, protecting the surface with crop residue, and reducing synthetic chemical inputs and mechanical compaction.

Regional consequences – the impact of global climate change varies from one region to another; some dry areas may become wetter, and another region may have less precipitation.

Regulating services (*sustainability*) – the benefits obtained from regulating ecosystem processes, including, for example, climate, water, or disease regulation.

Regulations – rules established by administrative agencies; that can be more important than *Statutory law* in managing resources.

Rehabilitate land – a utilitarian program to make an area useful to humans.

Rehabilitation – to rebuild elements of structure or function in an ecological system without necessarily achieving complete restoration to its original condition.

Relative – the relation of one thing to another, expressed as the ratio of the specified quantity to the total magnitude (as the value of a measured quantity) or the mean of all the quantities involved.

Relative humidity – at any given temperature, a comparison of the actual water content of the air with the amount of water that could be held at saturation.

Relative sea level rise – the increase in ocean water levels at a specific location considers global sea level rise and local factors, such as local subsidence and uplift. *Relative sea level rise is measured with respect to a specified vertical datum relative to the land, which may also change elevation over time.*

Relativists – those who believe moral principles are always dependent on the situation.

REM (*roentgen equivalent man*) – a unit in radiation protection to measure the amount of damage to human tissue from a dose of ionizing radiation. The amount of ionizing radiation required to produce the same biological effect as one "*rad*" of high-penetration x-rays. *An average American receives about 0.370 rems of radiation per year.*

Remediation – cleaning up chemical contaminants from a polluted area.

Removal unit (or *Kyoto unit*) – a tradable carbon credit represents an allowance to emit one metric ton of greenhouse gases absorbed by a removal or carbon sink activity in an Annex I country.

Renewable energy – any source of energy used without depleting its reserves. *These sources include sunlight (solar energy) and other sources such as wind, waves, biomass, geothermal, and hydro energy. Naturally replenishing energy such as biomass, hydro, geothermal, solar, wind, ocean thermal, wave action, and tidal action.*

Renewable energy certificates – Market trading mechanisms created through the *Renewable Energy (Electricity) Act 2000* in connection with the Canadian government's mandatory renewable energy target. *Provides a "premium" revenue stream for renewable sources.*

Renewable resources – resources typically replaced or replenished by natural processes; resources not depleted by moderate use (e.g., solar energy, biological resources such as forests and fisheries, biological organisms, and some biogeochemical cycles).

Renewable water supplies – annual freshwater surface runoff plus annual infiltration into underground freshwater aquifers that are accessible for human use.

Roentgen equivalent man (REM) – a unit in radiation protection to measure the amount of damage to human tissue from a dose of ionizing radiation. The amount of ionizing radiation required to produce the same biological effect as one "*rad*" of high-penetration x-rays. *An average American receives about 0.370 rems of radiation per year.*

Replacement level of fertility (or *zero population growth, ZPG*) – the number of births at which people are just replacing themselves.

Representative Concentration Pathways (RCP) – time series of emissions and concentrations of the suite of greenhouse gases, aerosols, and other chemically active gases, as well as land use/land cover. The word "representative" signifies that each RCP provides only one of many possible scenarios leading to the specific radiative forcing characteristics. The term "pathway" emphasizes that not only the long-term concentration levels are of interest but also the trajectory taken over time to reach that outcome.

Reprocessing (*waste*) – changing the physical structure and properties of waste that would otherwise have been sent to a landfill to add financial value to processed material; may involve a range of technologies, including composting, anaerobic digestion, and energy from waste technologies such as pyrolysis, gasification, and incineration.

Reservoir – a natural or artificial pond or lake for storing and regulating water.

Residence time – the time a component, such as an individual water molecule, will spend in a compartment or location before it moves on through a process or cycle. *The average time spent in a reservoir by an individual atom or molecule. For greenhouse gases, residence time refers to how long, on average, a particular molecule remains in the atmosphere. The residence time is approximately equal to the atmospheric lifetime for most gases other than methane and carbon dioxide.*

Residual waste – residue after separating recyclable materials (including *green waste*).

Residue – 1. material remaining; residues of some contaminants may remain after clean-up; 2. the part of a molecule that remains after a portion of its constituents is removed.

Resilience – 1. the ability of a community or ecosystem to recover from disturbances. 2. a capability to anticipate, prepare for, respond to, and recover from significant multi-hazard threats with minimum damage to social well-being, the economy, and the environment. *A capability to anticipate, prepare for, respond to, and recover from significant multi-hazard threats with minimum damage to social well-being, the economy, and the environment.*

Resistant – the ability of an individual or community to resist change by potentially disruptive events.

Resource – 1. a substance or object in the environment required by an organism for normal growth, maintenance, and reproduction. 2. in economic terms, anything with potential use in creating wealth or giving satisfaction.

Resource Conservation and Recovery Act (RCRA) – regulates the handling of waste from *cradle-to-grave. Establishes rules for handling such waste from its generation, while being packaged, stored, transported, and how it is disposed of, as well as the disposal sites themselves.*

Resource flow – the totality of changes in multiple resource stocks, or at least any pair of them, over a specified period

Resource intensity – the ratio of resource consumption relative to its economic or physical output; for example, liters of water used per dollar spent or liters of water used per ton of aluminum produced. *At the national level, energy intensity is the ratio of the total primary energy consumption of the country to either the gross domestic product or the physical output (total goods produced).*

Resource mismatch – decoupling a previously synchronized ecological relationship, such as changes in timing within a trophic (food-web) relationship.

Resource productivity – the output obtained for a given resource input.

Resource partitioning – in a biological community, various populations share environmental resources through specialization, thereby reducing direct competition. *The coexistence of two or more competing species that use the same natural resource differently.* See *ecological niche.*

Resource recovery (*waste*) – obtaining matter or energy from discarded materials.

Resource scarcity – a shortage or deficit in some *resource.*

Resource stock – the total amount of a resource often related to resource flow (the number of resources harvested or used per unit of time). *Stocks are measured in mass, volume, or energy and flow in mass, volume, or energy per unit of time. The harvest must not exceed the net production to harvest a resource stock sustainably.*

Respiration (*biology*) – 1. uptake by a living organism of oxygen from the air (or water), which is then used to oxidize organic matter or food; the outputs of this oxidation are usually CO_2 and H_2O. 2. the metabolic process by which organisms meet their internal energy needs and release CO_2.

Restoration – to bring something back to a former condition; ecological restoration involves active manipulation of nature to recreate the conditions that existed before human disturbance.

Restoration ecology – a branch of ecology that attempts to understand the ecological basis needed to restore impaired or damaged ecosystems. *Seeks to repair or reconstruct ecosystems damaged by human actions.*

Retail therapy – shopping to compensate for things psychologically and physically lacking.

Retrofit – to replace existing items with updated items.

Reuse – the second pillar of the waste hierarchy. Recovering value from a discarded resource without reprocessing or remanufacturing (e.g., clothes sold through opportunity shops represent a form of reuse *rather than recycling*).

Reverse osmosis – a process of desalinization where water is forced under pressure through a semipermeable membrane whose tiny pores allow water to pass but exclude most salts and minerals.

Riders – amendments attached to bills in the conference committee, often wholly unrelated to the bill to which they are added.

Rill erosion – the removal of thin layers of soil caused by little rivulets of running water cutting small channels in the soil.

Risk – 1. the probability that something undesirable happens due to hazard exposure. 2. threats to life, health and safety, the environment, economic well-being, and other things of value. *Risks are often evaluated in terms of how likely they are to occur (probability) and the damages that would result if they did happen (consequences).*

Risk assessment – evaluates short-term and long-term risks associated with an activity or hazard, usually compared to anticipated benefits in a cost-benefit analysis. Estimates the likelihood of specific events occurring and their potential positive or negative consequences.

Risk management – planning to manage the effects of climate change to increase positive and decrease negative impacts.

Risk perception – the psychological and emotional factors that affect people's behavior and beliefs about potential adverse hazards or consequences.

Risk-based framing – planning based on the pros and cons of a given set of possibilities includes assessment of a risk in terms of the likelihood of its occurrence and the magnitude of the impact associated with the risk.

RNA – Ribonucleic acid; nucleic acid used for transcription and translation of the genetic code found on DNA molecules.

Rock – a solid, cohesive aggregate of one or more crystalline minerals.

Rock cycle – the process whereby rocks are broken down by chemical and physical forces; sediments are moved by wind, water, and gravity, settle and reform into rock, and then eventually are crushed, folded, melted, and re-crystallized into new forms.

Roundwood (or *industrial timber*) – trees used for lumber, plywood, veneer, particleboard, chipboard, and paper.

Routinely monitored – regular, periodic testing.

r-selected species – a species selected for superiority in variable or unpredictable environments. Contrast *k-selected species*.

Ruminant animals – cud-chewing animals, such as cattle, sheep, goats, and buffalo, with multi-chambered stomachs in which cellulose is digested with the aid of bacteria.

Runoff – the flow of water over land from rain, melting snow, or other sources. *The excess of precipitation over evaporation; water that the ground cannot absorb. The main source of surface water and, broadly, the water available for human use.*

Run-of-the-river flow – ordinary river flow not accelerated by dams, flumes, etc.; some small, modern, high-efficiency turbines can generate useful power using only run-of-the-river flow, with a current of only a few kilometers per hour.

Runaway greenhouse effect – an ill-defined term associated with irreversible temperature rises.

Rural area – an area where most residents depend on agriculture or the harvesting of natural resources for their livelihood.

S

SF_6 – Sulfur hexafluoride

S curve (or *S-shaped curve*) – a curve that depicts logistic growth; called an S curve because of its shape. See *logistic growth*.

Saffir/Simpson – a scale to measure hurricanes based on wind speeds and air pressure.

Salinity (*ecology*) – 1. salt in water and soils, generally in the context of human activity such as clearing and planting for annual crops rather than perennial trees and shrubs. Can make soils infertile. 2. dissolved salts in water and soils, generally in the context of human activity such as clearing and planting for annual crops rather than perennial trees and shrubs, can make soils infertile.

Salinization – 1. the process by which land becomes salt–affected. 2. a process in which mineral salts accumulate in soil, killing plants. *Occurs when soil in dry climates are irrigated profusely.*

Salt domes – a solid mass of salt that was once fluid but has flowed into fractures in surrounding rock and geologic structures.

Saltwater intrusion – the movement of saltwater into freshwater aquifers in coastal areas where groundwater is withdrawn faster than replenished. *Fresh or ground water is displaced by the advance of salt water due to its greater density, usually in coastal and estuarine areas.*

Sanitary landfills – a landfill where refuse and municipal waste are buried daily under enough soil or fill to eliminate odors, vermin, and litter.

Saturation point – the maximum concentration of water vapors the air can hold at a given temperature.

Savanna – a tropical or subtropical grassland ecosystem with trees without a closed canopy.

Scale – the physical dimensions of phenomena or events in either space or time.

Scattered – few and far apart in distance or time.

Scavenger – an organism feeding on dead organisms.

Scenarios – 1. a plausible and often simplified description of how the future may develop based on a coherent and internally consistent set of assumptions about driving forces and key relationships. 2. sets of assumptions used to help understand potential future conditions such as population growth, land use, and sea level rise. *Scenarios are neither predictions nor forecasts. Scenarios are commonly used for planning purposes.*

Scientific method – a systematic, precise, objective study of a problem; generally, this requires observation, hypothesis development and testing, data gathering, and interpretation.

Scientific theory – an explanation supported by many tests that have come to be accepted by the consensus of scientists.

Scrubbers – an air pollution device that uses a spray of water or reactant or a dry process to trap pollutants in emissions.

Sea surface temperature (SST) – the top several feet of ocean measured by ships, buoys, and drifters.

Second law of thermodynamics – states that with each successive energy transfer or transformation in a system, less energy is available to do work.

Secondary energy – primary energies that are transformed in energy conversion processes to more convenient secondary forms, such as electrical energy or cleaner fuels.

Secondary pollutants – chemicals modified to a hazardous form after entering the air or formed by chemical reactions as components of the air mix and interact.

Secondary recovery technique – pumping pressurized gas, steam, or chemical-containing water into a well to squeeze more oil from a reservoir.

Secondary standards – the 1972 *Clean Air Act* regulations intended to protect materials, crops, visibility, climate, and personal comfort.

Secondary succession – a stage of ecological succession that occurs after the original community has been destroyed or disturbed, as with a forest fire. *Succession on a site where an existing community has been disrupted.*

Secondary treatment – bacterial decomposition of suspended particulates and dissolved organic compounds that remain after primary sewage treatment.

Sectors (*economics*) – economic groupings to generalize patterns of expenditure and use.

Secure landfill – a solid waste disposal site lined and capped with an impermeable barrier that prevents leakage or *leaching*; drain tiles, sampling wells, and vent systems provide monitoring and pollution control.

Sediment (*ecology*) – soil or other particles settling to the bottom of water bodies.

Sedimentary rock – deposited material that remains in place long enough or has been covered with enough material to compact into stone; examples include shale, sandstone, breccia, and conglomerates.

Sedimentation – the deposition of organic materials or minerals by chemical, physical or biological processes.

Seed sourcing – seed sources are taken from areas where the climate is like the predicted future climate in the planting location to assist with climate adaptation.

Seismic activity – describes the size, type, and frequency of earthquakes in an area over time.

Selective cutting – harvesting only mature trees of certain species and size; usually more expensive than clear-cutting, but it is less disruptive for wildlife and often better for forest regeneration.

Selfish herd – individuals in a group acting together without planned direction.

Self-organization – the process by which systems use energy to develop structure and organization.

Self-regulating – an internal mechanism by which a system or organism controls its functions.

Sensitivity – the degree to which a system is affected, either adversely or beneficially, by climate variability or change. The effect may be direct (e.g., a change in crop yield in response to a change in the mean, range, or variability of temperature) or indirect (e.g., damages caused by increased coastal flooding due to sea level rise).

Sentinel indicator (*ecology*) – captures the essence of the change process affecting a broad area of interest and is easily communicated.

Septic sewage – sewage in which anaerobic respiration occurs. *Characterized by a blackish color and the smell of hydrogen sulfide.*

Septic tank – a sedimentation tank in which the sludge is retained long enough for organic content to undergo anaerobic digestion, typically used for sewage from houses and premises too isolated for sewer connection.

Sequestration (*global warming*) – the removal of carbon dioxide from the Earth's atmosphere and storage in a sink, as when trees absorb CO_2 in photosynthesis and store it in their tissues.

Seriously undernourished – those who receive less than 80 percent of their minimum daily caloric requirements.

Sessile – permanently attached or established; not free to move about.

Sewage – water and raw effluent disposed of through toilets, kitchens, and bathrooms. *Includes water-borne wastes from domestic uses of water from households or similar uses in trade or industry.*

Sewer – a pipe conveying sewage.

Sewerage – a system of pipes and mechanical appliances for collecting and transporting domestic and industrial sewage.

Sewerage system (*infrastructure*) – the network of pipes, pumping stations, and treatment plants used to collect, transport, treat and discharge sewage.

Sewer-mining – tapping directly into a sewer (either before or after a sewage treatment plant) and extracting wastewater for treatment and use.

Sexual selection – a mode of natural selection in which members of one biological sex choose mates of the other sex to mate with and compete with members of the same sex for access to members of the opposite sex.

Shallow ecology – a critical term applied to superficial environmentalists who claim to be green but are quick to compromise and do little to bring about fundamental change.

Shantytowns – settlements created when people move onto undeveloped lands and build their shelter with cheap or discarded materials; some are illegal subdivisions where landowners rent land without city approval, and others are land invasions.

Sheet erosion – peeling off thin soil layers from the land surface; accomplished primarily by wind and water.

Short ton – standard measurement for a ton in the United States. A short ton equals 2,000 lbs. or 0.907 metric tons. See *metric ton.*

Short-wave radiation (or *solar radiation*) – emitted by the Sun. Solar radiation has a distinctive range of wavelengths (i.e., electromagnetic spectrum) determined by the temperature of the Sun. See *ultraviolet radiation, infrared radiation,* and *radiation.*

Shredder flock – the residue from shredded car bodies, white goods (i.e., large home appliances), and the like.

Sick Building Syndrome – a building whose occupants experience acute health or comfort effects that appear to be linked to the time spent there but where no specific illness or cause can be identified. *Complaints may be localized or spread throughout the building.*

Sign stimulus – a fixed action pattern such as a mating dance.

Silent Spring (Rachel Carson, 1962) – environmental science book that inspired the environmental movement and later led to the creation of the U.S. Environmental Protection Agency (EPA) in 1970.

Siltation – to become choked or obstructed with silt or mud.

Simple living – a lifestyle individuals pursue for a variety of motivations, such as spirituality, health, or ecology. Some explicitly reject "Westernized values," while others live more simply for personal taste, a sense of fairness, or personal economy. Others may choose simple living for social justice or rejection of consumerism. Simple living as a concept is distinguished from the simple lifestyles of those living in conditions of poverty in that its proponents consciously choose not to focus on wealth directly tied to money or cash–based economics.

Sinkholes – a large surface crater caused by the collapse of an underground channel or cavern; often triggered by groundwater withdrawal.

Sinks – 1. processes or places that remove or store gases, solutes, or solids; 2. any process, activity, or mechanism that results in the net removal of greenhouse gases, aerosols, or precursors of greenhouse gases from the atmosphere. *Any process, activity, or mechanism which removes a greenhouse gas, an aerosol, or a precursor of a greenhouse gas or aerosol from the atmosphere. A natural or technological process that removes and stores carbon from the atmosphere.*

Slash and burn – a form of deforestation used to clear fields for agricultural use.

Slow Food – movement founded in Italy in 1986 by Carlo Petrini to respond to the negative impact of international food industries. Slow Food is a counteracting force to Fast Food as it encourages using local seasonal produce, restoring time–honored production and preparation methods, and sharing food at communal tables. *Slow Food encourages environmentally sustainable production, ethical treatment of animals, and social justice. Slow Food members seek to defend biodiversity in the food supply, to appreciate better and improve understanding of the sensation of taste, and to celebrate the connection between plate and planet. Gatherings of Slow Food supporters are convivia.*

Sludge – 1. waste in a state between liquid and solid. 2. a semi-solid mixture of organic and inorganic materials that settle wastewater at a sewage treatment plant.

Slums – legal but inadequate multifamily tenements or rooming houses; some are custom-built for rent to poor people; others have been converted for some other use.

Smart growth – efficient use of land resources and existing urban infrastructure.

Smog – 1. (*photochemical*) air pollution produced by the action of sunlight on hydrocarbons, nitrogen oxides, and other pollutants; 2. (*industrial*) primarily a winter phenomenon that occurs when sulfur dioxide emissions and smoke particles react with water vapor; 3. describes the combination of industrial smoke (and automobile exhaust) and fog formerly in the stagnant air of London and the air of present-day Los Angeles.

Snowball Earth – a geohistorical hypothesis that proposes during one or more of Earth's icehouse climates, the planet's surface became entirely or nearly entirely frozen with no liquid oceanic or surface water exposed to the atmosphere.

Snowpack – a seasonal accumulation of slow-melting snow that accumulates over the winter and slowly melts to release water in spring and summer.

Snow water equivalent (SWE) – the amount of water held in a volume of snow, which depends on the density of the snow and other factors.

Soak away (or *absorption pit*) – a hole dug in permeable ground filled with broken stones or granular material and usually covered with earth, allowing collected water to soak into the ground.

Social behavior – the behavior of an individual organism towards other members of the population of its species.

Social ecology – a socialist/humanist philosophy based on the communitarian anarchism of the Russian geographer Peter Kropotkin; shares much with *Deep ecology* except that it is more humanist in its outlook.

Sociality – the degree to which animal population members associate in social groups and form cooperative societies.

Social justice – equitable access to resources and their benefits; a system that recognizes people's inalienable rights and adheres to what is fair, honest, and moral.

Sodicity (*ecology*) – measures the sodium content of soil. Sodic soils are dispersible and vulnerable to erosion. *An indicator of the suitability of water for use in agricultural irrigation, as determined from the concentrations of the main alkaline and earth alkaline cations present in the water.* See *sodium absorption ratio.*

Sodification – the build–up in soils of sodium relative to potassium and magnesium as exchangeable cations (i.e., *positively charged ions*) of clay fractions. *Sodic soils present challenges because they tend to have very poor structure which limits or prevents water infiltration and drainage.*

Sodium absorption ratio (SA) – an indicator of the suitability of water for use in agricultural irrigation, as determined from the concentrations of the main alkaline and earth alkaline cations present in the water. See *sodicity.*

Soil – the naturally occurring, unconsolidated, or loose covering of Earth's surface; part of the pedosphere. *A complex mixture of weathered mineral materials from rocks, partially decomposed organic molecules, and a host of living organisms.*

Soil acidification – reduction in pH, usually in soil. *Acidification can result in poorly structured or hard–setting topsoil that cannot support sufficient vegetation to prevent erosion.*

Soil bulk density – the relative density of soil measured by dividing dry weight of soil by its volume.

Soil carbon – a major component of terrestrial biosphere pools in the carbon cycle. *The amount of carbon in soil is a function of historical vegetative cover and productivity, dependent on climatic variables.*

Soil compaction – the degree of compression of soil. *Heavy compaction impedes plant growth.*

Soil conditioner – any composted or non–composted material of organic origin produced or distributed for adding to soils; it includes *soil amendment, soil additive, soil improver*, and similar materials. However, it excludes polymers that do not biodegrade, such as plastics, rubbers, and coatings.

Soil ecology – a branch of ecology that studies the pedosphere (i.e., soil mantle).

Soil horizons – horizontal layers analyzed to reveal a soil's history, characteristics, and usefulness.

Soil moisture deficit – the volume of water needed to raise the soil water content of the root zone to *field capacity* (i.e., amount of water held by soil after excess has drained).

Soil organic carbon (SOC) – the total organic carbon of a soil exclusive of carbon from undecayed plant and animal residue.

Soil organic matter (SOM) – the organic fraction of soil without undecayed plant and animal residues.

Soil structure – the way soil particles are aggregated into aggregates or *"crumbs,"* essential for air and water passage.

Soil water storage – the total amount of water stored in the soil in the plant root zone.

Solar energy – Sun's radiant energy, which can be converted into other forms of energy (e.g., heat or electricity).

Solar power – electricity generated from solar radiation (Sun's rays).

Solar radiation (or *short-wave radiation*) – emitted by the Sun. Solar radiation has a distinctive range of wavelengths (i.e., electromagnetic spectrum) determined by the temperature of the Sun. See *ultraviolet radiation, infrared radiation,* and *radiation.*

Solar variation – changes in the amount of radiant energy emitted by the Sun.

Solar wind – the stream of charged particles ejected from the Sun's upper atmosphere.

Solid industrial waste – generated from commercial, industrial, or trade activities, including factories, offices, schools, universities, State and Federal government operations, and commercial construction and demolition work. Excludes wastes prescribed under the *Environment Protection Act* (1970) and quarantine wastes.

Solid inert waste – hard waste and dry vegetative material that has a negligible activity or effect on the environment, such as demolition material, concrete, bricks, plastic, glass, metals, and shredded tires.

Solid waste – non–hazardous, non–prescribed solid waste ranging from municipal garbage to industrial waste, generally: domestic and municipal; commercial and industrial; construction and demolition.

Soluble – susceptible to being dissolved in a liquid, particularly in water.

Song system – discrete brain nuclei in songbirds used to learn and produce specific sequences.

Source separation (*waste*) – separation of recyclable material from other waste at the point and time the waste is generated (i.e., at its source). This includes the separation of recyclable material into its component categories, e.g., paper, glass, aluminum) Furthermore, it may include further separation within each category (e.g., paper into computer paper, office whites, and newsprint). The practice of segregating materials into discrete streams before collection by or delivery to reprocessing facilities.

Source-sink dynamics – a theoretical model used by ecologists to describe how variation in habitat quality may affect organisms' population growth or decline.

Southern pine forest – the United States coniferous forest ecosystem characterized by a warm, moist climate.

Special Report on Emissions Scenarios (SRES) – a set of emission scenarios from the IPCC Special Report on Emission Scenarios released in 2000 that describe a wide range of potential future socio-economic conditions and resulting emissions.

Specialist species – only thrive in a narrow range of environmental conditions or have a limited diet.

Speciation – the evolutionary process when new biological species emerge from a common ancestor.

Species – a taxonomic category subordinate to a genus (or subgenus) and superior to a subspecies or variety, composed of individuals possessing common characteristics and that can reproduce sexually among themselves but cannot produce fertile offspring when mated with other organisms, distinguishing them from other categories of individuals of the same taxonomic level. *In taxonomic nomenclature, species are designated by the genus name followed by a Latin or Latinized adjective or noun.*

Species diversity – the number and relative abundance of species in a community.

Species recovery plan – restoring an endangered species through protection, habitat management, captive breeding, disease control, or other techniques that increase populations and encourage survival.

Specific heat capacity – the amount of energy needed to increase the temperature of 1 kg of a substance by 1 °C. Measures resistance to temperature increase and essential for energy transfer.

Spectrum – an ordered array of the components of an emission or wave.

Spent fuel – the uranium cores taken out of the nuclear power plant.

Spillways – a passage permitting surplus water to run over or around an obstruction (such as a dam).

Spontaneous – 1. happening or arising without apparent external cause; self-generated; 2. arising from a natural inclination or impulse and not from any external incitement or constraint; 3. unconstrained and unstudied in manner or behavior; 4) plants growing without cultivation or human labor; indigenous.

Sport hunting – hunting animals, not just for food.

Sprawl – an unlimited outward extension of city boundaries that lowers population density, consumes open space, generates freeway congestion, and causes decay in central cities.

Spring overturn – 1. a springtime lake phenomenon that occurs when the surface ice melts, and the surface water temperature warms to its greatest density at 4 °C and then sinks, creating a convection current displacing the nutrient-rich bottom waters. 2. the mixing of lake water through the melting of ice cover, warming surface waters, convection currents, and wind action occurring in spring.

Squatter towns – *Shantytowns* that occupy land without the owner's permission; some are highly organized movements in defiance of authorities; others grow gradually.

Stability – 1. in ecological terms, a dynamic equilibrium among the physical and biological factors in an ecosystem or a community; 2. relative homeostasis.

Stable runoff – the fraction of water available year-round. *Usually more important than total runoff when determining human uses.*

Stack emissions – emissions of pollutants from a smokestack, including dioxin, furans, nitrogen oxides, and carbon.

Stakeholders – parties having an interest in a particular project or outcome. *An individual or group directly or indirectly affected by or interested in the outcomes of decisions.*

Standard Metropolitan Statistical Area (SMSA) – an urbanized region with at least 100,000 inhabitants with strong economic and social ties to a central city of at least 50,000 people.

Standing – the right to take part in legal proceedings.

State Environment Protection Policies – statutory instruments (e.g., legislation, rules) under the *Environment Protection Act* 1970 identifying beneficial uses of the environmental protection, established environmental indicators and objectives, and defines attainment programs to implement policies.

State of Environment Reporting – a scientific assessment of environmental conditions, focusing on the impacts of human activities, their significance for the environment, and social responses to the identified trends.

Stationary energy – that energy that is other than transport fuels and fugitive emissions; used mostly for producing electricity but also for manufacturing, processing and in, agriculture, fisheries, etc.

Statute law – formal documents or decrees enacted by the legislative branch of government.

Statutory law – rules passed by a state or national legislature.

Steady state – a constant pattern; a balance of inflows and outflows.

Steady-state economy – characterized by low birth and death rates, use of renewable energy sources, recycling of materials, and emphasis on durability, efficiency, and stability.

Steppe – a dry, grassy plain occurring in temperate climates between the tropics and polar regions. *Temperate regions have distinct seasonal temperature changes, with cold winters and warm summers.*

Sterilization – 1. making an organism barren or infertile (unable to reproduce); 2. clearing an object of living organisms by heating it or applying chemicals.

Stewardship – a philosophy that humans have a unique responsibility to manage, care for, and improve nature.

Storm surge – giant waves, often fifty miles wide and twenty-five feet or more high, that are caused by the force of a hurricane. An abnormal rise in sea level accompanying a hurricane or other intense storm, whose height is the difference between the observed sea surface level and the level that would have occurred without the cyclone. *For example, as the eye of the hurricane makes landfall, the wave comes sweeping across the coastline; aided by the hammering effect of the breaking of the waves, it acts like a giant bulldozer sweeping everything in its path.*

Stormwater – rainfall accumulating in natural or artificial systems after heavy rain; surface run–off or water sent to (stormwater) drains during heavy rain.

Stranded assets – assets that have suffered from unanticipated or premature write-downs, devaluations, or conversion to liabilities. A variety of environment-related risks can cause them.

Strategic Environmental Assessment (SEA) – a system of incorporating environmental considerations into policies, plans, and programs, especially in the European Union (EU).

Strategic Lawsuits Against Public Participation (SLAPP) – lawsuits that have no merit but are brought merely to intimidate and harass private citizens who act in the public interest.

Strategic metals and minerals – materials a country cannot produce but needs to use for essential materials or processes.

Stratification – the layering of water by temperature and density can occur in lakes or other bodies of water, often seasonally.

Stratosphere – the zone in the atmosphere extending from the tropopause to about 30 miles above the Earth's surface; temperatures are stable or rise slightly with altitude; has very little water vapor but is rich in ozone; above the *troposphere* and below the *mesosphere*. A region of the atmosphere between the troposphere and mesosphere, having a lower boundary of approximately 8 km at the poles to 15 km at the equator and an upper boundary of approximately 50 km. *Depending upon latitude and season, the temperature in the lower stratosphere can increase, be isothermal, or even decrease with altitude. However, the temperature in the upper stratosphere generally increases with height due to ozone's absorption of solar radiation.*

Stratospheric ozone – See *ozone layer*.

Stream – a flowing-water ecosystem that starts as a freshwater spring or melting snow.

Streamflow – the volume of water moving over a designated point within a fixed period. It is often expressed as cubic feet per second (ft^3/sec).

Stressor – something that influences people and natural, managed, and socio-economic systems. Multiple stressors can have compounded effects, such as when economic or market stress combines with drought to impact farmers negatively.

Strip cutting – harvesting trees in strips narrow enough to minimize edge effects and allow natural forest regeneration.

Strip farming – planting different kinds of crops in alternating strips along land contours; when one crop is harvested, the other remains in place to protect the soil and prevent water from running straight down a hill.

Strip mining – removing surface layers over coal seams using giant earth-moving equipment; creating a vast open pit from which enormous surface-operated machines scoop coal and transport it by trucks; an alternative to deep mines.

Structure – in ecological terms, patterns of organization, both spatial and functional, in a community.

Sublimation – the process by which water can move between solid and gaseous states without ever becoming liquid.

Subsidence – a settling of the ground surface caused by the collapse of porous formations that result from the withdrawal of large amounts of groundwater, oil, or other underground materials.

Subsiding/Subsidence – the downward settling of the Earth's crust relative to its surroundings.

Subsistence – 1. broadly refers to any human system that seeks to secure survival and flourishing within ecosystems. 2. in legal and policy contexts, used more narrowly to refer to the provision of food that is a necessary part of a household's or a community's regular diet or legal entitlements to harvesting rights in particular situations. 3. the harvest or use of naturally produced renewable resources for direct personal or family consumption as food, shelter, fuel, clothing, tools, transportation, or production of handicrafts for customary and traditional trade, barter, or sharing.

Subsoil – a layer of soil beneath the topsoil with lower organic content and higher concentrations of fine mineral particles. *Often contains soluble compounds and clay particles carried down by percolating water.*

Sulfate aerosols – particulate matter consists of compounds of sulfur formed by the interaction of sulfur dioxide and sulfur trioxide with other compounds in the atmosphere. Sulfate aerosols are injected into the atmosphere from the combustion of fossil fuels and the eruption of volcanoes like Mt. Pinatubo. Sulfate aerosols can lower the Earth's temperature by reflecting away solar radiation (negative radiative forcing). General Circulation Models, which incorporate the effects of sulfate aerosols, more accurately predict global temperature variations. See *particulate matter, aerosol,* and *general circulation models.*

Sulfur cycle – the chemical and physical reactions by which sulfur moves into or out of storage and through the environment.

Sulfur dioxide – a colorless, corrosive gas directly damaging plants and animals.

Sulfur hexafluoride (SF$_6$) – a colorless gas soluble in alcohol and ether, slightly soluble in water. A potent greenhouse gas used primarily in electrical transmission and distribution systems and as a dielectric in electronics. The global warming potential of SF$_6$ is 22,800. This GWP is from the IPCC's Fourth Assessment Report (AR4). See *global warming potential.*

Sulfur oxides – molecules formed by combining sulfur and oxygen (SOx).

Sullage – domestic wastewater from baths, showers, laundries and kitchens (but *not* from toilets).

Sunspot – a region on the Sun's surface (i.e., photosphere) marked by lower temperature than its surroundings and has intense magnetic activity, which inhibits convection, forming areas of low surface temperature.

Super city (or *megacity* and *megalopolis*) – an urban area with more than 10 million inhabitants.

Superfund (1980) – a U.S. federal program that funds the cleanup of sites contaminated with hazardous substances and pollutants. It was established as the *Comprehensive Environmental Response, Compensation, and Liability* Act of 1980 (CERCLA).

Supply – the quantity of a product offered for sale at various prices, other things being equal.

Supporting services (*sustainability*) – ecosystem services necessary for producing all other services. *For example, biomass production, production of atmospheric oxygen, soil formation, nutrient, and water cycling.*

Surface mining – when minerals are extracted from surface pits. See *strip mining.*

Surface runoff – rainfall passing out of an area into the drainage system.

Surface tension – when the water surface meets the air and acts as an elastic skin.

Survivorship – the percentage of a population reaching a given age or the proportion of the maximum lifespan of the species reached by any individual.

Survivorship curve – a graph showing the number or proportion of individuals surviving at each age for a given species.

Suspended particulate matter (SPM) (*aerosols*) – a suspension or dispersion of fine particles of a solid or liquid in a gas.

Suspended solids (SS) – solid particles suspended in water, an *indicator of water quality.*

Sustainability covenant (Section 49 of the Environment Protection Act of 1970) – a sustainability covenant is an agreement that a person or body undertakes to increase the resource use efficiency or reduce environmental impacts of activities, products, services, and production processes. *Parties can voluntarily enter into such agreements with the EPA or could be required to if they are declared by a Governor in Council (Canada), on the recommendation of the EPA or have the potential for a significant impact on the environment.*

Sustainability science – the multidisciplinary scientific study of sustainability, focusing primarily on the quantitative dynamic interactions between nature and society. *Its objective is a deeper and more fundamental understanding of the rapidly growing inter–dependence of the nature–society system and the intention to make this sustainable. It critically examines the tools used by sustainability accounting and the methods of sustainability governance.*

Sustainability triangle a graphic indication of the action needed to stabilize CO_2 levels below about 500 ppm. *It shows stabilization 'wedges' indicating savings per year using a particular strategy.*

Sustainable – meets the needs of the present without compromising the ability of future generations to meet their needs.

Sustainable agriculture – an ecologically sound, economically viable, socially just, and humane agricultural system; stewardship, soil conservation, and integrated pest management are essential for sustainability.

Sustainable consumption (or *sustainable resource use*) – a change to society's historical patterns of consumption and behavior enabling consumers to satisfy their needs with better–performing products or services using fewer resources, causing less pollution, and contributing to social progress worldwide.

Sustainable development – meets the needs of the present without compromising the ability of future generations to meet their own needs. *An increase in the well-being and standard of life for the average person maintained over the long term without degrading the environment or undermining the ability of future generations to meet their needs.*

Sustainable resource use (or *sustainable consumption*) – a change to society's historical patterns of consumption and behavior enabling consumers to satisfy their needs with better–performing products or services using fewer resources, causing less pollution, and contributing to social progress worldwide.

Sustained yield – utilization of a renewable resource at a rate that does not impair or damage its ability to be fully renewed long-term.

Swale – an open channel transporting surface run–off to a drainage system, usually grassed. *Swales promote infiltration, the filtration of sediment by plants, and offer ornamental interest.*

Swamp – a wetland with trees, such as the extensive swamp forests of the southeastern United States, especially Florida, and Louisiana.

Swidden agriculture – land cleared for cultivation, left to regenerate, and repeated. See *Milpa agriculture*.

Symbiosis – the intimate living together of members of two different species; includes mutualism, commensalism, and, in some classifications, parasitism.

Synecology (or *community ecology*) – studies the interactions between the species comprising an ecological community.

Synergistic effects – when an injury caused by exposure to two environmental factors is together greater than the sum of exposure to each factor separately would be.

Synfuels – synthetic gas or synthetic oil made from coal or other sources.

System – a set of parts organized into a whole, usually processing flow of energy. *A group of interacting, interrelated or interdependent elements forming a complex whole.*

Systemic – a condition or process that affects the whole body; many metabolic poisons are systemic.

T

Taiga in Siberia (or *boreal forest*) – 1. forest areas of the northern temperate zone, mainly consisting of conifers. 2. the northernmost edge of the boreal forest, including species-poor woodland and peat deposits, intergrading with the arctic tundra.

Tailings – mining waste left after mechanical or chemical separation of minerals from crushed ore.

Take-back – a concept commonly associated with product stewardship, placing responsibility on brand–owners, retailers, manufacturers, or supply chain partners to accept products returned by consumers at the end of their useful life. *Products may then be recycled, treated, or sent to landfills.*

Taking – unconstitutional confiscation of private property.

Tar sands – sand deposits containing petroleum or tar.

Tax incentive – reduction in taxes given to encourage specific behavior on the part of the recipient.

Technological optimists (or *Promethean environmentalism*) – those believing technology and human enterprise will find solutions for all problems.

Technosphere – synthetic and composite components and materials formed by human activity. *True technosphere materials, like plastics, are not biodegradable.*

Tectonic plates – huge blocks of the Earth's crust that slide slowly, pulling apart to open new ocean basins or crashing ponderously into each other to create new, larger landmasses.

Temperate – with moderate temperatures, weather, or climate; neither hot nor cold. *A mean annual temperature between 0 and 20 °C.*

Temperature climate – characterized by relatively moderate mean annual temperatures, with average monthly temperatures above 10 °C in their warmest months and above −3 °C in colder months. *In geography, the temperate climates of Earth occur in the middle latitudes, which span between the tropics and the polar regions of Earth.*

Temperate deciduous forest – any forest in a temperate zone whose trees shed their leaves during the cold season. See *deciduous broadleaf forest.*

Temperate rainforest – the cool, dense rainforest of the northern Pacific coast, shrouded in fog often, dominated by large conifers many hundreds of years old.

Temperature – a measure of the speed of motion of molecule in a substance.

Temperature inversions – an atmospheric condition in which a layer of warm air traps cooler air near the Earth's surface, preventing the normal rising of surface air.

Tennessee Valley Authority (TVA) – a federal corporation created by Congress in 1933 to operate Wilson Dam and to develop the Tennessee River and its tributaries in the interest of navigation, flood control, and the production and distribution of electricity; enactments include reforestation, industrial and community development, test-demonstration farming, the development of fertilizer and the establishment of recreational facilities; includes several dams for electricity and flood control.

Teragram – 1 trillion (1012) grams = 1 million (106) metric tons.

Teratogens – chemicals or other factors that specifically cause abnormalities during embryonic growth and development.

Terracing – shaping the land to create level shelves of Earth to hold water and soil; requires extensive hand labor or expensive machinery, but it enables farmers to farm very steep hillsides.

Territoriality – an intense form of intraspecific competition in which organisms define as theirs an area surrounding their home site or nesting site and defend it, primarily against other members of their species.

Territory – an area where individual organisms defend against competition from others.

Tertiary treatment – removing inorganic minerals and plant nutrients after primary and secondary sewage treatment.

Tetrafluoromethane (or *carbon tetrafluoride*) – the perfluorinated counterpart to the hydrocarbon methane. It can be classified as a haloalkane or halomethane. *Tetrafluoromethane is a useful refrigerant but also a potent greenhouse gas. It has a very high bond strength due to the nature of the carbon– fluorine bond.*

TEX-86 – a paleothermometer based on the composition of membrane lipids of the marine picoplankton Crenarchaeota.

Thermal ecology – the study of the relationship between temperature and organisms.

Thermal expansion – the increase in volume (and decrease in density) results from warming water. A warming of the ocean leads to an expansion of the ocean volume, which leads to an increase in sea level.

Thermohaline circulation – large-scale density-driven circulation in oceans caused by differences in temperature and salinity. *In the North Atlantic, the thermohaline circulation consists of warm surface water flowing northward and cold deep water flowing southward, resulting in net poleward heat transport. The surface water sinks in highly restricted sinking regions located in high latitudes.*

Thermal mass (*architecture*) – any mass that can absorb and store heat and therefore be used to buffer temperature change. *Concrete, bricks, and tiles need a lot of heat energy to change their temperature and therefore have high thermal mass; timber has low thermal mass.*

Thermal plume – a plume of hot water discharged into a stream or lake by a heat source, such as a power plant.

Thermal pollution – industrial discharge of heated water into a river, lake, or another body of water, causing a temperature rise that endangers aquatic life.

Thermocline (or *metalimnion* for lakes) – a layer within a body of water or air where the temperature changes rapidly with depth. *In oceans and lakes, a distinctive temperature transition zone separates an upper layer mixed by the wind (the epilimnion) and a colder, deeper layer not mixed (the hypolimnion).*

Theoretical ecology – the development of ecological theory, usually with mathematical, statistical, or computer modeling tools.

Thermodynamics – a branch of physics focused on energy transfers and conversions.

> *First law of thermodynamics*: energy can be transformed and transferred but cannot be destroyed or created.

> *Second law of thermodynamics*: with each successive energy transfer or transformation, less energy is available to do work.

Thermohaline circulation – the global density-driven circulation of the oceans.

Thermosphere – the highest atmospheric zone; a region of hot, diluted gases above the mesosphere extending to about 1,000 miles from Earth's surface.

Third pipe system – a third pipe, in addition to the standard water supply pipe and sewer disposal pipe, which carries recycled water for irrigation purposes.

Third World – less-developed countries that are neither capitalistic and industrialized (the First World) nor centrally-planned socialist economies (the Second World).

Threat display – a signal used by organisms of certain species that the user intends to attack.

Threatened species – while it may still be abundant in parts of its territorial range, a species that has declined significantly in numbers and may be on the verge of extinction in certain regions or localities.

Three Gorges Dam – near Yichang on the Yangtze River in China; helps control the flooding of the Yangtze River Valley; in addition, multiple river flows make the Three Gorges complex the largest electricity-generating facility in the world; a lake about 400 miles long was formed behind the dam, forcing the relocation of more than a million people and permanently submerging many historical sites.

Threshold (*ecology*) – a point that, when crossed, can bring rapid and sometimes unpredictable change in a trend. *An example would be the sudden altering of ocean currents due to ice melting at the poles.*

Tidal/ocean/wave energy – mechanical energy from water movement used to generate electricity.

Tidal station – a dam built across a narrow bay or estuary that traps tidewater in and out of the bay; water flowing through the dam spins turbines attached to electric generators.

Timberline – in the mountains, the highest-altitude edge of the forest that marks the beginning of the treeless alpine tundra.

Tipping fee – a fee for disposal of waste.

Tipping point (or *threshold*) – when a change in the climate triggers a significant environmental event, which may be permanent, such as widespread bleaching of corals or the melting of vast ice sheets.

Tipping points in the climate system – thresholds in the climate system that, when exceeded, can lead to significant changes in the system's state that are often irreversible.

Tolerance limits – maximum and minimum requirements in which an individual or system can maintain normal processes. See *limiting factors*.

Topography – a detailed map of the contours of surfaces of land.

Topsoil – 1. mostly fertile surface soil moved or introduced to top-dress gardens, road banks, lawns etc. 2. usually, the uppermost 3 to 10 inches of soil. However, its thickness ranges from a meter or more under virgin prairie to zero in some deserts, a layer in which organic material is mixed with mineral particles. *Topsoil is critical for agriculture.*

Tornado – a rotating column of air usually accompanied by a funnel-shaped downward extension of a cumulonimbus cloud and having a vortex several hundred yards in diameter whirling destructively at speeds of up to 500 miles per hour.

Tort law – civil court cases that seek compensation for damages.

Total energy use – combined direct and indirect energy use.

Total equivalent warming impact (TEWI) – the sum of the direct emissions (chemical) and indirect emissions (energy use) of greenhouse gases.

Total fertility rate – the number of children, on average, a woman would have in her lifetime at present age-specific fertility rates. *Calculated as the average number of children born per woman of every given age in a particular year and totaled for all ages.*

Total growth rate – the net population growth rate from births, deaths, immigration, and emigration.

Total maximum daily loads (TMDL) – the amount of a pollutant that a water body can receive from both point and non-point sources and still meet water quality standards.

Total water use – in water accounting, the *distributed water* use plus *self-extracted water* use plus *reuse water*. Water consumption here means total *direct* and *indirect* water use.

Town water – supplied by government or privately as mains or reticulated water supply.

Toxic – poisonous; a substance that reacts with specific cellular components to kill cells.

Toxic colonialism – shipping toxic wastes to a weaker or poorer nation.

Toxic Release Inventory – a program created by the *Superfund* Amendments and Reauthorization Act of 1984 requires manufacturing facilities, waste handling, and disposal sites to report annually on releases of more than 300 toxic materials.

Toxins – poisonous chemicals that react with specific cellular components to kill cells or alter growth or development in undesirable ways; often harmful, even in dilute concentrations.

Trace gas – any one of the less common gases found in the Earth's atmosphere. Nitrogen, oxygen, and argon comprise more than 99 percent of the Earth's atmosphere. *Other gases, such as carbon dioxide, water vapor, methane, nitrogen oxides, ozone, and ammonia, are trace gases. Although relatively unimportant in terms of their absolute volume, they significantly affect the Earth's weather and climate.*

Tradeable permits – pollution quotas or variances that can be bought or sold.

Traditional knowledge – information, practices, and beliefs handed down through generations.

Tragedy of the commons – an inexorable process of degradation of pooled resources due to the selfish self-interest of "free riders" who use or destroy more than their fair share of common property. See *open access system.*

Transfer station (*waste*) – allows drop–off and consolidation of refuse and a wide range of recyclable materials. *Transfer stations have become integral to municipal waste management, essential in materials recovery and improving transportation economics associated with municipal waste disposal.*

Transgenic plant – a plant into which genetic material (e.g., DNA) has been transferred by genetic engineering.

Transitional zone – where populations from two or more adjacent communities meet and overlap.

Transparent – a substance capable of transmitting light so that objects or images can be seen as clearly as if there were no intervening material.

Transpiration – the evaporation of water through plant leaves. *The process by which water is absorbed by the root system of plants, moves up through the plant, and then evaporates into the atmosphere as water vapor.*

Tree line – any delineation between habitats in which trees can grow and in which they are not capable of growing. *Tree lines are at the edges of habitats with suitable conditions for tree growth and* *development; trees cannot tolerate harsher environmental conditions beyond the tree line, usually because of frigid temperatures or insufficient moisture.*

Tributary – a small stream that empties into a bigger river.

Triple Bottom Line (*John Elkington*, 1994) – a form of sustainability accounting going beyond the financial 'bottom line' to consider *social, environmental, and economic consequences of an organization's activity.*

Trophic level – 1. a step in the movement of energy through an ecosystem; 2. an organism's position in the food chain in an ecosystem. *The position of an organism within a food chain: what it eats and what eats it.*

Trophic networks (*food chain, food webs, or food network*) – the feeding relationships between species within an ecosystem.

Trophic social network (or *food chain, food network, or web of life*) – the feeding relationships between species in each ecosystem.

Tropical – occurring in the tropics (the regions on *either side of the equator*); hot and humid with a mean annual temperature greater than 20 °C.

Tropical depression – brings about hurricanes due to weather, climate, altitude, latitude, or direction changes.

Tropical rainforests – a biome characterized by regular, heavy rainfall, a humidity of at least 80 percent, and incredible biodiversity. *Forests in which rainfall is abundant (more than 80 inches per year), and temperatures are warm to hot year-round.*

Tropical seasonal forest – semi-evergreen or partly deciduous forests tending toward open woodlands and grassy savannas dotted with scattered, drought-resistant tree species; has distinct wet and dry seasons and is hot year-round.

Tropopause – the boundary between the troposphere and stratosphere.

Troposphere – the layer of air nearest to Earth's surface; temperature and pressure usually decrease with increasing altitude (depending on specific latitude). It ranges from the surface to about 10 km in altitude in mid-latitudes (ranging from 9 km in high latitudes to 16 km in the tropics on average) where clouds and "weather" phenomena occur. In the troposphere, temperatures generally decrease with height. See *ozone precursors, stratosphere,* and *atmosphere.*

Tropospheric ozone (O₃) – See *ozone.*

Tropospheric ozone precursors – See *ozone precursors.*

Tsunami – giant seismic sea swells that move rapidly from the center of an earthquake; can be 32-65 feet (10-20 meters) high when they reach shorelines hundreds or even thousands of miles from their origin.

Tundra – 1. a permanently frozen, treeless expanse between the Arctic region's ice cap and tree line. 2. treeless arctic or alpine biome characterized by cold, harsh winters, a short growing season, and potential for frost any month. *Vegetation includes low-growing perennial plants, mosses, and lichens. A treeless, level, or gently undulating plain characteristic of the Arctic and sub-Arctic regions characterized by low temperatures and short growing seasons.*

Turbine – a machine for converting heat energy in steam or high–temperature gas into mechanical energy. In *a turbine, a high–velocity flow of steam or gas passes through successive rows of radial blades fastened to a central shaft.* See tidal energy.

Turbulence – an eddying motion of the atmosphere that disrupts the normal flow of wind.

Typhoon – a tropical cyclone occurring in the western Pacific or Indian oceans.

U

U-238 – an isotope of uranium (U) used in nuclear power plants.

UHI – Urban heat island

Ultraviolet (UV) radiation – radiation from the sun that can be useful or potentially harmful; UV rays from one part of the spectrum (UV-A) enhance plant life; UV rays from other parts of the spectrum (UV-B) can cause skin cancer or other tissue damage; the ozone layer in the atmosphere partly shields the Earth from ultraviolet rays reaching the Earth's surface. The energy range just beyond the violet end of the visible spectrum. *Although ultraviolet radiation constitutes only about 5 percent of the total energy emitted from the Sun, it is the major energy source for the stratosphere and mesosphere, playing a dominant role in energy balance and chemical composition. Most ultraviolet radiation is blocked by Earth's atmosphere, but some solar ultraviolet penetrates and aids in plant photosynthesis and helps produce vitamin D in humans. Too much ultraviolet radiation can burn the skin, cause skin cancer and cataracts, and damage vegetation.*

Umbrella species – a species selected for making conservation-related decisions because protecting it indirectly protects the many other species that make up the ecological community of its habitat. Compare *flagship species*.

Uncertainty – an expression of the degree to which future climate is unknown. *Uncertainty about the future climate arises from the complexity of the climate system and the ability of models to represent it,* *as well as the inability to predict the decisions that society will make. There is uncertainty about how climate change and other stressors will affect people and natural systems.*

Uncontrolled – not under control, discipline, or governance.

Unconventional air pollutants – toxic or hazardous substances, such as asbestos, benzene, beryllium, mercury, polychlorinated biphenyls, and vinyl chloride, not listed in the original *Clean Air Act* because they were then thought not to be released in large quantities. See *non-criteria pollutants*.

Unconventional oil – resources such as *shale oil* and *tar sands* liquefied and used as oil.

Undernourished – those who receive less than 90% of the minimum dietary intake over a long-term period; they lack energy for an active, productive life and are more susceptible to infectious diseases.

Underutilized – to utilize less than fully than or below its potential.

Undiscovered resources – speculative or inferred resources or those that haven't yet been thought of.

United Nations (1945) – an international organization based in New York and formed to promote international peace, security, and cooperation under a charter signed by 51 founding countries.

United Nations Framework Convention on Climate Change (UNFCCC) (March 1994) – the Convention on Climate Change sets an overall framework for intergovernmental efforts to address the challenges posed by climate change. *It recognizes that the climate system is a shared resource whose stability can be affected by industrial and other carbon dioxide emissions and other greenhouse gases. The Convention has near universal membership, with 189 countries having ratified. Under the Convention, governments:*

> report information on greenhouse gas emissions, national policies, and best practices.

> launch national strategies for addressing greenhouse gas emissions and expected impacts, including the provision of financial and technological support to developing countries.

> cooperate in preparing for adaptation to the impacts of climate change.

Universalists – those who believe that some fundamental ethical principles are universal and unchanging; to them, these principles are valid regardless of the context or situation.

Upstream – those processes necessary before a particular activity is completed. *For a manufactured product, this is extraction, transport of materials etc., needed prior to the process of manufacture.* Compare *downstream*.

Upwelling – wind-driven motion of cooler nutrient-rich ocean water towards the ocean's surface, which stimulates the growth of phytoplankton. *The movement of nutrient-rich bottom water to the ocean's surface can occur far from shore but usually along certain steep coastal areas, where the surface layer of ocean water is pushed away from shore and replaced by cold, nutrient-rich bottom water.*

Urban area – an area in which a majority of the people are not directly dependent on natural resource-based occupations.

Urban ecology – studies ecosystems in urban areas.

Urban heat island – any metropolitan area significantly warmer than its surroundings. The tendency for urban areas to have warmer air temperatures than the surrounding rural landscape due to the *low albedo* of streets, sidewalks, parking lots, and buildings. *These surfaces absorb solar radiation during the day and release it at night, resulting in higher temperatures. These surfaces absorb solar radiation during the day and release it at night, resulting in higher night temperatures; sparse vegetation and paved surfaces increase rain runoff, further reducing cooling effects; temperatures in cities are usually 3-5 °F hotter than the surrounding countryside.*

Urban heat island effect (or *heat island*) – the tendency for higher air temperatures to persist in urban areas because of heat absorbed and emitted by buildings and asphalt, tending to make cities warmer than the surrounding countryside.

Urban metabolism – the functional flow of materials and energy required by cities.

Urbanization – an increasing concentration of the population in cities and a transformation of land use to an urban pattern of organization.

Useful energy – available energy used to increase system production and efficiency.

Utilitarian conservation – a philosophy that resources should be used for the greatest good for the greatest number for the longest time.

Utilitarianism – a theory that states that the best moral action is also often the most utilitarian one, meaning maximizing the well-being of others. See *utilitarian conservation.*

V

Validate – to establish or verify accuracy. For example, using measurements of temperature or precipitation to determine the accuracy of climate model results.

Values – 1. (*economics*) an estimation of worth; 2. a set of ethical beliefs and preferences that determine our sense of right and wrong; beliefs or ideals individuals or society hold about what is essential or desirable.

Vector (*disease*) – an organism, such as an insect, that transmits disease-causing microorganisms such as viruses or bacteria. Vector-borne diseases include, for example, malaria, dengue fever, and Lyme disease. See *vector-borne disease.*

Vegetation – ground cover provided by plants.

Vegetation formation – a concept used to classify vegetation communities.

Veloway – cycle track; cycleway. Contrast *freeway*.

Vertical stratification – the vertical distribution of specific subcommunities within a community.

Village – a collection of rural households linked by culture, custom, and association with land.

Vinyl – a plastic (usually PVC) used to make beverage bottles, credit cards, pipes, and hoses.

Virtual water (*J.A. Allan*, early 1990s) – the volume of water required to produce a commodity or service. First coined by Professor J.A. Allan of the University of London, now widely known as *embodied water*.

Virus – a microscopic obligate intracellular parasite that infects and replicates exclusively within the living cells of host organisms.

Viscous – having a relatively high resistance to flow.

Visible light – a portion of the electromagnetic spectrum that includes the wavelengths used for photosynthesis.

Visual waste audit – observing and estimating data on waste streams and practices without physical weighing.

Vitamins – organic molecules essential for life that cannot be manufactured in the body but must be gotten from one's diet; they act as enzyme cofactors.

Volatile organic compounds (VOC) – molecules containing carbon and differing proportions of other elements such as hydrogen, oxygen, fluorine, and chlorine. *With sunlight and heat, they form ground–level ozone.*

Volcanism – the eruption of molten rock (magma) onto the surface of Earth or a solid-surface planet or moon, where lava, pyroclastic, and volcanic gases erupt through a break in the surface called a vent. *It includes all phenomena resulting from and causing magma within the crust or mantle of the body to rise through the crust and form volcanic rocks on the surface. Magmas that reach the surface and solidify form extrusive landforms.*

Volt or voltage V) – the potential difference between two points. One thousand volts equals 1 kilovolt (kV).

Voluntary simplicity – deliberately choosing to live at a lower level of consumption as a matter of personal and environmental health. See *simple living*.

Vortex – a spiral motion of fluid within a limited area, especially a whirling mass of water or air that sucks everything near it toward its center.

Vulnerability – the degree to which a system is susceptible to, or unable to cope with, adverse effects of climate change, including climate variability and extremes. *Vulnerability is a function of the character, magnitude, and rate of climate variation to which a system is exposed, its sensitivity, and its adaptive capacity.*

Vulnerability assessment (or *vulnerability analysis*) – an analysis of the degree to which a system is susceptible to or unable to cope with the adverse effects of climate change.

Vulnerable species – naturally rare organisms or species whose numbers have been so reduced by human activities that they are susceptible to actions that could push them into a threatened or endangered status.

W

WMO – World Meteorological Organization

Warm front – a long, wedge-shaped boundary caused when a warmer advancing air mass slides over neighboring cooler air parcels.

Warning coloration (or *aposematism*) –a warning signal consisting of brightly colored or starkly contrasting patterns used by a prey species to advertise its unprofitability to potential predator species.

Waste – any material (liquid, solid or gaseous) produced by domestic households and commercial, institutional, municipal, or industrial organizations that cannot be collected and recycled in any way for further use. *Solid waste involves materials currently entering landfills, even though some are potentially recyclable.*

Waste analysis – quantifying waste streams, recording, and detailing it as a proportion of the total waste stream, determining its destination, and recording details of waste practices.

Waste assessment (or audit) – observing, measuring, and recording data and collecting and analyzing waste samples. *Some practitioners consider an assessment where observations are carried out visually, without sorting and measuring individual streams (see visual waste audit).* See *visual waste audit.*

Waste avoidance – the primary pillar of the waste hierarchy; avoidance works on the principle that the greatest gains result from efficiency–centered actions remove or reduce the need to consume materials in the first place but deliver the same outcome.

Waste factors (*round-wood calculations*) – the ratio of one cubic meter of round wood used per cubic meter (or ton) of product.

Waste generation – unwanted materials, including recyclables as well as garbage. Waste generation equals materials recycled plus waste to landfill; waste generation = materials recycled + waste to landfill.

Waste hierarchy (or *waste management hierarchy*) – promoting waste avoidance ahead of recycling and disposal, often referred to in community education campaigns as 'reduce, reuse, recycle.' The waste hierarchy is recognized in the Environment Protection Act 1970, promoting the management of wastes in the order of preference: avoidance, reuse, recycling, energy recovery, treatment, containment, and disposal.

Waste lagoons – a blocked-off area used for the dumping of waste products.

Waste management – practices and procedures related to handling waste.

Waste minimization – 1. techniques to keep waste generation at a minimum level to divert materials from landfill and thereby reduce the requirement for waste collection, handling, and disposal to a landfill; 2. recycling and efforts to reduce waste going into the waste stream.

Waste reduction – measures to reduce the amount of waste generated by an individual, household, or organization.

Waste stream – materials that are either of a particular type (e.g., timber waste stream) or produced by a particular source (e.g., C & I waste stream). *The steady flow of varied wastes from domestic garbage and yard wastes to industrial, commercial and construction refuse.*

Waste treatment – where some additional processing is undertaken of a waste; may be done to reduce its toxicity or increase its degradability or compostability.

Wastewater – used water, generally not suitable for drinking.

Water consumption – in water accounting: distributed water use plus self–extracted water use plus reuse water use minus distributed water supplied to other users minus in–stream use (where applicable).

Water cycle (*hydrological cycle*) – 1. passage of water between oceans and water bodies, land, and atmosphere. 2. the recycling and utilization of water on Earth, including atmospheric, surface, and underground phases and biological and non-biological components. *The non-stop water circulation on, above, and below Earth's surface. Water changes states at different times during the cycle: liquid, vapor, and ice.*

Water droplet coalescence – a mechanism of condensation that occurs in clouds too warm for ice crystal formation.

Water entitlement – the benefit, as defined in a statutory water plan, to a share of water from a water source.

Water footprint – the total volume of fresh water required in each period to perform a particular task or to produce the goods and services consumed at any level of the action hierarchy. *Country water footprint is a concept introduced by Hoekstra in 2002 as a consumption–based indicator of water use – the volume of water needed to produce the goods and services consumed by the inhabitants of a country.*

Water harvesting (or *rainwater harvesting*) – collecting rainwater either in storage or the soil mainly close to where it falls; the attempt to increase rainwater productivity by storing it in ponds, wetlands etc., and helping to avoid the need for infrastructure to bring water from elsewhere. *Practiced on a large scale upstream, this reduces available water downstream.*

Water intensity – the volume of water used per unit of production or service delivery; this is generally further reduced to monetary unit return per given volume of water used. *Essentially equivalent to water productivity.*

Water neutral – a scientifically based calculator for individuals to be extended to cover the construction industry, the food and beverage sector, and other corporations or organizations. *The water offset calculators aimed at businesses and other organizations are being developed and will be launched with the Individual Water Offset Calculator.*

Water productivity (WP) – the efficiency of outcomes for water used; the quantity required to produce a given outcome. WP–field relates to crop output (e.g., kg of wheat produced per m^3 of water). *WP–basin relates to water productivity in the widest possible sense, including crops, fishery yield, environmental services, etc. Increasing WP means obtaining increasing value from the available water.*

Water quality – the microbiological, biological, physical, and chemical characteristics.

Water resources – water in various forms, such as groundwater, surface water, snow, and ice, at present in the land phase of the hydrological cycle—some parts may be renewable seasonally, but others may be effectively mined.

Water restrictions – mandatory restrictions on water use relative to water storage levels.

Water security – reliable availability of water in sufficient quantity and quality to sustain human health, livelihoods, and the environment.

Watershed – the land from which rain and melted snow drain downhill into a body of water (i.e., a river, lake, reservoir, estuary, wetland, sea, or ocean).

Water stress – when the demand for water by people and ecosystems exceeds the available supply. A situation when residents of a country or region do not have accessible enough high-quality water to meet their everyday needs.

Water table – upper level of water in saturated ground. The surface between the zone of saturation and the zone of aeration; water seeping down from rain-soaked surfaces will sink until it reaches an impermeable or water-tight layer of rock; the water will collect above this layer, filling all the pores and cracks of the permeable portions; the top of this area of water is called the water table.

Water trading – transactions involving water access entitlements or water allocations assigned to water access entitlements.

Water treatment – 1. converting raw, untreated water to a public water supply safe for human consumption; can involve various screening, initial disinfection, clarification, filtration, pH correction, and final disinfection. 2. where some additional processing is undertaken of a particular waste. This may be done to reduce its toxicity or increase its degradability or compostability.

Water vapor – the most abundant greenhouse gas is the water present in the atmosphere in gaseous form. Water vapor is an integral part of the natural greenhouse effect. *While humans are not significantly increasing their concentration through direct emissions, it contributes to the enhanced greenhouse effect because the warming influence of greenhouse gases leads to positive water vapor feedback. In addition to its role as a natural greenhouse gas, water vapor also affects the planet's temperature because clouds form when excess water vapor in the atmosphere condenses to form ice, water droplets, and precipitation.* See *greenhouse gas.* The gaseous state of water (H_2O). *Water vapor is a greenhouse gas because its presence in Earth's atmosphere contributes to the greenhouse effect.*

Waterlogging – water saturation of soil that fills all air spaces and causes plant roots to die from lack of oxygen; often the result of over-irrigation.

Watershed – a water catchment area (North America) or drainage divide (non–American usage). *The area of land that catches rain and snow and drains or seeps into a marsh, stream, river, lake, or groundwater; often contained in the area of land between two ridges of high land, which divide two areas that are drained by different river systems.*

Watt, Kilowatt – a unit of measure of electric power at a point in time as capacity or demand; 1 watt = 1 joule/second; 1 joule = energy spent in one second when a current of 1 amp flows through a resistance of 1 ohm; 1 kilowatt – 1000 watts.

Weather – the hourly/daily change in atmospheric conditions over a more extended period constitutes the climate of a region. 1. atmospheric conditions at any given time or place. It is measured in terms of wind, temperature, humidity, atmospheric pressure, cloudiness, and precipitation. In most places, weather can change from hour to hour, day to day, and season to season. 2. in a narrow sense, the climate is usually defined as the "average weather" or, more rigorously, as the statistical description regarding the mean and variability of relevant quantities over a period ranging from months to thousands or millions of years. The classical period is 30 years, as defined by the World Meteorological Organization (WMO). These quantities are often surface variables such as temperature, precipitation, and wind. 3. in the broader sense, the climate is the state of the climate system, including a statistical description. A simple way of remembering the difference is that *climate* is expected (e.g., cold winters), and *weather* is what results (e.g., a blizzard). See *climate.*

Weathering – 1. the degradation of rocks, soil, minerals, wood, and artificial materials through contact with the Earth's atmosphere, water, and biological organisms. 2. changes in rocks by exposure to air, water, changing temperatures, and reactive chemical agents.

Web of life (or *food chain, food network, trophic social network*) – the feeding relationships between species in each ecosystem.

Weed – a plant growing where it is not wanted, often at a high dispersal rate.

Well-being – a context–dependent physical and mental condition determined by the presence of basic materials for a good life, freedom and choice, health, good social relations, and security.

Wetlands – areas of permanent or intermittent inundation, whether natural or artificial, with static or flowing water, fresh, brackish, or salt, including areas of marine water not exceeding 6 m at low tide. An ecosystem consisting of land permanently or seasonally saturated with water; the habitat of aquatic plants. *Engineered wetlands* are becoming more frequent and are *constructed wetlands*. In urban areas, wetlands are referred to as the *kidney of a city*.

Whitegoods – household electrical appliances like refrigerators, washing machines, and dishwashers.

Wicked problems – problems with no simple right or wrong answer where there is no single, generally agreed-on definition of or solution for the particular issue.

Wicking (or *capillary action*) – water drawn through a medium by surface tension.

Wilderness – an area of undeveloped land affected primarily by the forces of nature; an area where humans are visitors who do not remain.

Wilderness Act – legislation of 1964 recognizing that leaving the land in its natural state may be the highest and best use of some areas.

Wildlife – plants, animals, and microbes that live independently of humans; plants, animals, and microbes that are not domesticated.

Wildlife corridor – a strip of land intended to facilitate the movement of wildlife species between separate areas of their habitat.

Wildlife refuges – areas set aside to shelter, feed, and protect wildlife; however, due to political and economic pressures, refuges often allow hunting, trapping, mineral exploitation, and other activities that threaten wildlife.

Wind – moving air, especially a natural and perceptible movement of air parallel to or along the ground.

Wind energy – the kinetic energy present in the motion of the wind. Wind energy can be converted to mechanical or electrical energy. A traditional mechanical windmill can be used for pumping water or grinding grain. A modern electrical wind turbine converts the force of the wind to electrical energy for consumption on–site or export to the electricity grid.

Wind farms – large numbers of windmills concentrated in a single area; usually owned by a utility or large-scale energy producer.

Wind turbines – a turbine with a large, fanned wheel that spins in the wind to generate electricity. See *wind energy*.

Windbreak – rows of trees or shrubs planted to block wind flow, reduce soil erosion, and protect sensitive crops from high winds.

Wise Use Groups – a coalition of ranchers, loggers, miners, industrialists, hunters, off-road vehicle users, land developers, and others who prefer unrestricted access to natural resources and public lands.

Withdrawal – a description of the total amount of water taken from a lake, river, or aquifer.

Woodland – a low-density forest. A forest where tree crowns cover less than 20 percent of the ground. See *open canopy*.

Work – 1. physical or mental effort; 2. a force exerted for a distance; 3. an energy transformation process that results in a change of concentration or form of energy.

World conservation strategy – a proposal for maintaining essential ecological processes, preserving genetic diversity, and ensuring that utilization of species and ecosystems is sustainable.

World Trade Organization (WTO) – an association of 135 nations that meet to regulate international trade.

X

Xeric – extremely dry, as of a landscape or habitat.

Xeriscaping – landscaping with drought-resistant plants that need no watering.

Xerocole – an animal adapted to live in a desert. The main challenges xerocoles must overcome are lack of water and excessive heat.

Xerophyte – a plant adapted to dry conditions.

Xylophagous – feeding on wood, as of an organism.

X-ray – very short wavelength in the electromagnetic spectrum; can penetrate soft tissue; although it is useful in medical diagnosis, it damages tissue and causes mutations.

Y

Yellowcake – the concentrate of 70 to 90% uranium oxide extracted from crushed ore.

Yellow rain – a powdery, poisonous, yellow substance reported dropping from the air in the eastern parts of China and Asia and found to be the excrement of wild honeybees contaminated by a fungal toxin.

Yucca Mountain, Nevada – the U.S. Department of Energy's potential underground geological repository for spent nuclear fuel and high-level radioactive waste.

Z

Zebra mussel [Latin, *Dreissena polymorpha*] – a European and Asian freshwater mussel regarded as a nuisance in the Great Lakes and surrounding waterways, where it was accidentally introduced.

Zero population growth (ZPG) (or *replacement level of fertility*) – the number of births at which people are just replacing themselves.

Zero tillage (or *no-till farming*) – a conservation tillage system. An agricultural technique for growing crops or pasture without disturbing the soil through tillage. *Zero tillage farming decreases soil erosion tillage caused in certain soils, especially in sandy and dry soils on sloping terrain. Benefits include an increase in the amount of water infiltrating into the soil, soil retention of organic matter, and nutrient cycling.*

Zero waste – turning waste into a resource; redesigning resource–use so waste can ultimately be reduced to zero; ensuring that by–products are used elsewhere, and goods are recycled, emulating the cycling of natural wastes.

Zone of aeration – the area immediately below the ground surface within which pore spaces are partly filled with water and air.

Zone of leaching – the layer of soil just beneath the topsoil where water percolates, removing soluble nutrients that accumulate in the subsoil.

Zone of saturation – lower levels of soil where all spaces are filled with water.

Zooplankton – the animal component of the planktonic community. Plankton are aquatic organisms that are unable to swim effectively against currents. Consequently, they drift or are carried along by currents in the ocean, or by currents in seas, lakes, or rivers.

Frank J. Addivinola, Ph.D.

The lead author and chief editor of this study guide is Dr. Frank Addivinola. With his outstanding education, laboratory research, and decades of university science teaching, Dr. Addivinola lent his expertise to develop this book.

Dr. Frank Addivinola conducted original research in developmental biology as a doctoral candidate and pre-IRTA fellow in Molecular and Cell Biology at the National Institutes of Health (NIH). His dissertation advisor was Nobel laureate Marshall W. Nirenberg, Chief of the Biochemical Genetics Laboratory at the National Heart, Lung, and Blood Institute (NHLBI). Before NIH, Dr. Addivinola researched prostate cancer in the Cell Growth and Regulation Laboratory of Dr. Arthur Pardee at the Dana Farber Cancer Institute of Harvard Medical School.

Dr. Addivinola holds an undergraduate degree in biology from Williams College. He completed his Masters at Harvard University, Masters in Biotechnology at Johns Hopkins University, and five other graduate degrees at the University of Maryland University College, Suffolk University, and Northeastern University.

During his extensive career, Dr. Addivinola held faculty positions at colleges and universities, including Harvard University, Johns Hopkins University, University of Maryland and Northeastern University, and taught numerous undergraduate and graduate-level courses in biology, biochemistry, organic chemistry, inorganic chemistry, anatomy and physiology, medical terminology, nutrition, and medical ethics. He received several awards for his research and presentations.

Essential Biology Self-Teaching Guides

Eukaryotic Cell & Cellular Metabolism

Molecular Biology & Genetics

Nervous & Endocrine Systems

Circulatory, Respiratory & Immune Systems

Digestive & Excretory Systems

Muscle, Skeletal & Integumentary Systems

Reproduction & Development

Microbiology

Plants & Photosynthesis

Evolution, Classification & Diversity

Ecology & Population Biology

Visit our Amazon store

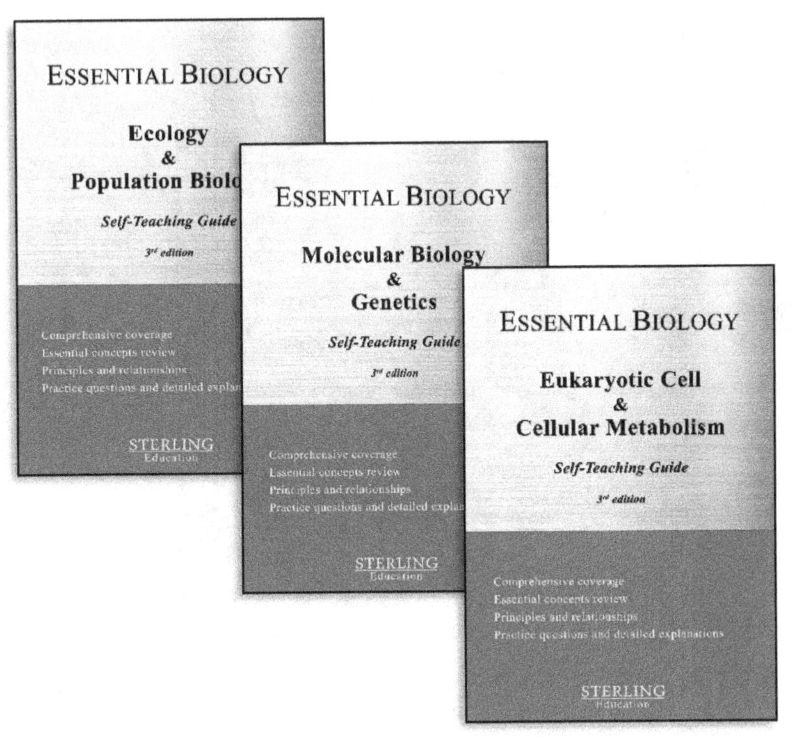

Electronic Structure & Periodic Table

Chemical Bonding

States of Matter & Phase Equilibria

Stoichiometry

Solution Chemistry

Chemical Kinetics & Equilibrium

Acids & Bases

Chemical Thermodynamics

Electrochemistry

Visit our Amazon store

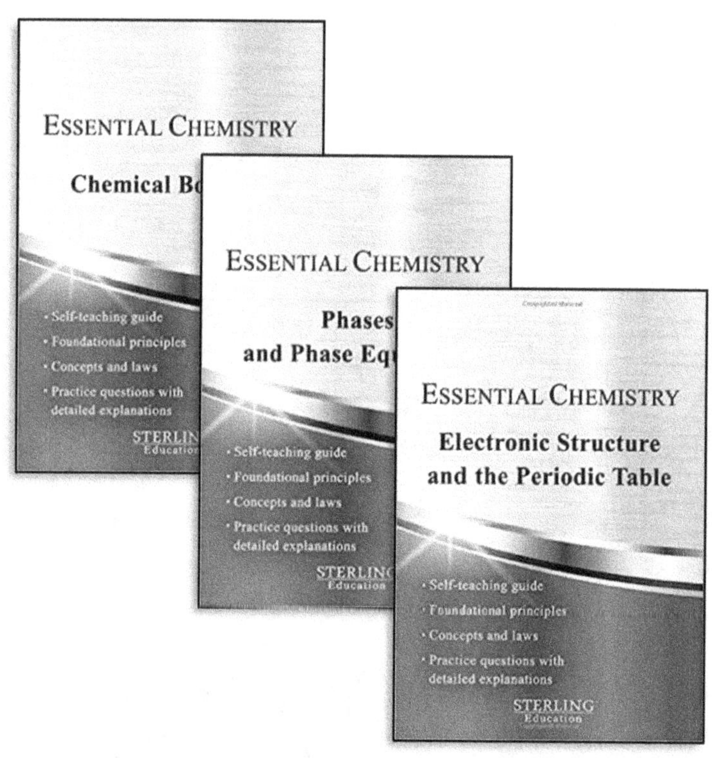